RURAL VIETNAM

T0330842

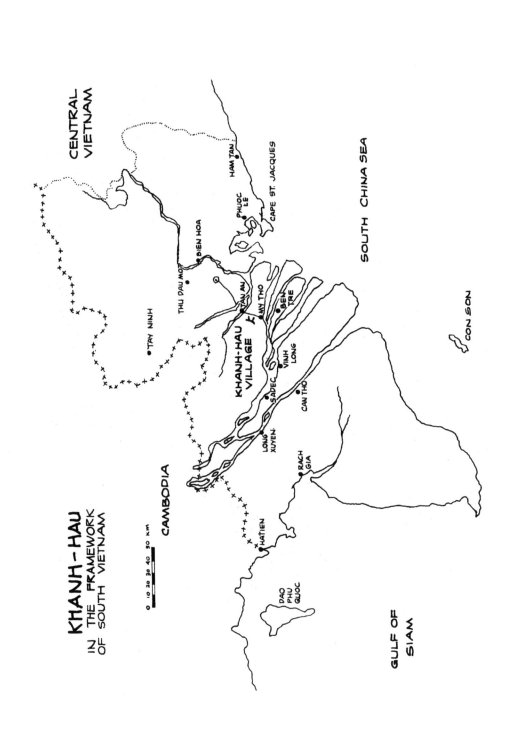

KHANH-HAU
IN THE FRAMEWORK
OF SOUTH VIETNAM

0 10 20 30 40 50 KM

CAMBODIA

CENTRAL
VIETNAM

TAY NINH

THU DAU MOT

BIEN HOA

TAN AN

MY THO

KHANH-HAU
VILLAGE

BEN
TRE

PHUOC
LE

HAM TAN

CAPE ST. JACQUES

VINH
LONG

SADEC

CAN THO

LONG
XUYEN

RACH
GIA

HATIEN

DAO
PHU
QUOC

SOUTH CHINA SEA

CON SON

GULF OF
SIAM

RURAL VIETNAM

The Small World of Khanh Hau

James B. Hendry

Routledge
Taylor & Francis Group

LONDON AND NEW YORK

First published 1964 by Transaction Publishers

Published 2017 by Routledge
4 Park Square, Milton Park, Abingdon, Oxon OX14 4RN
605 Third Avenue, New York, NY 10017

Routledge is an imprint of the Taylor & Francis Group, an informa business

Library of Congress Catalog Number: 2008039946

Library of Congress Cataloging-in-Publication Data

Hendry, James Bausch.
    [Small world of Khanh Hau]
    Rural Vietnam : the small world of Khanh Hau / James B. Hendry.
       p. cm.
    Originally published in 1964 under title: The small world of Khanh Hau.
    Includes index.
    ISBN 978-0-202-36299-1 (acid-free paper)
       1. Khanh Hau (Vietnam)--Economic conditions. I. Title.

HC444.Z7K415 2009
330.9597'8--dc22
                                                          2008039946

ISBN 13: 978-0-202-36299-1 (pbk)

CONTENTS

LIST OF FIGURES

FOREWORD

The material presented in *Rural Vietnam* was gathered in 1958-59 in the course of a program of joint research carried out by the Michigan State University Advisory Group in Viet Nam in cooperation with the National Institute of Administration. The purpose was to initiate a series of studies on the economic, social, and administrative problems in the rural areas of Viet Nam which would provide useful information to the students studying for the civil service at the National Institute of Administration, as well as to those actively concerned with framing policies of economic development. Although this objective was realized in part, deteriorating security conditions after 1959 severely hampered the continuation of the research program. Furthermore, government programs in the rural areas after 1959, such as the *agrovilles* and strategic hamlets, became essentially counter-insurgency measures, with rural development a somewhat subsidiary concern. Parts of Khanh Hau, in fact, were converted into a strategic hamlet. At the time this is being written, there are indications that the strategic hamlet program will be at least partially curtailed, because the enforced concentration of villagers for defensive purposes has been generating hostility rather than support for the government.

For this reason it seems probable that attempts to reshape the village life of South Viet Nam have had little lasting impact, and the observations made here on factors affecting economic activity have not been outdated by the events of the intervening years. The outcome of the struggle in Viet Nam is still far from certain, but if the disruption caused by incessant guerilla warfare can be eliminated, perhaps the country can make a start toward the promise of development which seems implicit in its land and its people.

The diacritical marks commonly used in written Vietnamese have been omitted in the interest of reducing publication problems. Since Vietnamese terms are not essential to the purpose of the book, this did not seem to pose a major deficiency as far as the general reader is concerned. Largely for this same reason, the index does not contain references in Vietnamese, with the exception of a very few terms in most common use. It is assumed that those with a reading knowledge of Vietnamese will be able to locate specific items by the English subject headings.

The title of The Small World of Khanh Hau was appropriated, without permission, from an article about the village studies which had been carried out by Francois Sully, correspondent for Newsweek Magazine. The article appeared in the Times of Viet Nam some time ago, and I hope Mr. Sully will forgive my high-handed use of his imaginative phrase-making.

I would like to express my thanks to the Rector of the National Institute of Administration, Mr. Vu Quoc Thong, and the Vice-Rector, Mr. Nghiem Dang, for their help in getting the project established, and to Professors Bui Quan An, Truong Ngoc Giau, and Cao Huu Dong of the Institute Faculty for their advice and cooperation during the period when field work was in progress. Thanks are also due to the USOM Field Service Division for their logistical support, and to the USOM Graphics Section for their help in preparing charts and maps used in the text. I am also grateful to a number of people who have worked in the project, or who have offered advice and help at various stages, including Messrs. Bui Quang Da, Nguyen Ngoc Yen, Le Due Gi, and Dang Van De of the Michigan State University Group staff, and Dr. J. Price Gittinger of USOM.

To my colleagues on the study, G. C. Hickey and L. W. Woodruff, I owe a special debt of gratitude for their continuous aid and assistance throughout and for the cordial and productive working relationships which existed at all times during the study. Each was working on a separate aspect of village life and activity, which was subsequently published in mimeographed form in Saigon, but the continual exchange of data, observations, and viewpoints was of enormous value in expanding what I could do alone and in placing my own findings in new perspectives. Mr. Nguyen Van Thuan also deserves special thanks for his patient, conscientious, sympathetic, and intelligent work as research assistant. One could not ask for better support than he provided.

Professor Frank Child, Chairman of the Department of Economics of the University of California at Davis, thoughtfully edited an earlier version and made numerous helpful suggestions. Typing of the final draft was ably done by Mrs. Shirley Finton, Mrs. Judith R. Kelly, and Miss JoEllen Rogers, all of whom patiently put up with the patches and scraps which constituted the original.

Finally, grateful acknowledgment must go to the Office of International Programs, Michigan State University, for a grant from the Ford Foundation gift to the University which facilitated publication, and to Professor Bert F. Hoselitz, Research Center in Economic Development and Cultural Change, University of Chicago, for his support and encouragement in making publication possible.

All errors of omission and commission in the book are, of course, entirely my own.

James B. Hendry

Dacca, East Pakistan

RURAL VIETNAM

1

THE SMALL WORLD OF KHANH HAU

Viet Nam is a land whose features change dramatically within very short distances, from mountains and high plateaus to coastal plains and inland swamps. To the south, the large delta formed by the Mekong and lesser river systems inches forward yearly into the South China Sea. This delta, while hardly typical of all Viet Nam, is one of the most fertile rice-producing regions of southeast asia. Its importance lies not only in the substantial contribution this area can, and will, make to the national economy of Viet Nam, but it is also the area of most recent settlement by the Vietnamese. The study of its institutions can, therefore, reveal much about the prospects for social and economic change, for they differ from those of the better known areas of central and northern Viet Nam.

The delta village chosen for this particular study bears the name of Khanh Hau, and is located approximately fifty kilometers south of Saigon in the province of Long An, not far from the chief provincial town of Tan An. Although the main highway passes through the village lands, the centers of village population are situated from one to two kilometers on either side of it, and in some cases are approachable only by footpath over the rice fields. There are five such centers, or hamlets, in the village—Ap Cau, Ap Nhon Hau, Ap Thu Tuu, Ap Moi, and Ap Dinh (see Figure 1.1). The latter has been recently divided into Ap Dinh "A" and Ap Dinh "B" for administrative purposes, but otherwise, it remains essentially a single unified hamlet as before.

The hamlets form a rough perimeter which follows the village boundaries, with most of the village rice fields inside these inhabited areas. The hamlets on the east side of the main highway—Ap Cau, Ap Nhon Hau and Ap Thu Tuu—are situated on sizeable streams which give them fairly good water facilities for fishing, transportation, and irrigation. Those on the west—Ap Dinh "A" and "B" and Ap Moi—have access only to a smaller stream, recently ex-

FIGURE 1.1

SETTLEMENT
PATTERN OF
KHÁNN-HẬU

SCALE: 1:25,000

tended by a canal. The village council house, the school, and the communal temple (*dinh*), where the cult of the village guardian spirit is celebrated, are all located in Ap Dinh, the most populous hamlet and the only one to have a street. This hamlet also contains the tomb of Marshal Nguyen Huynh Due, a hero of Vietnamese history from the early period of the Nguyen dynasty. A second *dinh* is located in Ap Nhon Hau, vestige of the time when the eastern portion of the present Khanh Hau was a separate village. The cult of this *dinh* is still actively celebrated, and in many respects this part of the village is more closely linked to neighboring villages than to other parts of Khanh Hau. Except for the one street in Ap Dinh, communication within and between hamlets is along footpaths which wind in and around the houses or meander across the rice fields on the earthen dikes which separate the holdings of individual farmers.

The land is the heavy, black clay of the delta, stretching flat in all directions. The hamlets have grown along the streams that lead to the main rivers, the houses hidden from view by the water palms and other foliage which grow thick along the banks. The chief village occupation is wet rice agriculture, carried on by methods which, with a few exceptions, have changed but little over the centuries. Tools and equipment are simple and locally made; secondary occupations are poorly developed. A great majority of the houses in the village are made wholly or in part of thatch and are surrounded by rough thickets of thorn and bamboo. The main highway, with its steady stream of buses and other vehicles, affords easy and inexpensive transportation to the larger towns, but no one in the village owns an automobile, and only a few have motorized bicycles or scooters. In many essentials, life is as it must have been one hundred and fifty years ago.

In terms of population size, the village is probably slightly smaller than other villages which surround it. An outside observer who stops to talk with village people will find polite reserve in their manner at first, but this usually changes to more open friendliness when the purpose of the visit is recognized as non-threatening. An invitation to have a cup of tea is a never-failing courtesy offered in every home, no matter how poor. The children, giggling and curious, often appear sturdy and alert, but many of the younger ones in particular, naked or clad only in a shirt, exhibit the distended stomachs and running noses that are symptomatic of malnutrition. The young women have a graceful carriage from carrying burdens on their heads and shoulders, but most of the old women appear stooped and thin from a lifetime of extremely hard physical labor. One is also struck by the incredibly bad teeth of the older people. The few still remaining to most of them are badly decayed and stained. Clothing, often in an advanced stage of disrepair, is largely a matter of black calico shirts and trousers for both men and women, with conical hats as protection from the sun. This is sometimes varied, particularly by the women, with bits of cast-off military uniforms or shirts of different cut and color. An exception is the all-white cotton garb worn by men of higher income and social standing, their clothing symbolizing their prestige position in the society.

The pace of village life is calm but not indolent. People are curious about things that are new and different, yet they are slow to register surprise or excitment. Meeting them, you gain an impression of people who are, on the whole, courteous, industrious, and able, tempered to some extent by the debilitating effects of poor diet and endemic ill health. It is also important to recognize that the events of recent years have had a profound effect on attitudes and temperament. The struggles for independence from France brought great pressures on people to ally themselves with one faction or another in that effort, and these divisions within the village have left their scars—friendships broken, property confiscated or destroyed, individuals imprisoned, fined, or physically harmed. Moreover, much the same conditions still prevail as the Vietnamese government vies with the communist guerilla forces (Viet Cong) for the support and loyalty of the population. Since the government cannot guarantee personal safety at all times, villagers dare not be openly hostile to the Viet Cong, who number some villagers among their underground supporters and whose patrols enter the village on irregular occasions. Conversely the government is in control of the area during daylight hours, and one cannot be an open adherent to the Viet Cong lest he become subject to the strict counter-subversive measures the government has imposed in its effort to destroy the guerilla forces and their indigenous supporters. To the typical peasant head of a household, the most pressing concerns are the material needs of his family, the maintenance of his obligations of ritual observances within the cult of the ancestors, and a strong desire to be left in peace. Broader political issues are usually of little concern, except when the struggle for political power directly involves him or members of his household adversely. Most villagers affect an attitude of political neutrality or indifference, are distrustful of strangers as a matter of course, and, more importantly, even appear distrustful of other villagers to an equal degree. This suspicion of others, thoroughly justified by the experiences of the past ten to fifteen years, turns the villagers toward the members of their imm ediate households as the only reliable elements in a changing and uncertain world. The expected conservatism of a peasant society is thus reinforced by the side effects of a power struggle that has its origins far beyond the borders even of Viet Nam itself.

Nothing definite is known of the dates when sections of the present village were first settled, or of the early history of the village. Vietnamese began to migrate into the delta of the Mekong River by the early part of the 18th century, but residents of Khanh Hau tend to fix the date of the establishment of the village as late as the first quarter of the 19th century. Isolated farmsteads existed in what is now village land before that time—the Marshal Nguyen Huynh Due, for example, was born there in 1746. However, a village as such cannot be said to have existed prior to the time the emperor named a guardian spirit for it. This act performed the double function of providing recognition of the establishment of a village and validating its existence as part of the imperial realm. It was not until the early part of the 19th century that the emperor Gia Long named guardian spirits for the villages of Tuong Khanh and Nhon Hau, and each constructed a *dinh* in which rituals honoring the guardian spirits could take place. In 1917, these two communities were combined into the administrative village unit which now bears the name of Khanh Hau. Although the separate communal houses and guardian spirits are still retained and the spirits honored in separate ceremonies, the *dinh* in the ham let of Ap Dinh has unofficially become the principal *dinh* of the village.

Villages in the delta generally supported the Viet Minh resistance movement against the French and Japanese during the years of World War II. After the Japanese withdrew from Viet Nam in 1945, the Viet MinL assumed authority and replaced the traditional village councils with administrative councils, elected by Viet Minh party members, in villages throughout the delta. The French, however, restored the village council when they returned to Viet Nam in 1946 and re-established the colonial administration of Cochinchina. The period which followed, 1946 to 1954, was the time of great insecurity mentioned earlier, but this has been only partially reduced since the Geneva Agreements were signed in in the latter year. Independence, under the present Republic of Viet Nam, has brought further changes in village administration and active efforts to introduce some economic reforms and stimulate economic activity, but it has not brought the peace and security necessary to the success of these programs.

Despite major changes—from colony to independent republic, a continuing struggle for power between the central government and the Viet Cong, the introduction of large-scale American economic and military aid—the world of Khanh Hau remains largely a world of limited horizons. There is some knowledge of events that take place beyond the boundaries of the village; there is awareness of the dependence on the outside world for markets and for goods which cannot be produced locally; and there is evidence of a receptivity to the infusion of new ideas. Still, the main focus is on events and personalities in the village, and the daily routine of activities proceeds in patterns that are little changed from the days of earliest settlement. Walking along the dirt lane which passes for the only street in the village, passing the houses of thatch and wood, watching people in their pursuit of daily tasks, it is not difficult to imagine oneself days removed from a city as modern as Saigon. In particular, the quiet of the village is impressive after the noise of the city, and it is hard to keep in mind that an atmosphere characterized by such serenity and calm has been, and to some extent still is, the arena of violent conflict.

This then is Khanh Hau, in most externals similar to any one of hundreds of villages that dot the delta region which lies south of Saigon, north of the Mekong, and east of the large swampy area that lines the Cambodian border. Its institutions, its problems, and its aspirations would be roughly those of villages elsewhere in the same region, although this description of life in Khanh Hau emphatically is not intended to be a portrait in miniature of rural life in all parts of Viet Nam. Institutional variations are as prevalent there as the topographical variations remarked upon at the outset.

2

THE RESOURCES OF POPULATION

Population Size and Composition

If one looks first at the data on the basic resource of the village, its people, impressions are apt to be mixed. Somewhat older and more literate than one might expect, the population also seems to be growing at an alarmingly high rate. While it would be incorrect to assume that it is a mobile population, there is evidence that mobility has taken place in the past and will probably continue to do so in the future under proper conditions. This, at least, is the view which the population data can give us, to be supplemented in due course by whatever can be said of the character, attitudes, and expectations of villagers based on subjective judgments and impressions of various kinds. It is the quantified data, however, which give an initial overview of the village population as a whole.

The data on the village population are taken from a house-to-house census which was conducted by village and school officials in September 1958. These are shown in Table 2.1, which gives not only the totals by hamlets, but also the number of families and the number of five-family groups in each hamlet in the village. The population for the five hamlets of Khanh Hau is 1958 was 3, 241 persons, of whom a bare majority (51.1 percent) were women.

A major portion of the population, although again by a slim margin, is also under 18 years of age (54.1 persent), but here the number of boys is slightly larger than the number of girls. The relative size of the hamlets is clearly indicated—Ap Dinh, the largest and the most important, contains 38.2 percent of the total population of the village. In contrast, its immediate neighbor to the south, Ap Moi, has only 11.5 percent of the total. To some extent, however, Ap Dinh "A" and "B" and Ap Moi represent a single concentration of population, because they are contiguous and because the people in Ap Moi have largely resettled from Ap Dinh. In terms of

TABLE 2.1
Population of Khanh Hau by Hamlets, 1958

Hamlet	No. of households	No. of five-family groups	Men over 18 years	Women over 18 years	Boys 18 years and under	Girls 18 years and under	Total
(1)	(2)	(3)	(4)	(5)	(6)	(7)	(8)
Ap Dinh "A"	142	29	258	309	363	309	1,239
Ap Dinh "B"	88	17	82	97	87	107	373
Ap Moi	69	15	101	110	129	124	464
Ap Cau	85	17	137	150	161	188	636
Ap Nhon Hau	144	23	112	132	156	129	529
Ap Thu Tuu	92	19					
Total	590	120	690	798	896	857	3,241

Source: Village Census of Khanh Hau, September 1958.

population, these hamlets comprise almost exactly half (49.7 percent) of the total population. Thus, Khanh Hau is divided not only geographically by the main highway; the same division also halves the population.

An average household in the village contains 5.5 persons, which is smaller than expected in light of the common belief that families and households in Viet Nam tend to be large (see Table 2.2). This household size is roughly true for each hamlet, with a range from the lowest average of 5.1 to the highest of 5.9, both extremes being found in Ap Dinh "A" and "B," which was formerly a single hamlet. The median size household is 6 persons, but there are 26 households in the village which have only one member, and one household that has as many as 16 members. Only 35 households have as many as 10 members or more.

TABLE 2.2
Household Size in Khanh Hau, by Hamlets, 1958

Household size (persons)	Ap Dinh "A"	Ap Dinh "B"	Ap Moi	Ap Cau	Ap Thu Tuu	Ap Nhon Hau	All hamlets
1	9	3	2	6	2	4	26
2	18	4	6	2	7	8	45
3	11	7	10	7	6	12	53
4	20	13	8	12	13	15	81
5	25	13	12	17	16	21	104
6	20	15	9	18	16	11	89
7	20	13	9	10	12	14	78
8	7	6	8	5	7	18	51
9	4	7	2	3	6	6	28
10	4	3	1	3	5	3	19
11	2	3	-	-	1	1	7
12	2	-	1	1	1	1	6
13	-	-	-	1	-	-	1
14	-	1	-	-	-	-	1
15	-	-	-	-	-	-	-
16	-	-	1	-	-	-	1
Total	142	88	69	85	92	114	590

Source: Village Census of Khanh Hau, September 1958.

The age and sex distribution of the village is shown in the population pyramids of Figures 2.1 to 2.6. In general terms, the pyramids for the hamlets and the village as a whole tend to have a broad base that narrows considerably at around age 20, and then extends vertically without much change past age 50. The youthful population which this reflects, foreshadows great population pressure in years to come unless subject to some kind of check.

The pyramid for the village indicated that births fell off 11 to 14 years ago, which would coincide with one of the major periods of political unrest and insecurity. This same pattern is found in all the hamlets, and to more or less the same degree. The abrupt narrowing of the pyramid at upper-age levels is also found in all hamlets, usually accompanied by a larger female than male population at most age levels above 20 years. Finally, there is actually a larger number of villagers in the age group 41 to 50 (345 persons) than there is in the age group 31 to 40 years (331 persons).

One would normally expect to find that more boys are born than girls, and therefore a majority of males in the low age brackets. The death rate among males is usually higher than that for females, so it would also be expected that there would be more females than males among the adult population. Both of these expectations hold true for Khanh Hau. However, the narrowing of the pyramid above age 20 suggests that the village population pattern has been affected by outside factors to a considerable degree. Since life expectancy in Viet Nam is assumed to be low, some of the sharp reduction in the size of age groups past 20 may be explained in terms of the poor health conditions which are generally prevalent, not just in Khanh Hau. The fact, however, that the middle-age group of persons, 41 to 50, is larger than the next youngest group must reflect something more than just poor health. If the comparison is made by sex, there are more men in the age group 41 to 50 (166 persons) than there are in either age group 31 to 40 (154 persons) or age 21 to 30 (158 persons). An important part of the explanation therefore seems to lie in the fact that young adult males have left, and are still leaving, in significant numbers.

The military has undoubtedly accounted for a good share

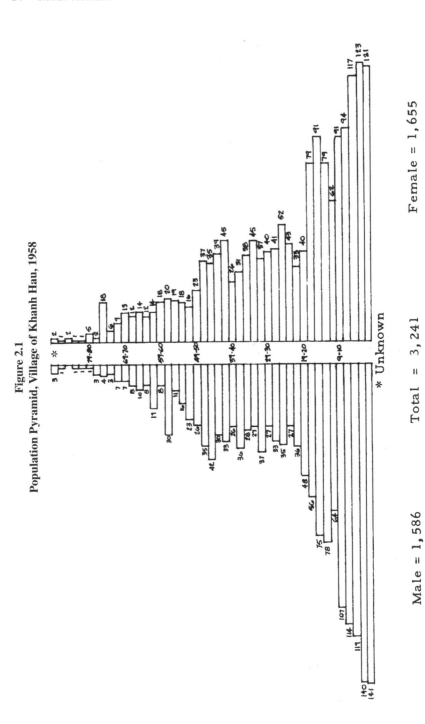

Figure 2.1
Population Pyramid, Village of Khanh Hau, 1958

* Unknown

Male = 1,586   Total = 3,241   Female = 1,655

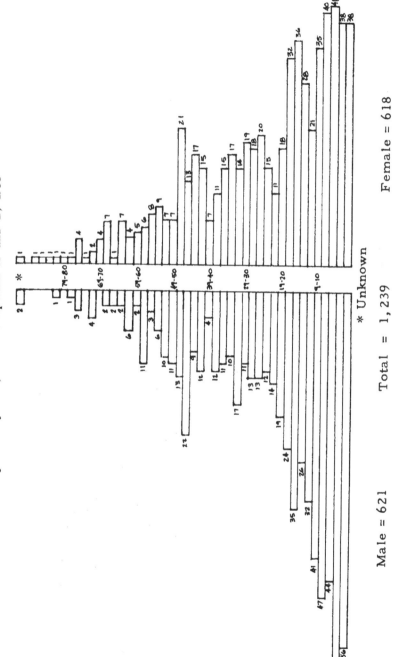

Figure 2.2
Population Pyramid, Hamlets of Ap Dinh "A" and "B," 1958

Male = 621   Total = 1,239   Female = 618

* Unknown

FIGURE 2.3
Population Pyramid, Hamlet of Ap Moi, 1958

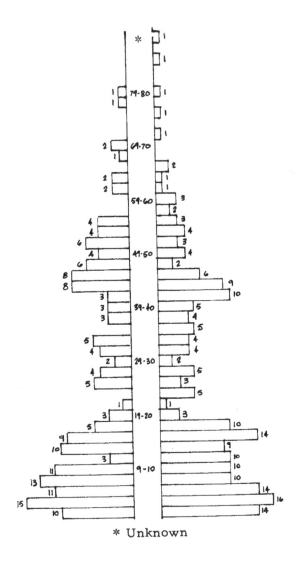

* Unknown

Male = 169   Total = 373   Female = 204

FIGURE 2.4
Population Pyramid, Hamlet of Ap Nhan Hau, 1958

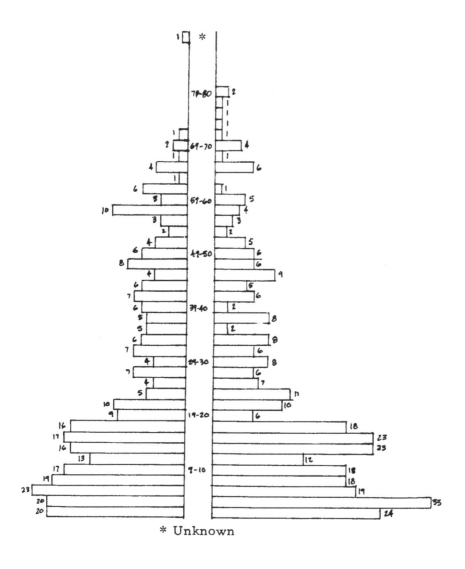

* Unknown

Male = 298   Total = 636   Female = 338

FIGURE 2.5
Population Pyramid, Hamlet of Ap Cau, 1958

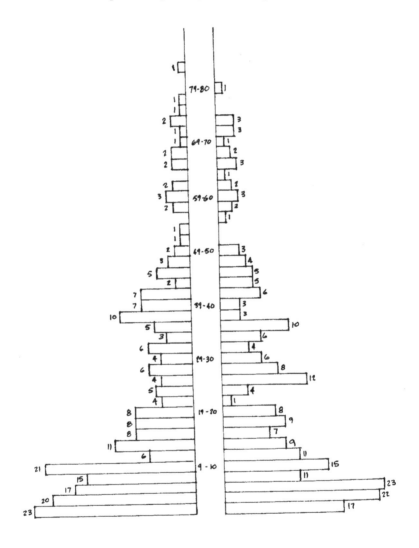

Male = 230   Total = 464   Female = 234

FIGURE 2.6
Population Pyramid, Hamlet of Ap Thu Tuu, 1958

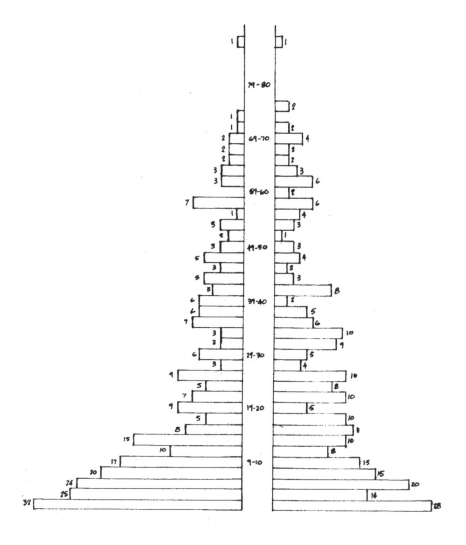

Male = 268   Total = 529   Female = 261

of this mobility out of the village. A conscription program is currently in effect which draws some young men into military service each year, but the relatively small numbers of men in age groups older than those now being called into service means that many who left during the past 15 years have not returned to the village. Some of these are still on active duty, but it is probably true that a larger number have found opportunities elsewhere and have preferred not to return. This indicates that mobility from the village may be greater than suspected, or at least that the drawing power of the village is not too great once the villager is away from it. There is also some mobility from the village by women who marry and move to the villages of their husbands, but this emigration is probably offset by immigration of women from other villages for the same reason. This does not explain why there are fewer women in the age group 31 to 40 (177 persons) than there are in the age group 41 to 50 (179 persons) but it suggests that women in the former age group have moved from Khanh Hau with the men whose emigration was noted above.

TABLE 2. 3
**Births, Deaths, and Marriages
in Khanh Hau, 1948-57**

Year	No. of births	No. of deaths	Excess of births over deaths	No. of marriages	Ratio of births to deaths
1948	83	18	65	22	4. 6:1
1949	94	20	74	14	4. 7:1
1950	90	17	73	25	5. 3:1
1951	98	21	77	22	4. 7:1
1952	99	16	83	17	6. 2:1
1953	180	35	145	34	5. 1:1
1954	123	37	86	28	3. 3:1
1955	166	27	139	41	6. 1:1
1956	176	26	150	17	6. 8:1
1957	177	33	144	17	5. 4:1

Source: Village records, Khanh Hau.

Since there is no record of births and deaths prior to 1948, there is little basis for estimating the long-run trend in the ratio of births to deaths. There is information for the period 1948 to 1957, however, and this is shown in Table 2.3. The same data are plotted in Figure 2.7 to illustrate the variation in the ratio from year to year and the trend which seems to express the change taking place. The ratio of births to deaths has averaged 5.2 to 1 over the ten-year period, and this is almost the same as the ratio in 1957, but there does appear to be a slightly rising trend in the ratio over time.

FIGURE 2.7
Ratio of Births to Deaths, Khanh Hau, 1948-57

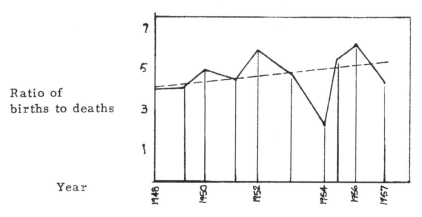

Source: Village records, Khanh Hau.

It is hard to evaluate the reliability of these data, for the earlier years in particular, and the village has no birth and death records which go back earlier than 1948. There may be under-reporting of both births and deaths, but it seems more likely that is would be the infant deaths that would go unreported, and these may be more or less offset by unreported births.

The slightly rising ratio of births to deaths may reflect an improvement in general health conditions, but a more probable explanation is the growing availability and acceptance of occidental medication. These medicines are being used increasingly, and some effects should therefore be expected.

The explosive element, however, is contained in the fact that each year there is an average of over five births for each death in the village. Based on the village population in 1958, the net increase in the population measured by the excess of births over deaths is proceeding at a rate of about 44 persons per thousand per year. In absolute terms, this promises an increase in the village population of nearly 1,500 persons over the next ten years, other things being equal.

As a check on the plausibility, if not the reliability, of these findings, the gross number of births per year can be compared with the number of women of child-bearing age and also the number of households in the village. In the case of the former, there were 479 females between the ages of 17 and 38 in the 1958 census. The total number of births was 176 in 1956 and 177 in 1957, or one child per 2.7 women of child-bearing age per year. Another way to express it would be to say that roughly 37 percent of the women of child-bearing age had children in 1956 and 1957. This estimate of the number of women of child-bearing age is a conservative one, and probably could be expanded by extending the age limits at each end, which would then lower the percentage of women of child-bearing age who had children each year. The age limits used above include the women most likely to bear children, however, without adding more doubtful age levels.

There are also polygamous households in the village, and a husband may keep his wives and their children in separate establishments. In this way married households should exceed the number of married men in the village, and the number of unmarried women of marriageable age (excluding widows) is probably quite small. Although polygamy has been banned in Viet Nam, the practice seemed to persist in the village to some degree among those who could afford the expense of separate households. The study did not attempt to measure the extent of polygamy because of its current illegal status, but knowledge of its existence adds to the plausibility of the birth rates given above.

The only offsetting factor to the growing population pressure is the apparent mobility among young adults indicated in the population pyramids for the village. If opportunities open in other parts of Viet Nam, and if young adults continue to relocate as a result of military service experience or for other reasons, there is some hope that population pressure on the limited land area may be checked to some extent. If such alternatives do not become available, however, village living standards will become further depressed, as the existing resources are stretched to provide for a rapidly increasing number of people.

Education and Literacy

Khanh Hau is well-provided with educational facilities, relative to villages in Viet Nam generally. It has a large elementary school located in the main hamlet of Ap Dinh that serves not only Khanh Hau but the neighboring village of Tan Huong as well. There is also a private secondary school in the village that accomodates a small number of students able to afford schooling beyond the elementary level. Finally, a UNESCO-sponsored Fundamental Education Center has established its training school on village land, although not in an inhabited part of the village, and students from all areas of Viet Nam are sent there to receive courses in education and in organizing community development projects. As part of this program, the Center has given adult education courses in home economics, health, craft skills, and reading and writing, and some of the villagers have attended these courses. The Center has also used its students to conduct surveys of various kinds in parts of the village, and this has given training to the students and provided much useful data about the village itself.

One of these surveys supplies the only information available on the literacy rate in the village, the results of which are summarized in Table 2.4. These figures are for one hamlet only, but it is the largest hamlet and also the one in which both the elementary school and the Fundamental Education Center are located. Thus, one would expect illiteracy to be lower in this hamlet than in any other in the village, and the findings should be discounted slightly on these grounds. Based on a census figure of 692 persons in Ap Dinh who are 15 years of age or more, the survey information indicates that slightly less than one-third (30.5 percent) of this population is illiterate. This percentage drops if only the age group 15 to 45 years is considered—

based on the census count of 479 persons, less than one-fifth (18.6 percent) of the people in this age group is illiterate. This indicates not only a surprisingly high degree of literacy at the village level in the age group 15 to 45 years, but also that important strides are being made to reduce illiteracy, because the rate of illiteracy is much higher among the older inhabitants. Children and young adults clearly have many more opportunities to acquire at least a minimum knowledge of reading and writing than were available to their parents. Officials at the provincial, district, and village levels maintain continuing pressure on those who are illiterate to attend literacy classes, and this pressure seems to be producing results.[1]

TABLE 2.4
Illiterate Persons, 15 Years of Age and Over, in the Hamlet of Ap Dinh, 1958

Age	Men	Women	Total
15 to 45	13	76	89
15 and over	43	168	211

Source: Survey conducted by Fundamental Education Center, Khanh Hau, 1958.

Over half the inhabitants of Ap Dinh (58.1 percent) aged 15 or over attended school for one year or more. The remaining 11.4 percent of that age group who could read and write were trained in adult literacy classes. This again is based on the survey conducted by students of the Fundamental Education Center. The findings, summarized in Table 2.5, show a pattern that is probably true throughout Viet Nam, i. e. , that there is a higher percentage of men than women among those who receive some formal education, and that the men generally attend school for a longer period of time than women. Among the men who had formal education, nearly half (48.0 percent) attended school for more than three years, but only 36.7 percent of the women attended that long. Only very small proportions of men or women had more than six years of school, and, in both cases, the percentages attending school this long were about the same.

TABLE 2.5
Years of Attendance by Inhabitants of Ap Dinh Receiving Formal
School Education

Years of attendance	Men No.	Men %	Women No.	Women %	Total No.	Total %
1	13	5.3	9	5.7	22	5.5
2	42	17.2	29	18.4	71	17.7
3	72	29.5	62	39.2	134	33.3
4	39	16.0	26	16.5	65	16.2
5	46	18.9	21	13.3	67	16.7
6	9	3.7	1	0.6	10	2.5
7	9	3.7	2	1.3	11	2.7
8	5	2.0	2	1.3	7	1.7
9	7	2.9	5	3.2	12	3.0
10	-	-	1	0.6	1	0.2
11	1	0.4	-	-	1	0.2
12	1	0.4	-	-	1	0.2
Total	244	100.0	158	100.0	402	99.9

Source: Survey conducted by Fundamental Education Center, Khanh Hau, 1958.

In terms of educational development, therefore, the prospects for the village appear fairly bright, although it should be kept in mind that this village is relatively well-provided with school facilities and that the data available refer only to the hamlet in which these facilities are located. Nevertheless, with this high degree of literacy, the learning process can continue and new ideas can be introduced through printed materials which people can use. Moreover, there is evidence that the campaign against illiteracy is making substantial progress, and, from all indications, the degree of illiteracy will continue to go down at a fairly rapid rate.

Mobility of the Village Population

In view of the apparent population pressure which Khanh Hau faces in the years to come, population mobility assumes great importance. For Viet Nam as a whole, it is equally important, for the willingness of people to move into new parts of the country, and in many cases, enter new kinds of occupations, will greatly influence the rate of economic growth. One of the more prevalent views of Vietnamese society regards the people as closely bound to their ancestral villages, reluctant to move no matter what incentives. The war years have altered this to some extent, for an unknown number of people did leave the villages to seek safety elsewhere. The most outstanding recent example of this, of course, was the flight of more than 800,000 refugees, many of them coming as entire villages from the north to the south at the end of hostilities. From a longer range point of view, the very existence of Vietnamese in the delta reflects their historical migration from the homelands in the north. Still, the question of whether or not people move freely under other than emergency conditions remains largely unexplored.

The survey conducted in Khanh Hau[2] sought to collect some information on mobility, and each household head was asked if he would be willing to move from the village. The initial replies seemed to bear out expectations; that is, 69 percent answered that they were not willing to move, and 31 percent responded that they were. The reasons given for the replies, however, do not all show a positive attachment to the village as such. Nearly half (46.7 percent) gave answers that reveal a link to the village in some respect, but they ranged from attachment to the village (6.7 percent) anddesire to be near the ancestral tombs (5.6 percent) to less strong statements, e. g. , the respondent was satisfied with his present life (12.2 percent), preferred farming (7.7 percent), liked rural life (14.4 percent), or was the only son (1.1 percent). Thus, for a majority, it is a preference for rural life, rather than identification with a particular village, that is the chief attraction. Over one-fourth of those who were unwilling to leave offered old age or physical weakness as their reason, and another fairly large group (14.4 percent) felt they had no hope of succeeding in a town or city. Significantly, all replies in this last category came from lower-class households. The balance of the replies indicated either a dislike of urban life or a dislike of change. In general, middle- and upper-class households heads gave replies that indicated a more positive attachment to the village than was true for the lower class, which would be the expected pattern of response.

In addition to asking if villagers would be willing to move the survey also asked if relatives of the households in the sample had moved and, if so, where and into what kinds of occupations. The replies showed that not quite half (44 percent) of the households had relatives who had emigrated from the village during the past fifteen years, totalling 67 persons for the 100 households in the sample.[3] For the village as a whole, this would mean upwards of 400 persons had emigrated, and probably morej since the replies usually did not include any members of the migrants'nuclear families. Projecting this same rate over the next ten yearss it would provide a sizeable offset to the probable population increase, but, even making allowance for the crudeness of the estimate, it does not seem large enough to fully counter it.

A majority of the households having emigrant relatives (61.4 percent) had only one in this category, and while 13.6 percent had three, none had more than that number. Most of these were sons or daughters, brothers or sisters. More distant relatives were not identified if they did in fact move from the village. The division between men and women was almost equal.

The occupations of those who have moved cover a wide range, but the largest and broadest category—private business— accounts for over two-fifths (43.2 percent) of them. This would include retailing, petty commerce, industry, and general private employment, of which petty commerce and the last-named are the most important. Only 7.4 percent have gone into industrial work. The army has taken 16.4 percent, but government employment has absorbed only 9 percent. Taxi and cyclo driving,"[4] domestic service, and students account for only small percentages in each case. The other large category (20.9 percent) consists of young girls leaving to marry into families living in nearby villages, which as remarked earlier is probably matched by an immigration of similar size, although this point was not specifically investigated.

In terms of destination of the emigrants, Saigon drew the largest group (40.3 percent), followed by the provincial capital of Tan An (28.3 percent), and other villages in South Viet Nam (22.4). Since Saigon is Only 50 kilometers from Khanh Hau, the radius of emigration from the village is not very large in this case—probably over three-fourths of those who have left Khan Hau have travelled less than 50 kilometers in doing so. The time pattern created by the emigrants shows no startling variation from year to year, largely because it is spread over a long period. Approximately half of them have left since 1950, which is mid-way in the period covered by the question. The only year to show an unusually high number of migrations is 1949, when nearly one-fifth of the total apparently moved from the village. This may have been a year of heavy exodus generally, but it is also possible that dates beyond the past three or four years are vague in the minds of the respondents. There was fighting and insecurity in the area in the late 1940's and early 1950's, so this is more likely a general, not a specific, time identification. In any event, with this one possible exception, movement away from the village seems to have taken place steadily over time. Though undoubtedly affected to some extent by unsettled conditions, it also reflects that many sought new opportunities and made efforts to move into new occupations.

In addition to those who have left the village to take up new homes elsewhere, there is some movement from the village on short trips. The survey found that 16 percent of the heads of households had never visited Saigon, but the rest make at least a few trips to the city during the course of a year. The largest group (59 percent) reported that they had gone to Saigon once or twice in the previous year, and one-fourth of all household heads went more often than that. The reasons for making these trips fell into three main categories, with pleasure accounting for about one-third, and business and visits to relatives taking slightly smaller shares. Together, these three three reasons covered nearly 90 percent of all trips to Saigon by villagers in the previous year.

This type of survey data provides at least a beginning perspective on the nature and extent of mobility from the village. On this basis, there appears to be resistance to mobility on the part of a majority of villagers, but even so, there is a substantial number of household heads who seem willing to move, and another substantial number of villagers who have already moved. Those who have moved have gone into non-farm pursuits for the most part, but without further detailed information it is hard to say how much of an adjustment the new occupations may have entailed. They have not travelled far, but this is partly because the largest group among them went to Saigon, which is not too far from the home village. Contact with Saigon by those remaining in the village is not frequent, but a majority of the villagers seem to get there at least once a year. General improvement in transportation conditions will probably increase the frequency of such visits in years to come. On the whole, therefore, the quantified picture is of a population that cannot be called highly mobile, but one which shows evidence of having a substantial margin within it who are wilting to move if conditions warrant and permit it.

There is some opportunity to obtain new land to the west along the Cambodian border. Word of this filters into the village via posters placed in the council house and by word of mouth from relatives and friends. In at least one case, relatives living in the new area were the major source of information. However, no two families seem to have the same version of what the opportunities actually are—different households held differing expectations of the amount of land and the amount of monetary aid that would be forthcoming from the government. This un certainty as to the facts tends to reinforce inclinations toward immobility. Many are too poor to take a trip to the area and investigate for themselves, so they wait for more positive news than has been available. The poorest households, and therefore the ones who would stand to benefit most from the move, feel they cannot risk a move into an unknown area without some means of supporting themselves until a start can be made. As bad as things may be in Khanh Hau for them, they prefer the known to the unknown.

Those who have left for the new area have tended to be

identified by one or both of two main characteristics. First, some have been without land in Khanh Hau, but owned buffalo and farm implements which they rented out to others. This advantage gave them extra confidence, and therefore, greater willingness to try a fresh start. The other identifiable characteristic was that some were fortunate enough to have relatives in the new area. These could at least provide a place to stay, help the newcomers obtain a grant of land, and make the start less hazardous in general. Thus, some equipment and on-the-spot contact emerged as important attributes and were commonly mentioned as prerequisites by those who expressed a desire to move but who felt uneasy about doing so.

A common attitude among those who have moved was the expectation that they would return to the village and retire when they could afford to do so. The new settlement areas are still raw frontier in many respects and most of the migrants left wives and families behind. Some said they hope to develop land in the west in order to have land to pass on to their children; others think in terms of saving enough from farming the new lands to be able to buy land in Khanh Hau. In either case, the migrant often thinks of his move as a temporary one. He tends to think of the opportunity as one which will some day enable him to re-establish himself in the village of his birth, and, to this end, he is reluctant to sever his ties of family and acquaintanceship. Not only is this true of those who have moved west to participate in the resettlement program, but is often mentioned in connection with those who have gone to Saigon and Tan An to work in commerce and industry.

Supplementing the earlier findings, therefore, mobility appears to depend to an important extent on the availablity of full and accurate information, assurance that means exist to support the migrant until he is reasonably settled, and preferably, the presence of relatives or friends to ease the adjustment to the new situation. The fact that the migrant may consider the move a temporary one is less important economically than that, for one reason or another, he moves from less to more productive opportunities.

A more subjective approach to this whole problem of mobility was provided by another portion of the survey data.

Heads of households were asked what ambitions they had for their children—an open-end question which could reveal the extent to which they hoped to see their children continue the patterns of village life which constituted their existence at the present time. Significant differences appeared in the replies of the different socio-economic classes, but from one-fifth to one-third of the respondents in all classes expressed a desire to see their children educated "as much as we can afford" or "as much as possible." A significantly larger proportion of middle- and lower-class families wanted vocational training or a factory job for their children, while over one-fourth of the upper-class families looked to government service as a desired occupation for their sons. Upwards of 10 percent in all classes condemned farming as an occupation and expressed positive desires that their children avoid it; less than 10 percent in all classes expressed a preference for it for their children. The other single most interesting result was the low priority given a military career, probably the most readily available means to economic advancement open to youth from the lowest income levels in the village.

These replies tend to show that there exists a desire to widen opportunities through education for the succeeding generation, and that a large majority prefer non-farm occupations for their children. Agains one is led to suspect that people would be willing to move from the village if known and easily available alternatives existed elsewhere. The chief problem is not one of immobility, but one of a lack of such alternatives.

3

THE RESOURCES OF THE LAND

Foreign visitors, comparing the size of the rice fields found in the delta region south of Saigon with those in other parts of south and southeast Asia, tend to be struck by their apparent extensiveness. The impression is enhanced if the visit is made during the months of November to January, when the rice is ready for harvest and the ripe grain hides the boundaries between the fields. Nevertheless, this appearance of spaciousness or lack of population pressure on the land is misleading, as examination of the tenure arrangements reveals.

The basic data on land ownership are provided by the tax rolls of the village for the year 1957, as amended in 1958, and the provincial land registers, and these are summarized in Tables 3.1 through 3.4. The total area of rice land in the village is 925. 91 hectares, or. 29 hectares per capita based on a population count of 3,241 persons in 1958. Communal land held by the village is relatively insignificant, and, together with one very small piece of land owned by a village pagoda, amounts to only 29 hectares. This corresponds with a general tendency in the southern part of Viet Nam for communal lands to be a very small proportion of the total cultivated area. One pre-war estimate put this proportion at only 3 percent, as contrasted with estimates of 25 percent and 21 percent of the total cultivated area in central and north Viet Nam respectively,[1] and in Khanh Hau communal land is actually 3.1 percent of the total rice land.

Land Ownership Patterns

The ownership of land is undergoing some change as a result of the government's agrarian reform program. To illustrate what effect this has had, Table 3.1 presents the ownership pattern that existed up to 1958, after which time the land belonging to the largest landowner in the village was redistributed.

TABLE 3.1
Ownership of Rice Land in Village of Khanh Hau, 1958

Area of holdings (hectares)	No. of land-owners[a]	% of total village land-owners	Cumulative % of total village land-owners	No. of hec-tares	% of total village hec-tares	Cumulative % of total village hectares	% of total village hectares excluding largest[b]	Cumulative % of total village hectares excluding largest[b]
Less than 2	60	46.2	46.2	52.23	5.6	5.6	8.7	8.7
2-3.9	25	19.2	65.4	70.82	7.6	13.2	11.8	20.5
4-5.9	14	10.8	76.2	69.71	7.5	20.7	11.6	32.1
6-7.9	11	8.5	84.7	75.71	8.2	28.9	12.6	44.7
8-9.9	6	4.6	89.3	54.03	5.8	34.7	9.0	53.7
10 or more	14	10.8	100.1	603.41	65.2	99.9	46.4	100.1
Total	130	100.1		925.91	99.9		100.1	

a. Includes communal and pagoda land.
b. Hectares of rice land, excluding those owned by the largest landowner, totaled 602. 05 hectares.
Source: 1958 tax rolls, village of Khanh Hau.

Prior to 1958 the rice land in Khanh Hau was owned by 130 land-owners of all sizes, of whom 31 were non-residents of the village and 99 were residents. The single largest landowner held 323. 86 hectares, or 35. 0 percent of all the rice lands in the village. Beyond this, the ownership of the land was divided into much smaller shares. For example, the average holding of all landowners was 7.1 hectares, but if the largest owner is excluded, this drops to 4.7 hectares. Under this ownership pattern slightly more than three-fourths of all landown-ers (76. 2 percent) owned about one-fifth (20. 8 percent) of the rice land, and all of these owned less than six hectares each. One-fourth of all landowners (25.4 percent) owned less than one hectare, and only 14 landowners (10.8 percent) owned more than ten hectares. Thus, aside from the one large village landlord, landownership meant fairly small holdings. The Lorenz curve in Figure 3.1 illustrates the degree of inequality in this pre-1958 pattern.

There does not seem to be any basic difference in the pattern of ownership between resident and non-resident landownersj once the biggest landowner (who was a non-resident) is excluded. Nearly half the landowners in each of these categories own less than two hectares, and over 90 percent own less than ten hectares. Tables 3.2 and 3.3 show the basic data for each type of landowner, butwith the largest landowner still included. If his holdings were excluded from consideration, resident landowners, comprising 76.7 percent of all landowners, would own 68.0 percent of all rice land, instead of the 44.2 percent shown in Table 3.2. Correspondingly, non-resi-dent landowners would hold 32 percent instead of the 55.8 percent shown in Table 3.3. Although non-resident landowners would thus still hold a slightly disproportionate share of the land in the village, it is not nearly as great as might be expected. Nothing in all this, however, should imply that land ownership was widespread among village residents, for the number of resident landowners represents only 16.8 percent of all households in the village in 1958, keep-ing in mind that this was before redistribution of land under the program of agrarian reform.

The land owned by non-residents is worked by tenants, but, as shown, the typical non-resident landlord in this village is not a large landowner. In general, he is someone

FIGURE 3.1
Lorenz Curve Distribution of Landownership Prior to Land Reform

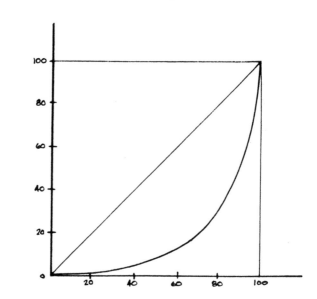

Percentage of total number of landowners

Source: Table 3.1.

living in a neighboring village or in the chief provincial town of Tan An, and in some cases, the land has come to him through inheritance. For example, a woman born in Khanh Hau may marry outside the village, and upon her parents' death may inherit a small piece of land in Khanh Hau. Typically, she and her husband will keep title to this land, but since they cannot conveniently work it themselves they will rent it to someone in Khanh Hau, often a sibling or other relative. People in Khanh Hau may also acquire land in other villages in the same way. However, some non-resident landowners purchased land as an investment and as a

TABLE 3.2

Ownership of Rice Land in Village of Khanh Hau, by Non-Resident Landowners, 1958

Area of holding (hectares)	No. of non-resident landowners	% of non-resident landowners	% of all village landowners	No. of hectares	% of area held by non-resident landowners	% of area held by all village landowners
Less than 2	14	45.2	10.8	18.12	3.5	2.0
2–3.9	1	3.2	0.7	3.24	0.6	0.3
4–5.9	5	16.1	3.8	26.38	5.1	2.8
6–7.9	4	12.9	3.1	29.14	5.6	3.2
8–9.9	1	3.2	0.7	8.43	1.6	0.9
10 or more	6	9.4	4.6	431.34	83.5	46.6
Total	31	100.0	23.7	516.65	99.9	55.8

Source: 1958 tax rolls, village of Khanh Hau.

TABLE 3.3

Ownership of Rice Land in Village of Khanh Hau, by Resident Landowners, 1958

Area of holding (hectares)	No. of resident landowners[a]	% of resident landowners[a]	% of all village landowners	No. of hectares	% of area held by resident landowners[a]	% of area held by all village landowners[a]
Less than 2	46	46.5	35.4	34.11	8.3	3.7
2–3.9	24	24.2	18.5	67.58	16.5	7.3
4–5.9	9	9.1	6.9	43.33	10.6	4.7
6–7.9	7	7.1	5.4	46.57	11.4	5.0
8–9.9	5	5.1	3.8	46.60	11.1	4.9
10 or more	8	8.1	6.2	172.07	42.0	18.6
Total	99	100.1	76.2	409.26	100.0	44.2

a. Includes communal and pagoda land
Source: 1958 tax rolls, village of Khanh Hau.

supplemental source of income. Several of the non-resident land-owners for Khanh Hau are retired school teachers or minor officials in the provincial government. But the total impact of all these owners is very small, for nearly two-thirds of them (64.5 percent) owned less than six hectares, and their total holdings were only 6 percent of the total rice land in the village.

Landownership prior to 1958 was therefore a matter of one large owner and many much smaller ones. Although the average size of holding by resident landowners was somewhat smaller than that for non-residents, the broad pattern in each case was much the same. In the village itself, only a small proportion of the households owned land, and the amounts held by most of these were small.

The Program of Agrarian Reform

Viet Nam is currently attempting to alter the basic land ownership pattern in rice lands under provisions contained in the ordinance on agrarian reform issued in October 1956.[2] Essentially, this limits the ownership of rice land to a maximum of 100 hectares per owner, and requires that owners who hold more than this sell the excess to the government.[3] The government reimburses the owners with a ten percent cash down payment and the balance in three percent government bonds, redeemable after twelve years or exchangeable for shares in government enterprises.

The government, in turn, undertakes to redistribute this land to the former tenants of the owners. The basic rule here is to permit each eligible tenant to buy the land he once rented, up to a maximum of 5 hectares.[4] The landowner is free to choose the 100 hectares he wants to keep, and these need not all be in one area or one village. After he has made his choice, the tenants on the remainder which will be redistributed may file applications to purchase the plots they have been leasing. Once his application is approved, a former tenant receives a temporary deed which will become permanent when he has completed payments on his new land. The government retains actual title, however, until the land is fully paid for. Payments vary with the estimated value of the land; in this village they ranged from VN\$ 12,000 to VN\$ 15,000 per hectare,[5] and are spread over a six-year period. The first installments are due at the end of the calendar year in which the first crops are harvested.

In the entire province of Long An, where Khanh Hau is located, there were 38 landowners who held more than 100 hectares at the time the land reform program went into effect. The size of these individual holdings ran from slightly more than 100 hectares to 2,300 hectares. Only one landowner in this group owned land in Khanh Hau, and 231.6 hectares of his land were made available for redistribution to his former tenants in the village. Applications were first made in November 1957, and temporary deeds were handed to the owners-to-be in June 1958. The results of the redistribution of land are shown in Table 3.4.

TABLE 3.4
Distribution of Land under the Agrarian Reform Program,
Village of Khanh Hau, 1958

Size of holding (hectares)	No. of recipients	% of total recipients	No. of hectares	% of total distributed
Less than 0.50	13	8.7	4.6	2.0
0.50-0.99	35	23.5	27.4	11.8
1.00-1.49	36	24.2	44.5	19.2
1.50-1.99	24	16.1	39.9	17.2
2.00-2.49	18	12.1	39.6	17.1
2.50-2-99	10	6.7	26.8	11.6
3.00-3.49	7	4.7	22.4	9.7
3.50-3.99	1	7.7	3.5	1.5
4.00-4.49	3	2.0	12.7	5.5
4.50-4.99	1	7.7	4.8	2.1
5.00 or more	1	7.7	5.4	2.3
Total	149	100.1	231.6	100.0

Source: Village records of land redistribution.

The 231.6 hectares of land were divided into 200 plots of varying size, and these were distributed among 149 former tenants. The average amount received was 1.6 hectares, and the median recipient had 1.4 hectares. Nearly three-fourths (72.5 percent) of these new owners received less than 2 hectares, and this accounted for almost exactly half (50.2 percent) of the total amount distributed.

While a majority received only one piece of land, about one-fourth (26.2 percent) received two pieces or more, and one person received as many as five pieces. This is probably a fairly good measure of the dispersion of land holdings among tenants. Of equal interest is the range in the size of parcels and amounts which were distributed. The smallest piece of land received was a minute .01 hectares, and the largest was 3.40 hectares, which may give an approximate idea of the size of the working units. In comparison, the smallest total amount of land received was .14 hectares and the largest was 5.4 hectares (slightly in excess of the announced legal maximum).

The land redistribution was therefore far from egalitarian, since it was based on the amounts the tenants had rented, but the degree of inequality in the redistribution was less than that among other landowners in the village, even when the holdings of the former largest landowner are excluded. This is seen in the Lorenz curve patterns of Figure 3.2. However, since most of the recipients did not own land before, and since most of them received small total quantities of land, the land reforms increased the number of land owners but had little effect in equalizing the over-all village land-owning pattern. This is seen in Figure 3.3, where Lorenz curves compare the degree of equality in landownership before and after the land redistribution. There the pre-reform curve is only slightly lower than that which represents landownership after redistribution. The glaring inequality due to the single largest landowner has been removed, but, since the land was redistributed with a pattern of inequality all its own, a large number of landowners still hold very small amounts of land. A large percentage of the landowners therefore still account for only a relatively small percentage of the total rice land in the village.

Village reaction to the land reform program varied

FIGURE 3.2
Lorenz Curve Distribution of Land Received
under the Agrarian Reform Program and the Land Ownership
Pattern in Khanh Hau
Prior to Redistribution, Largest Landowner Excluded

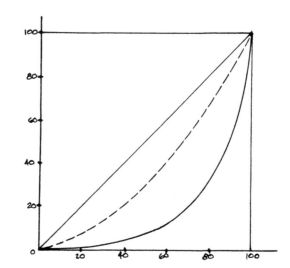

Percentage of total landowners-recipients

Key: Recipients of land under agrarian reform program Ownership prior to land redistribution.
Source: Tables 3.1 and 3.4

predictably with the status of the person being questioned. Most landowners had too little land to be worried over any further redistribution and did not identify themselves with the large owners who had been forced to divest themselves of some land. The fortunate tenants who received something through the reform program obviously were pleased with it. Since Viet Minh land reforms were never carried out in the area in which the village is located, there was no

FIGURE 3.3

**Lorenz Curve Comparison of Landownership before and after
Land Redistribution**

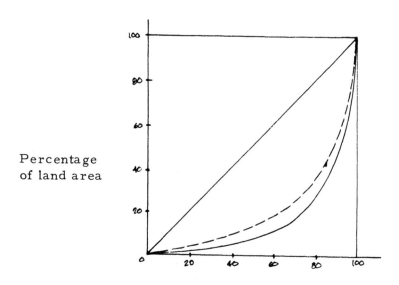

Percentage of total landowners

Key: After land redistribution
        Before land redistribution
Source: Tables 3.1 and 3.4.

resistance to paying for the land. Such resistance has occurred in places where the Viet Minh had given land to farmers at an earlier date. There also did not seem to be any pressure to sabotage the program by refusing to take land that was offered, again a problem which has arisen in other parts of Viet Nam. The criticism one did encounter came mostly from the landless laborers and tenants who did not benefit from the land redistribution, and who still comprise a majority of the village population. This took various forms, but usually it reflected bitterness at being left out, together with a feeling that the land reform did nothing to help them, the poorest of the village householders.[6]

Fragmentation and Inheritance of Land

Because the delta is an area of "recent" settlement, fragmentation of the land has become a problem only in the last decade or two. In fact, the villagers themselves tend not to regard it as a problem even at the present time. During the 1930's, some of the larger landowners began to sell portions of their land, often to their former tenants, and this process was somewhat accelerated during the war years. Landownership patterns of the present time are beginning to reflect the division and re-division of land by heirs to this recently acquired land. Since some people hold adjacent pieces of property, any spatial fragmentation that may occur through inheritance does not seem an irremediable affair. Instead, the main effect of inheritance has been to reduce the size of the land units that are passed on from one generation to the next.

Inheritance practices with respect to land do not appear rigid or fixed by strong tradition. Land is usually divided equally among all children, male and female, but this mayvary. Villagers report that younger sons are often favored over other children, and that they tend to inherit not only the family house, but also the largest or choicest piece of land. Even in the custodianship of the *Huong Hoa*,[7] the land dedicated to the maintenance of the cult of the ancestors, oldest sons may be passed over in favor of other children. Thus, while it is not possible to measure the quantitative importance of the different inheritance practices, there is ample evidence that the oldest sons do not inevitably occupy the favored position in the family, and nothing approaching primogeniture seems to exist.

When the number of children is large, and the land to be divided between them is small, adjustments must be made to deal with the situation. Most people leave some kind of will, but unless a great deal of property is involved, it is not considered worthwhile to register the will in the provincial office. Wills usually set forth the general conditions of the distribution, but they do not make detailed statements of what each heir will receive. The adjustments, therefore, are made by the heirs through agreement among themselves. In the kind of situation just referred to, a farmer may leave a small piece of property to one child with the stipulation that he give the other children some rice from each year's harvest, the amount to be decided by agreement among all the children.

Another variation is multiple use of the land. If no specific plots are willed, the heirs sometimes set out markers indicating each one's portion, and each then farms his own share. There are almost no instances of heirs pooling land and labor and operating a joint enterprise. Where the land area is too small to share and work individually, the heirs sometimes rotate the use of land from year to year. The person working the land during any given year keeps all the proceeds of the land; those who do not have the use of the land for that year make their living in any way available to them, usually as farm labor. If the land area is too small to divide or to work on even a rotation basis, the heirs may decide to sell it, either to some member of the family or to an outsider. This would happen, for example, when the already small shares in a small plot of land are passed on to the next generation of children, in which case there would be too many people to rotate use of the land or to benefit much from renting it. Much of the ill feeling existing between and within some village families can be traced to disputes over land. In spite of this, most village landowners continue to leave wills whose provisions are general and somewhat vague, thereby providing fuel for future difficulties.

Considering the bits of evidence available, it seems probable that fragmentation, both spatially and in terms of size of land holding, has been increasing in the village over the last thirty years. One indication of this is in the survey finding that over two-fifths of all farm households in the village report they operate less land now than when they first began, but less than 10 percent report increases in the amount of land they operate. While this is not due to inheritance in all cases, it supports the general impression that land per household or per capita is declining. This would be expected with the growth in landownership which has taken place and the tendency for villagers to divide their holdings more or less equally among the children. Offsetting this are such factors as the ability of a few families to acquire more Land than they inherited, some migration from the village, and a high death rate among the children of some families. On balance, however, the trend toward fragmentation is greater than the offsetting factors.

Farm Tenancy

The basic data on farm tenancy were taken from the rent contract records of the village and apply to a period before the agrarian reform program went into effect. An over-all view, shown in Table 3.5, gives the distribution of tenant holdings and the cumulative percentages of tenants who rent less than the indicated amounts. For the village as a whole, the average tenant rents 2.4 hectares, but the median tenant has only 1.7 hectares. Before agrarian reform, 642.13 hectares were rented to tenants, amounting to 69.4 percent of the rice land in the village.

TABLE 3.5
Size of Tenant Holdings, Khanh Hau, 1955-56

Size of holding (hectares)	No. of tenants	Cumu- lative % of tenants	No. of hectares	Cumu- lative % of hectares
0 - . 9 9	47	17.60	31.94	5.1
1.00-1.99	93	52.43	115.94	22.9
2.00- 2.99	48	70.41	109.63	40.0
3.00-3. 99	25	79.77	83.66	53.0
4.00- 4.99	22	88.05	93.45	67.6
5.00-5.99	14	93.25	73.03	79.0
6.00- 6.99	11	97.37	70.00	89.9
7.00- 7.99	2	98.12	14.60	92.2
8.00- 8.99	1	98.87	8.68	93.6
9.00-9.99	3	99.62	28.20	98.0
10.00 or more	1	100.0	13.75	100.1
Total	267		642.13	

Source: Rent contract records, Khanh Hau village.

Looked at from the other side, the typical landlord was also small-scale, as shown in Table 3.6. The average landlord rented out 12.6 hectares, but if the single largest landlord and the communal lands are both excluded from the totals, the average drops to 7.2 hectares. The median figure is 4.0 hectares if the same two landlords are excluded. Before land reform, the single largest landlord accounted for 41.2 percent of all the rice land that was leased to tenants.

The degree of inequality in the distribution of tenant rights can be seen from the cumulative percentages of tenants and the area of land they lease, shown in Table 3.5. The same thing appears graphically in the Lorenz curve in Figure 3.4. Although the degree of inequality is less pronounced than in the case of landownership, a few of the larger tenants have a disproportionately large share of the rice land that

TABLE 3.6
Size of Ricefields Rented to Tenants by Landlords, Khanh Hau, 1955-56

Size of area rented (hectares)	No. of landlords	Cumulative no. of landlords	Cumulative % of landlords
0 -1.99	8	8	16
2. 00-3.99	12	20	40
4. 00-5.99	14	34	68
6. 00-7.99	2	36	72
8. 00-9. 99	4	40	80
10. 00-11.99	-	40	80
12. 00-13.99	2	42	84
14. 00-15.99	2	44	88
16. 00-17.99	1	45	90
18. 00- 19.99	2	47	94
20. 00 or more	4	51	100

Source: Rent contract records, village of Khanh Hau.

FIGURE 3.4
Lorenz Curve Distribution of Holdings by Farm Tenants Prior
to Land Redistribution

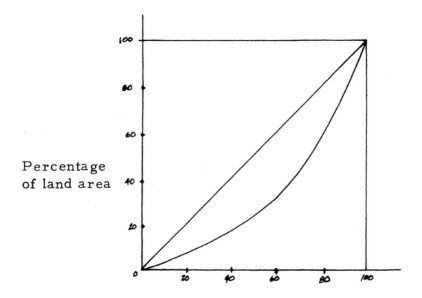

Percentage of total farm tenants

Source: Table 3. 5.

is rented. For example, over half the tenants (52.4 percent) rent less than two hectares each, and this amounts to less than one-fourth (22.9 percent) of all the land that is rented. At the other end of the scale, the upper 12 percent of tenants account for nearly one-third of the total rice land that is rented.

The typical tenant has only one landlord, but some have more. For the village as a whole, 15.7 percent have two or more landlords, and one has as many as four, but this is clearly not a common practice. On the other hand, probably a slight majority of landlords have more than .one tenant, although this is simply an inference drawn by comparing the size of typical tenant holdings with the median amounts rented out by landlords. In a sample of fifty tenant households in the village, over one-third (36 percent) replied they rented part or all of their land from relatives. Thus kinship factors effect the landlord-tenant relationship of a substantial proportion of the tenant population of the village, but there is some evidence that this is not necessarily advantageous to the tenant.

Land Values and the Rent of Agricultural Land

There are no firm data on land values in the village because land changes hands through sale only infrequently, and when it does no record is kept of the price of the sale. Approximations must therefore be made from the recollections of villagers who have knowledge of past sales, and also from the estimated values owners and tenants place on their own lands. The latter method was used in the sample survey in which each respondent was asked to estimate the value of farm land he either owned or rented.

The replies produced a range of values of from VN$ 12,000 to VN$ 30,000 per hectare, the amount in each case depending mainly on the productivity of the land and, to a lesser extent, its location. The median value of two-crop land was VN$ 25,000, or about one-third more than the median estimated value of one-crop land of VN$ 19,000 per hectare. This corresponds closely with estimates obtained in conversations and interviews outside the sample suvey, and the tendency for replies to bunch around the two figures of VN$ 20,000 and VN$ 25,000 per hectare offers some grounds for confidence that actual land values are of this order of magnitude.

As noted earlier, values set on the land redistributed under the agrarian reform program and paid by the government varied only from VN$ 12,000 to VN$ 15,000 per hectare, depending on the relative quality of the land. The top price of VN$ 15,000 was paid for land as good as the most productive found in the village. Using the estimated values from the survey, the best land redistributed brought the owner only fifty percent of its probable market value, but the poorest pieces of land probably brought anywhere from seventy percent to their full market value. Land reform therefore resulted not only in a loss of income to the large landowners, but also the forced sale may well have cost them one-third or more of the current market value of land affected by the sale.

The measurement of rents actually paid on rice land in the village presents several problems. Here data are available in the rent contracts, a record of which is kept on file with the village council. However, for reasons to be given below, the annual rents given in these records are probably subject to some degree of error. Under the agrarian reform law, the area of each plot of land that is rented is recorded along with the expected main crop yield of the land, and up to 25 percent of this main crop yield may be stipulated in kind as the annual rent payable to the landlord. Actually, every rent contract in the village sets the rent at 25 percent of the main crop yield. Payment may be made either in cash at the market value of the paddy, or in kind, at the option of the landlord. Provision is also made for a scheduled reduction in rents during poor crop years.

Although rents were reported to be as high as 40 percent or more of the main crop yield in pre-war years, conditions in the countryside during the period prior to independence did much to temper the attitude of landlords toward their tenants. In many areas no rents were collected for several years, the lives of landlords were threatened, and in some places land was confiscated and redistributed to the former tenants by the Viet Minh. The agrarian reform program of the present government does less violence to the landlords' interests, but the main purpose remains protection of the tenants against their landlords, and as administered at the village level the tenants' interests generally receive greater weight. For all these reasons, the leverage of the landlords has been steadily reduced.

It has not been completely eliminated, however, for tenants are still anxious to retain their tenant rights. These rights have traditionally been fairly secure, and current rental contracts generally run for five years with an option to renew. Still they can be discontinued after that time, and, under certain conditions, they may even be terminated upon as little as six months notice.[8] This leaves some bargaining advantage still in the hands of the landlords, and villagers report that many landlords and tenants reach private agreements on rents which differ from the formal contract conditions. As might be expected, attempts to measure the extent and nature of these undercover arrangements met with considerable evasiveness, despite a general willingness to admit that they did exist.

One approach to this was to abandon percentage estimates and instead ask individual tenants the actual amounts of paddy they paid in rents, later converting these to rough percentage estimates based on the probable normal yields of all types of production in each case. This resulted in rent estimates that ranged from 15 to 25 percent of total yield, not just the main crop, fully as often as it did in estimates above 25 percent. To illustrate this, a few farmers were able to grow vegetables on paddy land before or after the rice crop, but paid rent only on the normal yield of the main paddy crop. Tenants renting land from non-resident landlords frequently reported themselves particularly fortunate because such landlords were generally less well informed on actual yields and accepted lower rents than resident landlords would accept. It was also the practice of some resident landlords to fix rents at 30 to 35 percent of the first crop, but to exact no payment from a second crop if the tenant raised one. Thus tenants who reported paying rents of 35 percent of the main crop may have actually paid 25 percent or less on the total yield for the crop year. Finally, over one-third of the tenants rented land from relatives, and since some in this group actually received the use of land rent-free, the average rent paid by this group is probably somewhat below the legal maximum of 25 percent of the main crop. To complicate matters further, the paddy harvest of 1958-59, the period during which field work for this study was carried out, was badly hit by drought and plant disease, with the result that many landlords reduced rents by 25 to 40 percent in cases where tenants had lost a large portion of the harvest. The foregoing comments on rents, therefore, reflect the recollections of village residents of conditions during previous periods.

Taking all these factors into account, and assuming that landlords still retain a certain amoung of leverage in dealing with their tenants, actual rents in this village probably run between 25 and 30 percent of the main crop, but a smaller percentage of total yields. A few tenants may pay more than this, but a larger number probably pay something less.

Summary

Although there is variation in the land tenure arrangements found in different parts of Viet Nam, the data for the village used in this study should be typical of an important part of the rice-producing region. They tend to show that most farm households, whether tenant or landowner, have relatively small pieces of land with which to work, and this basic pattern has not been significantly changed by the program of agrarian reform. In this village, the largest landowner has been forced to redistribute a major portion of his lands to his former tenants, and the average recipients in this case had been renting less land than average tenants in the village. Land reform has therefore affected some of the poorest tenants, and this should ultimately result in greater net incomes per household. Aside from the small amounts of land which they are able to rent, farm tenants are not subject to many of the limitations found in other underdeveloped areas. The land reform program seems to have had some effect in keeping rents in check, and the prevailing political climate plus the provisions of the rent contracts make tenure relatively secure against arbitrary eviction by the landlords.

4

RICE PRODUCTION IN KHANH HAU

Preparation for the Planting

From November to May or June, the village lands lie brown and arid, the wells are dry, the streams brackish and low. The thick black clay hardens, cracks, and turns to a fine dust that filters everywhere. It is a time of inactivity, barring a few desultory pursuits, and the lack of income from agriculture production brings idleness to the non-agricultural sector as well. The importance of the single resource, land, in the thinking of the villagers imposes a severe seasonal limitation to their conception of the alternative occupations available to them. Although many look for laboring jobs in the nearby towns, the chances for success are limited. When their land is unproductive, they can find few ways to productively employ their existing capital goods or labor; their expectations are therefore almost totally bound up in their hopes for a heavy crop of rice in the year ahead. There are several things which reinforce this kind of outlook, but the traditional reliance on the yield of the land is undoubtedly the main factor in the villagers' acceptance of the seasonal idleness enforced by the lack of water.

It would be inaccurate to say that the advent of the rainy season is accompanied by a large flurry of activity—few aspects of village life could be described in those terms. However, as the villagers begin to prepare for the coming crop, they give increased attention to such matters as repairing the bundings[1] and readying the various farm implements for use. If the rainy season is late, as it was during the years 1957 and 1958, there is great concern that the crop will suffer thereby, and the waiting is accompanied by increasing tension and anxiety. Until the month of April, however, a lack of rain is accepted with equanimity. Part of the village land can produce two crops of rice a year, and those who farm these lands are particularly anxious to see the rains arrive. A late rain will possibly eliminate one of the crops and reduce their total yield by anywhere from one-third to one-half. For this reason, those who have double-crop land may anticipate the rains and begin the seeding process after the first few rainfalls in the hope that the steady, regular rains will follow soon after. This can be a costly gamble, but it is undertaken by many. As a rule, however, the actual work on the farms begins with the first clear indication that the rainy season has finally arrived.

One of the first aspects of the production process one notices is its individualistic character. Farming is a household affair, and the nuclear family is the basic working unit. This does not mean that farmers rely only on the labor of the nuclear family for the rice crop, but that fully cooperative effort on the scale of more than a single household is relatively rare. One example of rather rigid organization into nuclear family working units involved two brothers who, together with their families, lived under the same roof. Despite this, the brothers maintained separate kitchens and worked their adjoining land individually. They were relatively poor and did help each other in some of the farm work such as irrigation of the fields, but they kept their incomes separate and felt basically responsible only for their own fields. This is not a typical situation, but it illustrates the extremes to which a nuclear family orientation can be carried. When siblings own or rent adjoining pieces of land, they occasionally remove the bundings separating their land in order to permit joint irrigation. However, markers are used to identify the boundaries of the land, and aside from this rather minor gesture in the direction of cooperation, the rest of the operations are carried on separately and the harvest divided in accordance with the individual property claims and rights.

Although farmers are inclined to use the seed rice of the previous year, the decision on what varieties of rice to produce in the growing season ahead rests on other factors as well, all of them variable to some extent. Perhaps the most important of all is the quality and level of the land which each farmer has at his disposal. Since water control is the key to the production of rice, the farmer whose land is "high" relative to the fields surrounding it must face the fact that water will drain from his land first. This means that his alternatives

methods employed, a digression on the availability of capital equipment is in order. Survey data provide some basis for measurement
of capital accumulation, as well as the distribution of its ownership.
Table 4.1 shows ownership of the main kinds of tools and implements among landowners, landowner/tenants, and tenants, as well
as for the village as a whole. According to the findings tabulated
there, most farmers in all tenure categories have the small tools
and implements they need but are much less well equipped in large
items such as plows and harrows, threshing sledges, rollers, water
wheels, and winnowing machines. The best equipped group, the
landowner/tenants who own some land and also rent some land,
come from both the middle and upper socio-economic classes, but
they are not a very numerous group, and the full significance of
their apparent superior position in terms of capital accumulation is
therefore uncertain. On a straight socio-economic class distribution,
however, middle class households appear to be equipped as well
as or better than upper class households.

Less than one-fourth of all village households own major implements, but eliminating those who do not have land to farm, it is
probable that around one-third of the farm households own them.
This bears out the observation that many farmers, even some of the
largest, do not own their own equipment but instead hire others to
supply the labor and implements for such things as plowing and
harrowing. For the well-to-do farmer, this is probably a matter of
choice, but for the others it probably represents inability to purchase. Ownership of major implements is linked with ownership of
draft animals, usually water buffalo, for the services of animals and
implements are rented together, and it is pointless to own a plow,
for example, if you must rent the services of a buffalo to pull it.

In another sample of twenty householdss established for the
purpose of making a study of family budgets, about one-third of the
households reported annual expenditures of around VN$ 1,000 for new
farm equipment. Since most farm tools are made primarily of wood, they
wear out rapidly, and these annual expenditures represent cash outlays
to replace worn-out equipment rather than net additions to the stock
of capital goods. Minor repairs are generally done by the farmer

TABLE 4.1
Ownership of Farm Tools and Implements, by Land Tenure Category
Village of Khanh Hau, 1958

Implements	% of land-owners	% of tenants	% of landowner / tenants	% of all villagers
Plow (Vietnamese)	12.5	11.3	33.3	10.0
Plow (Cambodian)	25.0	31.8	66.6	22.0
Harrow	31.2	38.6	83.3	28.0
Waterwheel	31.2	18.1	83.3	18.0
Winnowing machine	43.7	11.3	50.0	15.0
Rice mill (hand-operated)	37.5	13.6	50.0	15.0
Digging tools	81.2	75.0	83.0	51.0
Hoe	81.2	79.5	66.6	52.0
Saw	81.2	75.0	66.6	51.0
Hammer	81.2	84.0	83.3	55.0
Axe	81.2	88.6	66.6	57.0
Sickles	87.5	84.0	100.0	58.0
Threshing sledge	43.7	61.3	100.0	40.0
Mortar	31.2	18.1	83.3	18.0
Roller	37.5	31.8	66.6	24.0

himself, and he does not consider them as a maintenance cost in any sense. Replacement occurs at different times for different pieces of equipment. For example, those purchasing new plows reported that they expect them to last from three to five years, after which time the wooden parts will require replacement. Water wheels last only two years and need rather constant maintenance during that time because the narrow-width paddles on the wheel break frequently. Harrows last longer, most farmers reporting that they are not replaced more often than every seven years. Small tools wear out in two or three years, and threshing sledges last about the same length of time. The mats used inside the threshing sledges, however, are replaced every year.

Outside of these simple, locally made implements, there are no other important pieces of farm capital in the village, with the exception of one gasoline pump used for irrigation. Mechanization of farm operations has not proceeded very far in Khanh Hau, and not only has little been introduced, but most farmers believe that the size of their fields makes the obvious kinds of mechanization, such as tractor plowing, unsuited to their situation.

Besides farming, there is some investment in rice mill machinery several households own manually operated sewing machines, one household owns a cart and another a small motorcycle bus, the artisans all own their tools, and storekeepers maintain inventories of consumer goods. Little of this is versatile in the sense of being useful in several different occupations. Further, there is little indication that the stock of these capital items is increasing over time, or that larger numbers of people are becoming familiar with their use.

Thus, the means of production are simple, limited in terms of variety, and in the case of major farm implements owned by less than a majority of the households who use them. However, ownership is not a function of land tenure statuss and tenants as well as landowners buy their implements if they can. It has never been customary for landowners in this area to supply their tenants with tools, nor have they been used collectively to any great extent. In terms of experience, therefore, private ownership of the means of production is an established practice at all levels in the society.

Plowing and Planting

Having settled upon a planting design which will take into account the above-named variables, the coming of the rains permits the actual work to begin. When the ground has become soft enough, the farmers start the preparation of the seed beds. This operation is undertaken with great care in order to bring the composition of the soil to a very fine consistency. This often requires that a seed bed be plowed and harrowed, given a two-day rest to "air" the soil, and then plowed and harrowed a second time. It is also sometimes rolled with long rollers which seem to break up the ground further and leave it smooth for the planting. When the soil has been broken up and worked into the desired condition, most of the water standing in the seed bed is drawn off, leaving a smooth, muddy surface on which the seed will be sown broadcast.

Plowing, harrowing, and rolling are done with basically wooden implements drawn by a pair of water buffalo. The kind of plow now in common use has a metal plowshare, but the rest is made entirely of wood. The harrow looks much like a large wooden rake with short wooden teeth on its broad crossbar and is drawn flat against the ground. Those who must rent the plowing and harrowing service do so at rates and under conditions which appear to be uniform throughout the village. The standard working day for a pair of buffalo is five hours, from six in the morning until eleven, and for this, plus the services of the owner as plowman and the use of a plow or harrow, the current charge is sixty piasters. This limit of a five-hour day is designed to protect the strength and general health of the buffalo, but the farmers, too, complain of the heavy nature of this kind of work and seemingly welcome the limitation for themselves fully as much as for their animals.

There is one other variation in the organization of the plowing and harrowing work, open to the landowners who hire labor to work their fields for them. Generally, these men own their own buffalo and their own implements but hire farm labor to use them on their land. For this they pay the straight rates for general labor, i. e. , thirty piasters a day plus two meals, but they stay in the fields themselves to supervise the work directly for much of the working period. Nowhere was there evidence of cooperative use of buffalo or pooling arrangements to eliminate the need to pay cash for plowing and harrowing services.

The size of the seed bed seems to bear no special relationship to the size of the rice fields, but the amount of seed used per hectare is fairly standard. Farmers in this village use approximately one *gia*[3] of rice seed for every one-and-a-half hectares of mature rice plants, which compares with the former ratio of three *gia* of seed for every one-and-a-half hectares of plants which was typical during the period before the widespread use of fertilizer.

Before sowing the seed rice, the grains are soaked in water and allowed to stand for two or three days until they begin to germinate. During this time they are kept damp but do not stand in water. When they have begun to sprout they are ready to be sown, and at that time the seed beds are drained. The bed is not allowed to fill with water until the plants are well established, usually several days after sowing.

In plowing the seed bed, prior to seeding, the farmers tend to prefer shallow plowing to deep plowing and try to limit the depth to around five centimeters. This differs from their practice in plowing the larger fields, but it essentially reflects their concern that the top layers of the soil be broken up very fine so that the seedlings will be able to grow quickly and take root firmly. This means easier plowing, but the saving in time is partially offset by the need to plow the seed beds more than once.

After the seed beds have been planted, and while the seedlings are growing large enough to be transplanted, the farmer begins to plow his main fields. Once again the crucial problem of water intervenes to affect decisions on the timing of activity and cash outlays. Ideally, the steady, soaking rains should have arrived by early June, and the seedlings for the first crops of rice should be ready for transplanting by the end of June or early July. For best plowing conditions, the farmers like the land to be moist and easy to handle, but not covered with water. A good deal of plowing is done when the fields are completely covered with water, but this is regarded as a sign that the farmer was caught by a sudden heavy rain or was slow in getting his plowing started. In 1957, as again in 1958, the rains came late, and although the seedlings were ready for transplanting, the ground in the main fields was still hard and dry.

Some of the villagers began to plow their land, even though it was still dry, in the hope that the rains would come and they could then begin to transplant immediately. Still others began to pull their seedlings in the hope of selling them in neighboring villages where some transplanting could take place. When this was attempted, however, a large portion of the seedlings were destroyed, because the hard earth held them fast, and pulling them out destroyed the root system. In addition, many seedlings had acquired a kind of rot from staying closely packed in the seed bed for too long a period. As a result, few of the first seedlings were really in saleable condition, and the market opportunities for even these were extremely limited because the same dry conditions were widespread in the Long An area. In many cases, the village cattle were allowed to graze in the seed beds, there being little else to do with the plants. Finally, a few of the farmers who held lands adjacent to the streams or canals attempted to irrigate their fields, plow them, and then transplant. Once again the lateness of the rains thwarted these attempts to save the crop, for the lack of rain kept the streams brackish and heavily salted. The transplanted seedlings irrigated with this water promptly died.

These events vividly illustrate how vulnerable the villages in this area are and how critical is their dependence on adequate and timely water supplies. During the dry season the underground supplies of water lie so far beneath the surface that irrigation wells are not feasible. The principal river system, to which the streams and canals in the vicinity flow, is the Vaico (see Figure 1.1), but since it is affected by tides it is an unreliable source of fresh water through the year. With only minimum amounts of rain, the heavy clay soils of the village remain too hard to permit much in the way of substitution of crops other than rice. Two or three bad years in a row can easily wipe out the meager reserves of the villagers and reduce their living standards to pitifully low levels. Still, given their basic resources, there is little they can do on their own to alter this dependence on the rains or to minimize the disastrous effects of their tardiness.

When the year is a normal one, and the rains arrive on schedule, the plowing is geared to the time when the seedlings are expected to be ready for transplanting. Most of the villagers appear to prefer to plow their fields to a depth of eight to ten centimeters, although this is by no means unanimous. Some express the belief that even deeper furrows would be desirable but feel that to plow any deeper would be too great a strain on the draft animals and the men. Others tend to regard the eight to ten centimeter depth as optimum, tested over time and justified by extensive experience. There is obvious concern about this problem of depth of the furrow and awareness that it can affect the size of the yield. A common complaint raised by those who must rent the animals and plowing service from others is that the hired service is inferior to that performed by a farmer for himself. Those renting their animals and labor to others will try to minimize the effort and plow only half the desired depth unless closely watched. Shallow plowing of this kind is widely believed to effectively reduce the potential yield of a farmer's crop. Men who have conscientiously built a reputation for plowing at proper depths are, therefore, in great demand.

The preparation of the main fields for transplanting is much less carefully done than for the seed beds. Fields are plowed only once, although they are harrowed twice—the second time at right angles to the first. The length of time it takes to complete the plowing and harrowing depends to some extent on such factors as the condition of the buffalo, the depth of the furrow, the condition of the soil, the plowing skill of the farmer, and the speed at which he pushes his animals. However, a normally strong pair of buffalo will be able to plow one hectare in five or six days, according to most of the estimates which were made. There was somewhat greater variation in the estimates of the time required to complete the harrowing, and the answers here ranged from one to three days per hectare.

When the plowing and harrowing have been completed, the farmer must decide the proper time to transplant the seedlings, assuming that conditions are "normal" and that some element of choice remains to him. To a minor extent this is tied to an interpretation of omens, for the lunar calendar lists certain days as unlucky or unpropitious for the conduct of affairs. While the major concern is the condition of the land and the seedlings, the farmer if possible will avoid starting his transplanting on a day marked as unlucky on the calendar. Actually, there are not too many of these days spread throughout the year, and the avoidance of them will not seriously handicap a farmer to the point, say, of jeopardizing the success of his crop. The only other ritual observation, excluding the major agricultural festivals held by the village as a whole, is the practice observed by some farmers of making a small token sacrifice of rice and cakes just before sowing the seed beds. This is not universal practice in the village, although a majority of the villagers probably observe this minor ritual.

The "Descent to the Fields"

The stark dependence of man upon nature is painfully evident in a rice village like Khanh Hau, and while as individuals the villagers do not go to great ritual lengths to secure the favor or protection of heaven at the start of the planting season, the village as a whole does make an effort to insure that the spiritual forces are propitiated and benevolently inclined. This takes expression in three major village rituals honoring the god of agriculture (*Ong Than Nong*), the first of which occurs regularly on the 15th day of the 6th lunar month at the *dinhs* of both Ap Nhon Hau and Ap Dinh "A." Ideally, this should fall after the first rains have come and after the first seedlings are well established and nearly ready for transplanting, but sometimes, as in 1958, the rains have not yet arrived by the date set for this ritual. It is considered unlucky at such times to talk about the lack of rain, but the general concern that is felt by all adds a note of urgency and anxiety to the ceremonies that the outside observer senses rather than hears explicitly, and, in a sense, the affair almost becomes a rain-making ceremony.

This first festival, the "descent to the fields" (*Ha Dien*), is intended to officially open the planting season and to request the god of agriculture for good crops. A cement altar dedicated to this diety is located behind the *dinh*, flanked by a smaller altar on each side, and it is here the ceremony takes place. All the traditional ceremonial accoutrements (altar tables, candlesticks, weapons, urns, etc.) are brought outside for the occasion, and the long cement slab that forms the main part of the altar is completely covered with offerings of food. The ceremonies start at noon and follow the same ritual form as the festival of the village guardian spirit (*Cau An*). Village notables present their respects before the altar of the god in order of precedence according to rank and follow this by a brief visit to the sanctuary inside the *dinh*, which is specially opened for the occasion. Since this ceremony takes place at the same time on the same day in both hamlets, village officials cannot be present at both. In actual practice, therefore, the hamlet chiefs of Ap Nhon Hau and Ap Cau participate as representatives of the village council at the Ap Nhon Hau *dinh*, while the members of the village council attend the ritual at Ap Dinh "A." The ceremonies are soon completed, and the participants return to their homes after the feast which follows has ended. Unlike the *Cau An*, the "descent to the fields" does not attract onlookers, and there is no attempt to make the ceremony an occasion for general celebration—e. g., no opera performances or other amusements are provided. This, together with the brevity of the ceremony and the time of day at which it is held, makes the occasion seem a lesser one, but it is probably accurate to regard it as a dignified and serious affair that is in keeping with the importance which attaches to the success of village agricultural activity.

Transplanting

When the seedlings are ready for transplanting, a small crew of men goes to the seed beds and begins pulling the young plants and preparing them for transport to the fields. Usually the farmer and two or three helpers are all that is needed, but this varies with the size of the fields to be planted and the need for speed in getting the job done. The main part of the task is to uproot the plants, usually twenty to thirty at a time. Holding them in a single bunch, the farmer slaps them sharply against the leg or foot to remove the loose mud that clings to the plants. This done, he binds them together with a piece of straw which he takes from a bundle carried at the waist and sets the plants in a neat central pile nearby.

One of the men in the group will be assigned the job of carrying the plants to the rice fields, usually one of the younger men. Several bunches are then tied together and carted away on a shoulder board. Once in the field, the young plants are left in sizeable piles scattered about the field in a pattern which will make it convenient for the transplanting. The young plants will survive for three days out of the seed bed, and they are often uprooted one day and moved on the next. Leaving them in the water of the field, however, offers some protection from the hot sun. The uprooting and carrying to the field can therefore move faster than the transplanting with some margin of safety for the plants.

Most of the transplanting done in the village is carried out by women and young girls organized into teams of varying size, again depending on the size of the job and the need for speed. Some farmers, working the smallest fields, transplant with family labor alone or with the help of neighbors, but most of them, both tenants and landowners, hire transplanting help. Cooperation exists, but it is not the most common pattern of organization.

The usual work day for women is from six to eleven o'clock in the morning and from two to five o'clock in the afternoon, but women sometimes work in the fields well into the middle of the day, or in the evening until dusk. Assuming the normal working day of eight hours, it requires ten to twelve women to transplant one hectare of land, or an out-of-pocket cost to the farmer of from VN$ 200 to VN$ 240 per hectare, plus the cost of the meals.

The transplanting job itself is tedious work, and during the summer months of July and August lines of young women, knee-deep in the water of the paddy field, are seen everywhere bending to the task of setting the plants in the black ooze. Their conical hats bob up and down in the steady rhythm of their work; their faces are almost completely hidden in the towels they use to protect themselves from the sun. Villagers say it was once the custom to sing planting songs as they worked, but this practice has died out in recent years. Even without it, the scene typifies, if any single activity can, the traditional, toil-demanding peasant world of southeast Asia.

There is a certain amount of variation in the spacing of the plants, because the women transplant them four at a time a single pace apart, which works out to from eighteen to twenty-five centimeters between plants. While the transplanting is going on, most farmers are on hand much of the day to supervise the work. The contractor for the transplanting teams is responsible for the quality of the work done by the women and will personally supervise his workers in the fields. Even so, farmers complain that the women sometimes become careless and do not set the plants in the ground firmly enough or do not space the plants properly. The pace of the work is well enough established that there are no complaints about slowness or idling on the job, but, as in the case of plowing services, the concern is over careless and sloppy work.

The Use of Fertilizers

Once a field is plowed and harrowed and the seedlings have been transplanted it receives relatively limited care. Small landowners and tenants and their families find work as laborers on the fields of others which are not yet fully prepared or transplanted. Because there is great difference within the village in terms of the varieties of rice grown, the kinds of land available, and access to water for irrigation, and therefore opportunities for double-cropping, there is almost continual activity from the time that farmers first begin to plant. While some farmers are transplanting seedlings, others are just beginning to prepare seed beds for the late-starting, longer-maturing varieties; still others are at the plowing and harrowing stage. The activity of the villagers at this stage shifts from their own fields to those of others and back, according to the particular phase of cultivation in each, but the over-all effect is one of steady work on the crop in a village-wide sense.

The single most important concern for the crop after transplantation centers around the use of fertilizer, and it would be difficult to overemphasize the importance which the villagers attach to this activity. The precise date at which fertilizer was first introduced into the village cannot be fixed with accuracy, but in the fifteen to twenty years during which it has been widely used there, it has become thoroughly established. The farmers believe that it is indispensable to the success of their crop, favorable conditions prevailing, and it is used by even the very poorest tenant farmers. Some villagers have stated that their land has become so used to fertilizer that they could grow nothing without it. Whether they believe this literally or not, the example they chose to use indicates the complete acceptance chemical fertilizers have won.

While the use of chemical fertilizer is virtually universal, the manner in which it is applied reflects a number of interrelated considerations. In questioning the villagers about their use of fertilizer, it quickly became evident that their present techniques are the result of local experimentation over time rather than any specific technical advice received. As far as can be determined, no study of the soils in the village has ever been made for the purpose of recommending kinds or amounts of fertilizer to be used. The merchants who first introduced fertilizer in the area may have had some idea of what kinds would have suited the soils found there and perhaps offered general advice on quantities to be applied, but this is all. Some importing firms handling chemical fertilizers have prepared pamphlets of instruction in the use of their products.'[4] Unfortunately, these often use only the chemical terms and are probably not widely understood at all. Farmers know only the brand names or commonly used general terms.

Whatever the instructions or the conditions under which fertilizers were first introduced, their present use in the village represents an adjustment to past experience. Farmers are aware that the quality and composition of the soil varies from place to place and that all fertilizers do not perform equally well in all situations. There is also a tendency to vary the time at which the fertilizer is applied, depending on the kind of soil and the variety of rice being grown on it. At present, the two kinds of chemical fertilizer most commonly used are ammonium sulphate and phosphate tricalcique. The phosphate tricalcique is regarded as the best for most areas, and it is by far the most popular. Moreover, there is a strong loyalty to particular brands, and fertilizers are identified by their brand names rather than by their chemical compositions.[5]

Although the villagers have carefully observed and

compared results in arriving at their present methods of application, actual use of chemical fertilizer depends heavily on financial considerations. A farmer may feel that he should use more than he does but settles for a smaller quantity which represents all he can finance by borrowing or from savings. The villagers do not fertilize early in the growing season, so their need for fertilizer comes late, at a time when their reserves of paddy or cash are at the lowest level. In past years, the price of fertilizer in the local market has risen over 400 percent by the latter part of the growing season, reflecting the very low price elasticity of demand for this product in this area. Villagers are fully aware of this meteoric rise in the price—it has been a regular occurrence for years—but most of them are powerless to anticipate or forestall it. The reasons for this are dealt with more fully in the section on credit, but briefly, this seems due both to the efforts of merchants to take advantage of short supplies locally and the generally poor credit facilities available to small farmers. The situation was substantially improved in 1958 when fertilizer became available in the village through two programs of aid. These had the effect of somewhat holding down the price of fertilizer in Tan An and other market centers, and those unable to benefit from the aid programs directly had the advantage of an indirect increase in the local supply of fertilizer. However, these programs may not continue to function on a regular basis, in which case the relief granted in this one year may have been only temporary.

Recognizing that actual use depends partly on past experience and partly on financial factors, and that these vary with the individuals concerned, there are some general patterns which the villagers follow in applying chemical fertilizers. The most common method seems to be one application of phosphate shortly after transplanting, and one application of ammonium sulphate a month or so before the harvest. Some vary this by reducing slightly the amount of phosphate used after transplanting and adding a second application midway in the growing season. The date for using the ammonium sulphate is also subject to some variation. Farmers described their preference in terms such as "just before ears of grain appear," or "when the plants are about one meter high," as well as "a month or so before harvest. " In some cases, farmers mix the phosphate and ammonium sulphate together, in a ratio of two-thirds phosphate and one-third ammonium sulphate, and use it in a single application at the same time the ammonium sulphate is normally applied by itself, e.g., before the harvest. This practice, however, is limited to fields where the lowest quality rice is being grown.

Most farmers mix the phosphate with rice husks and also with ashes when they are available. The ammonium sulphate is not mixed with either rice husks or ashes but is scattered in the fields directly. There is a general feeling that more fertilizer brings larger crops and that the villagers are not able to buy as much as they could profitably use. This attitude, coupled with the financial limitations already noted, brings wide swings in the amounts used per farm year. Specific examples of use in this case are not particularly meaningful, although they may be indicative of what is done within a broad range. For example, some report they use as little as 100 kilos of phosphate and 25 kilos of ammonium sulphate to the hectare; others state they use 250 kilos of phosphate and 150 kilos of ammonium sulphate to the hectare. The ratio between phosphate and ammonium sulphate, however, generally ranges between two to one and three to one, with relatively more phosphate being used on the good land and relatively more ammonium sulphate going into the poorer land.

Slightly before the introduction of chemical fertilizers, the villagers sometimes used a mixture of buffalo manure, ashes, straw, and dead leaves on their rice fields, although it is hard to estimate the extent to which this was done. These natural fertilizers are not now used to supplement chemical fertilizers in the rice fields, although they are still used in village gardens. Contrary to the practice in much of Asia, villagers have never used night soil in fields and use it only to a limited extent on their gardens. Most farmers do not use it at all. This seems to be due more to the fact that there was never enough available for use on a wide scale than to objections on grounds of health or cultural inhibition. Present-day use of animal manure is restricted to the quantity they can collect themselves, and villagers do not buy large amounts from others. In fact, there is some surplus in the village which is sold for use in the vicinity of My Tho, where gardening opportunities are greater.

Water Control

In addition to the application of fertilizer, which does not require a great deal of work time despite its importance in the minds of the villagers, only one other activity is considered critically important between the time of transplanting and the time of harvesting. This is the control of the level of water in the fields, and the farmers hold definite opinions on what the proper level should be. If the rains continue steadily through the months of a normal rainy season, water control becomes a relatively simple matter of permitting it to drain away until the proper level is reached, around ten centimeters in depth. The villagers believe that more water than this will prevent the full growth of the rice plants; less than this will cause the plants to dry out. If the rains are too generous, the drainage problem can become serious, because the water level in the streams and canals will rise to that of the adjacent fields.

In recent years, however, the problem has been that of too little rain, and to maintain the proper level in the fields water must be lifted from streams and canals by some mechanical means. Three methods are in use at the present time—the scoop or basket lift (*gau*), the water wheel (*quat nuoc*), and, for the past two years, one gasoline pump. The use of each of these is essentially a function of the kind of water problem an individual farmer happens to have, although use of the automatic pump is also related to ability to rent a service which is quite costly.

If the water has to be raised a half-meter in height or less, from source to the field itself, the locally made wooden water wheel is the most efficient and economic means available at the present time. Its use is somewhat inflexible, however, because the diameter of the wheels most commonly made in the village and the surrounding area will permit a maximum lift of only one-half meter. When the level of the streams or canals drops, or where the fields to be irrigated are particularly high, other methods become necessary. Traditionally, this has meant using the scoop or basket lift, operated either singly or by two men.

In a one-man operation, a long triangular scoop is suspended from a tripod and put in place over the source of water. The operator stands behind the scoop and literally shovels the water into the irrigation ditch which leads into his fields. The height to which water can be lifted by this device is limited by the height of the tripod from which the scoop is hung. Generally, this will be a little higher than the water wheel, but it is less efficient than the basket lift operated by two men. This latter consists of a single conical basket, waterproofed with shellac, with double ropes attached to each side. The operators stand on high ground next to the source of water, usually on a bunding, and dropping the basket into the water, they will fill it, lift it, and then swing it so that it empties into the higher fields. The men work in unison, the basket suspended midway between them on the ropes that each one holds. They work rhythmically, quickly, and with apparent ease. The whole operation resembles children turning the ends of a skipping rope, with the difference being that the rope in this case never makes a complete revolution. The height to which water can be raised by this method is limited by the length of the ropes attached to the basket and the distance separating the two men who operate it. Still, it is effective under most situations which are likely to occur. The chief drawback is its slowness and the greater physical effort needed to irrigate a given piece of land.

The main contribution of the mechanical pump so far has been as a substitute for the scoop or basket lift. The length of the intake hose on the pump gives it the flexibility needed to raise the water to any height needed. The capacity to deliver water is limited by the diameter of the hose, but it requires no human effort beyond that needed to carry it to the water sources. On fields located some distance from the water source, it can throw a stream of water farther and with far greater force than other methods, but it is also the most expensive way to irrigate. The single pump available in the village rents at a rate of sixty piasters per hour, but despite its cost it is in almost constant use during times when its particular features are needed.

Comparing the mechanical pump with the water wheel under those conditions where the water wheel can operate, the latter currently gives superior performance. The capacity of the water wheel could be changed by altering the diameter of the wheel and width of the spillway, but even with the dimensions of those commonly in use, it can lift more water per time period (e. g. , an hour) than pumps with a hose diameter of ten centimeters. This means not only a faster irrigation job but a cheaper one as well. The operation of a water wheel generally requires two teams of two men each. A team peddles the axle of the wheel, thus turning the wheel, and the blades attached to the wheel lift a steady stream of water into a spillway which empties into the higher field. The alternate team rests while the first is at work, and the teams exchange each hour during the working day. This type of work is considered heavier than general farm labor and is therefore paid at a slightly higher daily wage rate. Reports on this vary, but the most commonly quoted wage is forty piasters a day plus two meals. Assuming an eight-hour day, the cost of lifting water by the water wheel would be VN$ 160 plus the cost of eight meals. Eight hours rental for the mechanical pump would cost VN$ 480, and the volume of water lifted would be less than that of the water wheel, again assuming the capacities which prevailed in the village at the time of the study. Clearly, the mechanical pump offers no advantages, other than the saving of physical labor, in those situations where a water wheel can be used.

Village farmers use several methods of getting water from the source to where it is needed. When the field to be irrigated is next to the stream there is no problem, and the water is spilled directly into it. But when the fields are located some distance away the procedures become more complex. Sometimes the fields closest to the stream or canal are irrigated first, and the bundings separating them from the field to be irrigated are breached so that the water may pass from the first field to the one beyond it. At other times, a temporary narrow trench will be built by mounding up a new bunding parallel to the more permanent one. The water is then pumped or spilled into this trench and carried to the distant field. This method has the advantage of enabling the water to be brought to the far field more quickly, since it does not require filling one field to irrigate another. It has the disadvantage, however, of requiring the work necessary to build the temporary bunding, and the owners of the fields closest to the water source are sometimes opposed to having these built in their fields.

Maintaining the proper levels in the different fields

requires a certain degree of common planning and common agreement. Irrigating only the high fields, and then letting them drain into the lower adjoining fields to provide an optimum level of water in all, would minimize the costs of irrigation in terms of both physical effort and money outlay. Coordination of efforts, however, does not always function smoothly. Village officials say there are numerous disputes each year over water problems, although village records do not support their statement that many of these are brought to the village council for settlement. Still, considering the importance of water to the success of the rice crop, together with the pattern of conflicting land claims and varying land use, friction over water use seems inevitable, particularly in view of the relatively weak sense of cooperation and community identification evidenced in this and other village activities.

Other Types of Intermediate Care

Applying fertilizer and maintaining the proper level of water in the fields are the main concerns during the growing season, but some farmers also spend time repairing bundings and doing a minimum amount of weeding. Villagers say that many of the fields in the village never require weeding, and observation confirms this claim. Fields in this category appear neat and well tended, although nothing in particular has been done to keep them that way. Even if weeds grow, farmers do not bother to take them out if the water level in the fields is high. With adequate water they feel that the rice plants will grow even with weeds. If the water level is low, however, farmers will weed the fields once, when the rice plants are about one-and-a-half to two feet tall. It would be very difficult to weed after this, but when the water is down the farmers feel one weeding is necessary to protect their crop. What weeding is done is performed by women, and the weeds themselves are used as fodder when collected.

In addition to weeding, a certain amount of time is devoted to setting the young plants more firmly in the earth after the transplanting has been completed. The transplanters do not always exercise uniform care when setting out the plants, and after a few days some of them become loose and require extra attention to root them more firmly in the field.

A week or ten days after transplanting, the plants that have failed to survive are replaced with new young plants. This may be due to plant disease or to poor handling, and while the need for replacement may vary a good deal, a certain amount is always necessary. The time spent on this seems to average two to three days per hectare.

Types of Crop Damage

Although weeding is not considered a particularly important problem at the present time, village farmers are becoming increasingly concerned over two sources of crop damage—insects and plant disease. The chief insect damage is caused by a small green winged insect, about the size of a rice grain, known locally as the *con ray*, and also by a small worm or borer known by the general terms *con sau* or *con bo*. In its adult stage, the *ray* attacks the leaves and stem of the rice plant, and the worm lives inside the stem and gradually rots the plant. Older farmers say that there was no trouble from insects twenty years ago or more and seem to feel that they became more numerous about the time they first began to use chemical fertilizers. They say they do not believe that the fertilizer is entirely responsible and would not give up its use as a means of eliminating insects, but they have noted an apparent coincidence of these two factors. The villagers have no traditional remedies to control insects, and before insecticides were introduced into this part of Viet Nam they relied on sudden and very heavy rains to rid their fields of insects.

The use of chemical insecticides is of very recent origin, within the last few years. At the present time they are used only by the more progressive farmers who generally have large cultivated areas to protect. Small farmers say insect damage in their fields is too slight to worry about, and they have not used insecticides very extensively. The insecticides used are purchased in bulk from the market in Tan An. The Fundamental Education Center has placed a portable sprayer at the disposal of the villagers, but aside from this there has been no special effort to either encourage or instruct the farmers in the use of insecticides. The insecticides seem to be effective against the *con ray* but not against the *con sau*.

The villagers believe this is because the *con sau* stays protected inside the stem of the plant, while the *con ray* is more exposed. Some farmers, however, doubt that the insecticides are effective against either.

The only plant disease that has been troublesome is a rust known by the Vietnamese term *tim*. Where this strikes, the leaves of the rice plant turn brownish-red in color, and plants affected fail to mature. It was particularly severe during the 1958-59 growing season, and an estimated seventy percent of village fields were hit by it. The result was a village-wide average decrease in yield to one-half of normal amounts, within even greater loss in individual cases. The combined effect of lack of rain and late rain, with a corresponding reduction in opportunities to grow two crops, and the attack of *tim* was disastrous for many. Fields located near streams or along the main highway (where there is more water than elsewhere) seemed to be less affected than fields located anywhere else in the village, but all varieties of rice were susceptible, and the incidence of the disease does not seem to be related to such factors as fertilizer use or plowing depths.

The villagers do not know the cause of the disease, but they do have several explanations for it. One is that it is related to the time of transplanting. Fields transplanted early in the season do not seem to be affected as much as those transplanted later. When the rains arrive late in the spring the transplanting is delayed, and these fields seem affected to a greater extent. This would also be consistent with the observation that the fields close to water are relatively free of infection, since these would be the first fields planted. Another explanation is that the disease is caused by ground that is "too cold. " This does not refer to the temperature of the air, which was hot and sunny for the growing season, but to the temperature of the ground which, in some unexplained way, was thought to be unusually cold during the night. Still another linked the plant disease with the damage caused by the *con sau*, while others held that atomic bomb testing was partly responsible.

It is significant that plant disease and insect damage were never linked to the specific actions of supernatural forces, and there was no reliance on ritualistic remedies as a primary defense against them. There does seem to be a strong belief that these kinds of crop damage can be controlled by means known to foreign technicians and that their cause lies in the soils, the weather, the farming methods, or some similar factor.

Just as there is no common understanding of the cause, there is no agreement on the remedy to be applied. For the most part, villagers do not attempt to do anything to stop the disease. A few have tried increasing the amount of fertilizer but without noticeable effect. The disease is a relatively new thing, and people are just beginning to appreciate the damage it can bring. Its impact on the village during the 1957-58 growing season was much less than in 1958-59, and before that the disease was of minor importance. Its sudden and crippling effects on production have aroused a great desire for knowledge to combat the disease, and while villagers resign themselves to the fact that their present knowledge is inadequate, almost every conversation brought a request for outside help.

Harvesting

The first crops to be harvested have usually ripened by mid-September, and from this date on harvesting is an almost continual activity throughout the village. The organization of this stage of production is, as in the earlier stages, essentially an individual household affair. This does not imply that families rely exclusively on the labor supplied by family members, but it does mean that harvesting is not a community-wide or cooperative affair as it is normally carried out.

If a family cannot provide enough labor to complete the harvesting by itself, it will hire additional labor for the job. In doing so, however, it will either apply through the Labor groups used to obtain labor for transplanting or will choose and hire directly. Farm labor is paid in kind at harvest time, and the rate of pay is one *gia* of paddy for each ten *gia* that a harvest team cuts and threshes. Outside of rent payments and the bride price, this is the only important non-monetary payment regularly made in the village at the present time.

A harvesting team usually consists of three persons, although in small fields there may be fewer than this, and in large fields there may be several teams. The team divides into those who cut the grain and one who threshes it on the spot. Threshing is almost always done by both men and women. Reapers cut the plants one at a time and then place fifteen to twenty plants together in a large bundle for the thresher.

Depending on whether the harvest will be threshed by hand or by buffalo, the reapers use one of two kinds of sickle for their work. A small curved sickle is most commonly used, because it is functionally related to the more prevalent hand threshing. It is crudely fashioned and set in a rough wooden handle, with a blade no more than eight or nine inches in length. If threshing is to be done by buffalo, the grain is cut shorter, near the ears, and a longer bladed sickle of unique design is used. The blade is attached to the handle in a "V" type connection, and the stem is literally wrapped around the blade as it is cut. Actually, the former is replacing the latter implement because the hand threshing technique, which has become almost universal, requires a longer stem on the plants, and the sickle can cut closer to the ground.

Threshing is done in the fields themselves, which is a change from the traditional method in which the grain was brought to the house and threshed in the farmer's yard by buffalo. A few families still use this old method, but they are a very small minority. The newer threshing device consists of a wooden sledge—a hard wood and bamboo frame about five feet long, set on wooden runners. Reed mats are placed inside this on the bottom and around each of the four sides of the sledge. A wooden grill is then set inside the box formed by the four sides and about four or five inches from the bottom. The thresher picks up a bundle of grain, holding the ears of grain away from him, and swings the bundle down partially on the edge of the sledge and partially on the wooden grill. By beating the grain in this way, the kernels of paddy are jarred loose and fall through the grill onto the mat which lines the bottom. Usually three or four swings are necessary to get enough grain from each bundle to satisfy the thresher. Since he is paid in kind in proportion to the amount he harvests, it is to his direct advantage to get as much from the threshing process as possible. Finally, a screen of mats seven or eight feet high is placed around three sides of the sledge to block the wind and prevent grain from being blown out of the sledge during the threshing. Traveling through the countryside at harvest time, the visual effect is one of numerous small sail boats bobbing about in a brownish-yellow sea.

It is difficult to estimate the efficiency of the threshing under these conditions. Examination of sheaves of grain that have been threshed shows that many retain a few good grains. This loss is partially offset by the work of the gleaners who comb the fields for stalks with grain still on them and thereby reduce some of the waste, even though the farmer himself does not regain it. The gleaners are usually children from the village, together with a few old people from the poorest families. Farmers do not restrict this activity, and it is not reserved for any families or groups in particular. The traditional method of threshing with buffalo ensures a larger yield, but it also increases the proportion of empty husks included For this reason, paddy threshed with buffalo brings a lower price per *gia*.

As the paddy collects in the threshing sledge, it is emptied regularly and measured by standard containers of one *gia*. After measurement, to determine the amount to be paid the-harvesters, the paddy is emptied into baskets and carried to the farmer's home to be dried. Women or girls, usually members of the family, do the carrying.

As the paddy is measured, a small amount may spill on the ground. Some attempt is made to clean this up before removing the paddy, but it is usually possible to tell where the grain was transferred from measure to basket by the kernels which remain on the ground. This would indicate that even though life is iiard and living standards low, acute hardship is uncommon in the village. Another such sign is that cultivation does not extend to all areas in the village which could grow something. Also the rice straw that remains after threshing is often disposed of casually. If the farmer does not own buffalo, or if he has more than enough straw to meet his needs for fodder, he may give the straw to anyone who wants it and will carry it away. It is true that some farmers sell the straw, but many do not bother.

A good three-man harvesting team can produce from eighteen to twenty *gia* of paddy per day, working from six to eleven o'clock in the morning and from two to five o'clock in the afternoon. The men exchange the job of threshing because it is tiring work, and an effort is made to keep the threshing at a pace which matches the reapers. In large fields more than one team must be used to complete the job within a few days' time. When the grain is ready for harvest, a sudden rain may flatten the crop, leaving the field a tangled mat of plants. This causes no concern and is not considered a serious problem. There may be small losses of grain, and the reaping may be a bit more difficult, but the farmers do not fear spoilage or rot in the fields. Similarly, grain may be cut and left in the field for a day or so, even when the fields are wet, without fear of damage.

When the paddy arrives at the house of the farmer, it is dried before it is stored. Most houses have a drying surface in front of the house for this purpose. If the family is well-to-do it will be made of brick or cement, but if the family is poor it will be simply a smooth, raised surface of dried earth. The drying process is a simple one of raking the paddy over and over under the bright sun until the farmer feels it has attained a uniform degree of dryness. Many villagers have abandoned the practice of winnowing the paddy, and the raking constitutes the only cleaning it gets. This is not as effective as winnowing, but it is easier. Crude winnowing is done by the simple expendient of standing on a chair and letting the paddy slowly pour onto the ground. The wind catches the chaff and blows it to one side, leaving a pile of clean paddy directly in front of the person performing the operation. Some of the wealthier farmers own hand-operated winnowing machines, but this is available to only 15 percent of the village households. These machines are constructed locally of wood and perform the most thorough cleaning job of all methods used. Clean paddy brings a slightly higher price, but this is offset by the fact that thorough cleaning reduces the volume.

After the paddy is dry enough to satisfy the farmer, it is stored inside the house in cylindrical bins made of reed mats. In some houses, efforts are made to protect the paddy from dampness by providing a mat floor, a layer of rice straw, or even better, a raised wooden floor that rests on wood or brick supports'. Many farmers, however, make no effort to provide a protection layer for their paddy and simply pour the paddy onto the bare earth floor inside the mat bins. Although storage practices are not uniform, there is apparently very little spoilage of paddy and only small loss due to rodents and to the fact that chickens are allowed free access to the storage bins.

Seed rice is carefully set aside at this time for probable use the following year, and the farmers select the best of the paddy for seed purposes. This method of obtaining seed does not seem to have had any adverse effects on productivity or quality. However, it perpetuates an abundance of varieties, and the absence of standardizing tendencies may have long run effects on the kind of rice which Viet Nam can provide for the export market.

Rice merchants complain that farmers often do not know how to dry their paddy properly, with the result that the rice which is milled from it has a high percentage of broken grains. Too rapid drying is partly due to the pressure to sell paddy which many farmers feel The need for cash can be extremely acute at harvest time, and farmers are apt to hurry the drying in order to sell at the first opportunity. However, it may also be due to ignorance of the fact that improperly dried paddy results in poor milling.

The Second Crop

The planting and care of a second crop of rice closely parallels that of the first, with a few minor exceptions. There is no plowing and harrowing of the fields before transplanting the second crop, for example. Instead, the farmers use a roller which knocks over the stubble remaining from the first crop, and the fields are then transplanted without any further preparation. Villagers also allow a little extra time to complete the transplanting, because extra care is exercised in handling the plants. Since the first crop has removed some of the fertility of the soil, a second crop requires larger amounts of fertilizer than the first, and farmers explain that for this reason a second crop costs more to produce. In all other respects the steps involved in production are the same for both crops.

The decision to grow a second crop is not always simply tied to the question of adequate water supply or level of field. A second crop is considered by most villagers as a very risky venture that frequently fails to cover the marginal costs. More fertilizer is needed, which means drawing on cash accumulations or finding new credit. If the rainy season is shorter than normal, there will be large costs for irrigation to carry the crop through to harvests and this will be a further drain on cash or credit. The yields of a second crop are also generally lower than the first—ten to fifteen percent lower—and only the average or low quality varieties of rice can be grown as a second crop. These factors taken together mean that the marginal revenues for a second crop are lower at a time when the marginal costs are rising. Add to this the risks of crop damage due to increased likelihood of plant disease, insects, or water shortage, and you have a prospect which, for many farmers, is too uncertain of success. The result is that the village as a whole can probably produce more rice each year than it actually does.

The description of the major activities within the production cycle is now complete. As the lunar new year approaches, more and more fields turn to brown stubble, and the buffalo and cattle again graze widely for bits of vegetation which may still remain. By March there are still some fields that have not been harvested—the low fields where a second crop has been planted. But these, too, are soon done, and the dry season sets in once again with its burden of inactivity, boredom, and for some, hardship. It will be three or four months until the rains begin and seven months until the first harvest of the new season. For those who have had a poor year, the wait will be a long one.

Costs of Production

The preceding section has described the production process in terms of techniques used, timing of different operations, and the general organization of production. But this leaves a picture that is incomplete, because an important element, production costs, has been omitted. By assembling an estimated per hectare cost to a farmer operating under assumed "normal" or "typical" conditions,[6] and dividing into cash, non-cash, and imputed categories, the relative importance of different kinds of costs emerges, as well as the beginning of an insight into the factors which account for living standards in the village.

The estimates given in Table 4.2 show the range of costs which farmers may encounter, depending on whether

TABLE 4.2

Estimated Costs of Rice Production per Hectare, Village of Khanh Hau, 1958

	Landowners		Tenants	
Category of cost	With NACO loan[a]	Without NACO loan[b]	With NACO loan[a]	Without NACO loan[b]
Payments in Cash (in VN$)				
1. Plowing 6 days at $60/day	360	360	360	360
2. Harrowing 1 day at $60/day	60	60	60	60
3. Transplanting 10 days at $20/day	200	200	200	200
4. Uprooting, carrying 5 days at $30/day	150	150	150	150
5. Irrigation 8 days at $40/day	320	320	320	320
6. Miscellaneous labor 8 days at $30/day	240	240	240	240
7. Transporting paddy 2 days at $20/day	40	40	40	40
8. Fertilizer				
a. Ammonium sulphate, 100 kilos[c]	350	350	350	350
b. Phosphate tricalcique, 200 kilos	480	480	480	480
9. Interest, $2,000 loan for 6 months	120	600	120	120
10. Taxes	98	98	-	-
Total cash payments	2,418	2,898	2,320	2,800

TABLE 4.2 (cont.)

Payments in Kind				
1. Transplanting, food at $20/day	200	200	200	200
2. Uprooting, carrying, food at $20/day	100	100	100	100
3. Irrigation, food at $20/day	160	160	160	160
4. Miscellaneous labor, food at $20/day	160	160	160	160
5. Transporting paddy, food at $20/day	40	40	40	40
6. Harvesting, 9 percent of yield[d]	540	540	540	540
7. Rent, 25 percent of yield[d]	-	1,500	1,500	1,500
Total payments in kind	1,200	1,200	2,700	2,700
Total costs	2,618	4,098	5,020	5,500

a. Interest on NACO loans is 12 percent per annum.
b. Interest on private loans is estimated at 5 percent per month.
c. Based on fertilizer prices, Tan An, December 1958.
d. One hectare is assumed to yield 120 *gia* of paddy, and one *gia* of paddy is valued at VN$ 50.

they are landowners or tenants, and whether they borrow money privately or through the government program of agricultural loans. Since all other costs are held constant as between the major categories of landowner and tenant, the comparison in all cases shows the advantage held by landowners. For example, a tenant's actual cost of production is probably 40 to 50 percent higher than a landowner's by virtue of the fact that he must pay rent. This can also be considered the opportunity cost of the landowner, but it does not mean any out-of-pocket payments by him. Rent is considered a fixed cost here because it is a contractual amount, based on one-quarter of the estimated yields in normal years and payable in kind at the end of the harvest. This type of cost estimate has been used in Table 4.2, although there is some reason to believe that the actual rents which tenants pay are five to ten percent higher than the official rent ceiling.[7] Taxes on the land, here based on the tax rate for "exceptional grade" (*ngoai hang*) land, obviously do not begin to compare with rent as a major element of cost.

The importance of interest as a cost of production is also shown by these estimates. The amount estimated as a "typical" loan figure, VN$ 2,000, is the median amount which farmers in this village borrowed from the National Agricultural Credit Office (NACO), as shown by village NACO loan records. It is impossible to get a clear measure of the volume of private lending for crop production alone, since private credit transactions often involve borrowing for several purposes at the same time. In any event, the figure of VN$ 2,000 is a conservative minimum estimate of borrowing by those farmers who must borrow. A conventional private loan of VN$ 2,000 would bear an interest charge of VN$ 600 for a six-month period, making it the third largest cost item, surpassed only by rent and fertilizer. A NACO loan for the same amount and same period of time would cost only VN$ 120 in interest, reducing this to the least expensive cost item except for taxes.

Interest and rent, major concerns of the peasant farmer in mostundeveloped areas of the world, begin to fall into perspective on the basis of cost estimates such as these. Together, they comprise nearly 40 percent of the costs of the "typical" tenant farmer who relies on private loans but who is assumed to have the advantage of a 25 percent rent ceiling. If the interest rates, amount of loans, or actual rents are greater, and other costs are considered irreducible minima in each case, their importance is obviously greater. At the other extreme, the small landowner who has access to government credit pays interest and taxes amounting to only six percent of his total costs of production.

The estimates assume that the yield of the "typical" hectare is 120 *gia* of paddy, and that this paddy sells for VN$ 50 per *gia*. This is a somewhat lower estimated yield than the average or median figures given on the rent contract records, but these figures are probably inflated. The price used is the price villagers reported they were receiving for paddy of average quality in December 1958. The net return, in money terms, to the "typical" farmer therefore ranges from around VN$ 2,300 per hectare for the landowner having access to NACO credit, to only VN$ 500 per hectare for the tenant farmer who was forced to borrow privately. The accuracy of the picture presented here can be tested only by relating it to income from other sources and the composition of family expenditures, but as a first approximation it seems clear that rice farming alone is an insufficient way for a small tenant farmer to earn a livelihood. It can barely provide his family with enough rice to meet their consumption needs for the year, let alone provide him with the cash outlays for food and other consumer items that his family budget indicates he actually spends.

Another check on the cost estimates presented here is to compare them with cost figures for rice production in other parts of southeast Asia. A recent study of a village in Thailand[8] provides cost figures on both weight and area of land bases. For example, the average cost of 1 *tang* of paddy is given as 6.7 *baht*.[9] Using the conversion ratios of 1 *tang* equal to 11 kilos, and 20 *baht* equal to US$ 1, this puts the cost of one kilo of Thailand rice at 3.1 US cents. For a comparable measure of the cost of rice in Khanh Hau, the figures in Table 4.1 can be converted by the ratios of 1 *gia* equal to 19 kilos and VN$ 70 equal to US$ 1, the "free market" rate, of exchange. This gives a cost range of 2.2 to 3.4 US cents per kilo in Khanh Hau, as against 3.1 US cents in Thailand, or roughly the same in each country.

Similarly, average costs per *rai*, a unit of land area equal to .16 hectares, were 215 *baht* or approximately US$ 67 per hectare.[10] This compares with an estimated range of US$ 51.67 to US$ 78. 57 per hectare in Khanh Hau, using the same exchange rates as those in the preceding example.

In making comparisons of this kind, a number of more or less arbitrary decisions canradically affect the results obtained. For one thing, the original estimates in each case were made by different methods, and while the conceptual bases are similar, there is not exact comparability between the two. For another, the choice of a rate of exchange in each case is arbitrary. Viet Nam uses a set of multiple exchange rates, with a special rate for rice exports that falls between the official rate and the free market rate. Thailand has also used multiple exchange rates and subsidies to rice export-ers from time to time. The use of the free market rates in making these comparisons rests on the assumption that price levels in each country are probably reflected more accurately by these rates than any other. Finally, the Thailand data are for the year 1948, while those for Khanh Hau reflect conditions in 1958.

A more direct comparison can be made by using the percentage breakdown of the various components in each of the two villages, as shown in Table 4.3. At first glance, the major differences be-tween the two villages occur in the categories of labor and rent. Rents in Khanh Hau are much higher than those in Bangchan, both absolutely and proportionately. The quoted going rate for 1948-49 rent in kind is 6.2 *tang* per *rai*,[11] or the equivalent of about 22 *gia* per hectare, which is about one-fourth less than the rent in kind es-timated for Khanh Hau. Eent of rice land in the Thai village is also a lower proportion of the average yield. For example, rents there came to only 21.5 percent of the average yield,[12] compared with the 25 percent maximum set by the agrarian reform program in Viet Nam. In fact, actual rental payments in Khanh Hau probably exceed this by five to ten percent in most cases. Rent comparisons between the two villages are not affected by price differentials, for the price of rice used in the Thailand study is the same as that for Khanh Hau when converted into US dollar prices per kilo, i. e., about 3.6 cents.

The labor cost in the Thai village is very similar to that

TABLE 4.3
Comparison of Rice Production Cost Components, Bangchan, Thailand, and
Khanh Hau, Viet Nam

Category of cost	%, Bangchan[a]	Khanh Hau %, tenant with NACO loan	%, tenant without NACO loan
Rent			
Actual	13.1		
Imputed	9.3	29.9	27.3
Subtotal	22.4	29.9	27.3
Labor			
Actual	6.7		
Imputed	44.6	51.2	46.7
Subtotal	51.3	51.2	46.7
Capital			
Seed and materials	5.6	16.5	15.1
Depreciation	9.6	-	-
Interest			
On investment	11.1	-	-
On loans		2.4	10.9
Subtotal	26.3	18.9	26.0
Total	100.0	100.0	100.0

a. Janlekha, *op. cit.*, p. 123.

computed for Khanh Hau. In the Bangchan study, this is largely an imputed element covering the cost of labor supplied by the family itself. As such, there is some flexibility in the amount which could have been assigned to this category. On the other hand, the Khanh Hau estimates are based on actual work days required to do the main farm operations, and since they are conservatively drawn, they represent the minimum amount of actual labor time used in production figured at going wage rates. This could perhaps be raised further by some small amount, since no attempt was made to account specifically for time spent during the year on supervision, weeding, spraying, repairing dikes, and similar tasks. However, observation of work habits during the growing season supports an estimate of eight man-days per hectare spent on these relatively minor activities, and this was added as "miscellaneous labor." Since the present estimates include an allowance of eight man-days for the cost of irrigation, although this is not necessary in years when rainfall is sufficient, total labor costs are probably not understated by very much—perhaps no more than three or four percent at most. On balance, therefore, proportionate labor costs in this part of Viet Nam emerge as about the same as those in a central Thailand village. In fact, it is surprising that the shares estimated for labor are as close as they are, given the different bases on which they were calculated.

Looking at the capital costs of the two villages, the totals are again similar, but the component parts differ widely. One of the important reasons for this difference is that the Bangchan villagers do not use chemical fertilizers to any great extent, with the result that seed and materials comprise a very small proportion of their total costs. In Khanh Hau, where fertilizer is an important item, these costs are about three times greater.

The Bangchan estimates contain items for depreciation of equipment and for interest on the investment in land and equipment. The Khanh Hau estimates contain only an estimate of interest payments on loans. Since the latter include, as elements of cost, payments made for plowing, harrowing, harvesting, and threshing, at the rates paid for the rent of such services, it is assumed that these rents include an amount equivalent to the annual depreciation on the equipment and animals used in these activities. Therefore, no additional allowance for depreciation is made. The Bangchan study did not make any assumption that farmers borrowed funds for putting in their crop, although nearly 60 percent of the farmers in that village were in debt, according to a companion study.[13] Failure to make any allowance for debt in Bangchan is offset by failure to include an allowance for return on investment in Khanh Hau, with the result that the two estimates counter each other to some extent and both probably understate the importance of capital costs in total production cost.

There are a number of things which can be emphasized in summarizing the significance of these findings on costs of rice production. For one thing, from the standpoint of the farmer, his actual out-of-pocket costs vary considerably according to his particular situation. A farmer who has a larger number of grown children and who owns buffalo and farm implements will be less dependent on others and have less need to hire outside farm labor and service. The tenant-landowner and debtor-creditor alternatives provide other possible combinations which affect the size of the money obligations which must be paid out. In other words, the amount a farmer can draw directly from his land varies widely, because the size of his fixed commitment to others is affected by so many different factors. Some farmers can absorb price drops or poor harvest with much less strain than others.

In the short run, price-cost relationships seem to have little effect in allocating resources or in changing production methods This is not so much due to the disinterest of the farmers as to their ignorance of other alternatives and their inability to undertake certain changes on their own. Limited responses can be expected, such as shifts from one rice variety to another as a result of prices which were in effect the previous year, but a rise in the general price of paddy would not bring forth a significant increase in production to take advantage of it. Nor is there any evidence of the reverse response which is sometimes claimed to prevail in agriculture, i. e., that low prie-es in one year will spur production in the following year. Instead, the margin of return is so small that it seems safe to conclude that all farmers try to increase production in all years and will adopt any method or new practice which will help them do so. Increases in rice production will therefore depend on such factors as the amount of fertilizer brought in under the commercial import program and the way in which it is made available to farmers.

At the assumed exchange rates, rice production in this part of Viet Nam is as efficient in terms of cost per hectare or cost per kilo as that of central Thailand, and the proportionate distribution of costs is also roughly the same in both cases. At the rate of exchange actually applied to rice exports (VN$ 48 = US$ 1), this would not be true, and in US dollar equivalents Thailand rice would appear to be produced much more cheaply. Devaluation possibly could result in some increase in the piaster price of paddy and an increase in the return which farmers would receive from their rice production. It would not lead to increased production of rice in the village, for reasons touched on above, although on a nationwide scale production might increase as new lands were planted. Further, increased returns from production, due to higher paddy prices, would probably go first for debt repayment and the purchase of more fertilizer, but thereafter items of consumption (improving graves of ancestors, better homes, more elaborate festivals) would begin to take precedence over other expenditures. At the village level, therefore, devaluation would probably bring some generally beneficial effects, but it would be unlikely that devaluation as such can stimulate production in the village or bring a shift in production methods. Changes of this kind depend far more on factors outside the village and are unrelated to foreseeable adjustments due to price-cost relationships.

5

SECONDARY FARM PRODUCTION

Fruit and Vegetable Raising

The organization of vegetable cultivation—In an agricultural community such as Khanh Hau, one would expect a considerable amount of supplementary farm activity such as fruit and vegetable raising, fishing, and poultry and livestock breeding. This is especially so where, as in Khanh Hau, the typical villager has a fairly small amount of land at his disposal, and where he tends to live at or near subsistence levels. Under these circumstances the additional production would be vital to the households. Yet a substantial number of households do not engage in such pursuits. An overall picture of fruit and vegetable raising in three hamlets of Ap Dinh "A" and "B" and Ap Moi is given by the data shown in Table 5.1. Judging from this sample, approximately half the households raise both to some degree, but 22 percent do not raise either. Moreover, it is much more common among middle and upper class households in the sample to raise vegetables or fruit or both, whereas all but one of those households raising neither fell into the lower class. Thus, the households seem at a disadvantage in terms of opportunity to raise fruit and/or vegetables; this is coupled with access to the smallest amounts of rice land, for the latter was the main basis on which households were assigned to the various socio-economic categories.

In terms of vegetable raising alone, the same survey provided data which showed that 66 percent of the households in these three hamlets raised vegetables, while 34 percent did not. Again the same pattern appeared, the upper and middle class households being more likely to have vegetable gardens than the lower class. A majority of those who raise vegetables (62.1 percent) do so for home use only, and do not derive any cash income from them.

For the minority who sell some portion of their garden produce, the cash income is not very large in even the

TABLE 5.1

Vegetable and Fruit Growing, by Socio-Economic Class, Village of Khanh Hau, 1959

	Upper Class		Middle Class		Lower Class		All Classes	
	No.	%	No.	%	No.	%	No.	%
Vegetables only	1	8.3	1	5.6	11	15.7	13	13.0
Fruit	1	8.3	4	22.2	9	12.9	14	14.0
Vegetables and fruit	9	75.0	13	72.2	29	41.4	51	51.0
Neither	1	8.3	-	-	21	30.0	22	22.0
Total	12	99.9	18	100.0	70	100.0	100	100.0

best years. Over two-fifths of these households (44.0 percent) report they receive Less than VN$ 500 per year from this source, and over four-fifths (84.0 percent) receive less than VN$ 1,500. In a poor year, over three-fourths of them (76.0 percent) receive less than VN$ 500. In a "good" year they sell from one-third to two-thirds of the total output, in bad years slightly less. A small minority (16.0 percent) specialize more heavily in gardening than the others, and in these cases the annual gross receipts from this activity may run from VN$ 7,000 to VN$ 10,000.

In general, therefore, while a majority of the households have gardens, only a minority of these sell even a portion of their output, and their cash income is relatively small. Further, upper and middle class households are more likely to have gardens than lower class households, but the size of the money income realized by those who sell vegetables does not seem to vary significantly from one class to another.

A large variety of vegetables is grown in the village, but most households have a narrow selection in their gardens. The most commonly grown items include cucumbers, several kinds of melons, onions, red peppers, beans, tomatoes, several types of squash and gourds, lettuce, cabbage, spinach, and manioc. In addition, some yams, corn, sweet potatoes, and white potatoes are grown, but except for white potatoes these are considered inferior foods, and their cultivation and use are not very extensive. A fairly complete list of vegetables grown is given in Table 5.2.

The limiting factors in the cultivation of vegetables appear to be availability of proper soil and a home plot large enough to permit a garden. The best area for vegetables is in the central portions of the hamlets of Ap Dinh "A" and "B" and Ap Moi and was formerly a sandy stream bed. The heavy clay of other parts of the village does not provide as good a base for vegetables, although they are grown in the areas near the streams that flow through Ap Cau, Ap Nhon Hau and Ap Thu Tuu. In the Ap Dinh-Ap Moi area, a few of the farmers are beginning to raise one crop of vegetables on the land they use for growing rice, since the sandy soil there is good for vegetables but is too far from the stream or canal to have enough water for two crops of rice. As yet there seems to be no standard timing or sequence for this type of double-cropping. Some farmers plant an early crop of rice and then put in vegetables in October, after the rice harvest, to be harvested in turn around February. Others follow what they claim is a more traditional order, planting vegetables first and rice second. Some vegetables are planted in mid-April, for example sweet potatoes, while manioc and beans are planted early in June and tomatoes late in June. Depending on the time it takes different vegetables to mature, these fields will be available for rice planting from late July through November.

With the exception of leafy vegetables such as lettuce, celery, and cabbage, most households use seed from the previous year's crop. In some cases, this leads to interesting results. Farmers report, for example, that they sell or use the largest sweet potatoes and keep the small ones for seed purposes. Over a three-year period this consistent selection of the poorest stock for seed gradually reduces the size of potatoes from their garden patches, and they usually must buy new seed every four years. There is also a general feeling among villagers that non-Vietnamese strains do not do well, and they are somewhat reluctant to experiment with them. At times over the past three years what are referred to as "American" varieties of tomatoes and corn were introduced through the village council on a trial basis, but the results were apparently unsuccessful. Villagers found that the "American" variety of corn produced as many ears as the local varieties, but each ear had fewer grains and the taste seemed inferior. Tomatoes were also disappointing; yields from the new strains were less than normally could be obtained using regular local seed. Most people felt that newly-introduced plants were not suited to the temperature, soil, and rainfall combinations in the village, although they were willing to believe that they do thrive in other situations. Another factor reported was that the particular corn seed which was given the villagers contained a high proportion of rotten seed or seed partially eaten by insects.

Planting and cultivating practices differ with different types of plant and also from household to household. However, most prepare the ground by turning it with shovel or

TABLE 5.2
List of Vegetables Grown in Khanh Hau

cai thia	Chinese cabbage
cai salade	Lettuce
cai xanh	cole, kale
cai bap	cabbage
ca chua	tomato
dua leo xanh	gherkin
dua gang	melon
dua hau	watermelon
thorn (dua)	pineapple
hanh	onion
he	(criboule) Welsh onion
rau can	celery
rau can tau	Chinese celery
rau can nuoc	water celery
rau den	a variety of spinach
rau mung toi	basella
muop ngot	sweet cucumber
muop dang	bitter cucumber
muop khia	flavor cucumber
bau ngan	a short variety of gourd
bau dai	a long variety of gourd
bi dao	
bi xanh	varieties of gourd or squash
ca rot	carrot
trai kho qua	prickly melon

(continued on next page)

TABLE 5.2 (cont)

bi do	a variety of squash
ca nau	brown eggplant
dau phung	peanut
khoai mi (san)	manioc
khoai mon	India potato, yam
khoai mo	varieties of sweet potato
khoai tu	
xu hao	turnip
dau que xanh	green beans
dau haricot trang	white French beans
dau haricot ve (dau mong chim)	a variety of green beans
rau muong	spinach, bindweed
rau hung	
rau que, rau hung cho, rau ram	varieties of thyme
ngo or bap	maize
ot	red pepper
chou-fleur	cauliflower
trai bau	long melon

pickaxe, then mounding it in rows so that water will collect between them and the moisture will be retained. There is practically no use of draft animals on garden plots. Chemical fertilizers are used if farmers can afford it, but otherwise they use buffalo manure, ashes, and on rare occasions, night soil. Most people deny they use it, but if questioned further they will also say that some other households use it occasionally.

One common practice is to spread ashes on the ground after it has been turned, and leave this for a period of 20 days before planting. Just prior to planting, a second treatment of ash is added, sometimes together with chemical fertilizer and sometimes with buffalo manure Both phosphate tricalcique and ammonium sulphate are used, but there seems to be a preference for the former. Buffalo manure is collected by individual households if they are poor, or purchased if the family can afford to do so. The manure is sometimes mixed with ashes and straw, but it is often applied directly to the garden plot. The timing of fertilizer applications also varies, for farmers add fertilizer throughout the growing season as they feel there is need for it.

Most gardens receive intensive care, although one gets an impression that garden plots are not always as large as they could be, and that a certain amount of home plot land is not fully utilized. Young plants are protected from the sun by individual shades made from bark or banana leaves, and sometimes branches of thorn are placed over plants to protect them from grazing animals and birds. Wooden racks are built for gourds, squash, beans, and tomatoes so that they will grow up from the ground and yield more and larger produce. Most gardens are carefully weeded and kept well watered at all times.

There were two attempts at innovation in garden practices during 1958, and while both were moderately successful it is still too early to tell if the example will result in any major change in gardening practices throughout the village. One of these was the construction of a large irrigation pond approximately 65 feet long, 20 feet wide, and 15 feet deep, at one end of a ricefield in the former stream bed portion of Ap Dinh. This was dug during the dry season and was designed to serve as a receptacle for water once the rains began. Too shallow to tap any underground sources of water, it nevertheless retained water after the rains stopped, and this was used to irrigate the vegetables which were planted after the early crop of rice had been harvested. The owner of this garden, who undertook this experiment on his own initiative and without outside advice or assistance, said he wanted to reverse the usual order of double-cropping because vegetables grown late in the season would bring better prices than those grown earlier. Although the garden itself was successful, the marginal benefits do not seem to have been great enough to stir much interest or generate a desire to emulate the experiment on the part of others.

The other experiment was more consciously designed to serve as a model and to introduce new techniques to the villagers. Installed on land rented from the village chief, it was set up at a cost of VN$ 40,000, donated by the Asia Foundation and administered by a member of the staff of the Fundamental Education Center. The work was done by a voluntary committee of four men who kept any profit from the garden as payment for their effort.

The plants and trees in the garden were purchased at a government nursery at Mytho, so the original stock was of high quality. An irrigation ditch was dug to connect the garden area with the nearest stream, and within the garden the water was distributed through deep ditches dug between "islands" on which the plants are grown. These large ditch areas thus provide room for raising fish as well as water for irrigation. Banana trees were planted along the edges of the island areas, and inside these there were vegetables, corn, mango trees, lime trees, quava trees, and grapefruit trees located in different sections of the garden. The banana trees grow quickly and provide shade for the others, which mature more slowly.

In setting out the fruit trees, buffalo hide was placed in the empty holes, and compost which was provided locally was added before putting in the young trees—a technique advocated by the government nurseries from which the trees were purchased. In addition to this, bone meal was used as fertilizer on the fruit trees, small amounts of it being placed in holes dug around each tree. Vegetable patches were fertilized with a mixture of phosphate tricalcique and water which was poured over the plants. In ali, this provided an example of intensive use of garden land, yielding a variety of fruits and vegetables which mature at different times to provide crops for cash sale or home use over a fairly long period of time. As such it is a useful model for the village, but it suffers from the fact that the initial cost was very high by village standards, even for a garden half the size of this one. Several of the plants—mango, lime, guava, and grapefruit—require much chemical fertilizer and a great deal of care. Thus, while the villagers are interested in the experiment, initial reactions have been to consider it as something beyond their ability to finance for themselves. In time, perhaps some of the ideas on spacing and irrigation will be adopted by a growing number of households, but there was little evidence of it after one year.

Fruit production—Around two-thirds of the households either raise fruit alone or in combination with vegetables, which leaves about one-third without any fruit trees at all. Once again there is a strong relationship between socio-economic class and fruit cultivation, for over ninety percent of upper and middle class households raise fruit, but nearly half (45.7 percent) of lower class households do not; thus, those families with the least, or no, land for rice are also less fortunate with respect to opportunities to raise fruit.

A list of fruit trees grown in the village is given in Table 5.3, but of these, bananas, papaya, and coconuts are the most commonly grown. By and large, fruit growing is less extensively carried on than vegetable cultivation, in terms of both its importance as a source of additional cash income and the amount of land or effort devoted to it. Although specific data were not collected on this point, it seems true that interest in fruit growing is less than that in vegetables. There are, for example, no households who make a major effort to raise fruit trees on a large scale, but there are some who do have large vegetable gardens. This is not to say that people are disinterested in fruit raising, but rather that it is considered of secondary importance to vegetable cultivation and provides less cash income.

Banana and papaya trees are probably the easiest to raise. Both require little care, need no fertilizer, grow rapidly, and produce fruit quickly. Some is sold, but most of it is consumed locally. Bananas are sometimes dried in the sun and, with a sprinkling of sesame seeds on top, are later sold in the market towns as a kind of candy. Areca palms and betel plant, which flourish particularly in the well-watered hamlet of Ap Cau, are also grown. These also require very little care, the produce is in large demand, and farmers sell it within the village and also in nearby markets.

Coconuts are grown everywhere in the village, but the hamlets of Ap Cau and Ap Nhon Hau, with better water resources, produce more than elsewhere. Very little copra comes from the village, however, because few farmers raise enough coconuts to make collection and preparation worth while. Most of the coconuts marketed are sold as whole fruit. Villagers serve the milk to guests, and it is also prized for use in preparing glutinous rice. People use the meat in cooking, in cakes, and in the preparation of a soup called *che*. The trees are given relatively little care, but it is five years before a tree begins to bear fruit.

Fruit trees such as grapefruit, mango, guava, and lime are grown, but they take much care and require chemical fertilizer for best results and are therefore not found in many households. People living on the banks of streams cultivate water palms for use in thatching roofs. These are grown in all hamlets, but the best ones are thought to grow in the hamlet of Ap Thu Tuu. These require little care, and mature about one year after planting. Finally, there are a number of fruit-bearing trees which apparently grow wild along the village paths or in the areas around graves, and in season you can find village children on almost any day knocking the fruit from these trees with long bamboo poles.

Both vegetable and fruit cultivation could probably be expanded in the village, but the limitations of soil and water availability are such that any foreseeable increase would not be too great. Without sources of fresh water for irrigation vegetables cannot be grown during the long dry season, and village canal-digging cannot meet this need. New varieties of fruit trees require chemical fertilizers, so there is another financial limitation in these cases. In short, it does not appear that additional income could be added easily or quickly by enlarging these productive activities, for the means to do so do not rest essentially with the villagers themselves.

TABLE 5.3
List of Fruit Trees Grown in Khanh Hau

dua	coconut palm
buoi	grapefruit
cam	orange
quyt	tangerine
oi	guava
chanh	lemon
mit	jack-fruit
soai	mango
vu sua	milk apple
mang cau (na)	anona or custard apple
chuoi	banana
long nhan	Longan
khe	carambole tree
me chua	tamarind (wild)
dao	apricot
man (roi)	jambose
du du	papaya
le-ki-ma	le-ki-ma
dau	mulberry, blackberry
cau	acreca nut
trau	betel
binh linh	type of tea substitute (wild)
o-moi	black fruit (wild)

The Organization of Fishing and Fish Raising

Fish raising—The large number of rivers and streams in the delta region of southern Viet Nam make fishing and fish raising important supplementary activities in many places and fish an important source of protein in local diets. Fishing is carried on actively in all the hamlets of Khanh Hau. Fish raising is more successful in Ap Cau, Ap Nhon Hau, and Ap Thu Tuu, all of which, unlike Ap Dinh "A" and "B" and Ap Moi, are served by large streams. In the latter hamlets, fish raising has not been very extensive. Although this is not typical of the area, there are many communities in the delta which face similar problems, and analysis of the factors which have deterred the raising of fish in these three hamlets can perhaps show some of the reasons why this allegedly common and widespread activity has not been developed more fully.

In the hamlets of Ap Dinh "A" and "B" and Ap Moi, only about one-fifth of all households raise fish as a regular activity, and only one household does so on a scale large enough to be considered a 'commercial' enterprise. A larger proportion of middle and upper class households raise fish than is true for lower class households, and while this may not be a significant difference, it is still not an activity engaged in by a majority of any socio-economic class.

Those who do not raise fish were asked to indicate the main reasons for not doing so. The replies were overwhelmingly a reflection of inadequate water resources. Many indicated their homeplots were too far from the stream, and they could not divert the water to maintain a pond throughout the year. Others said their land was too high, and that water would drain out of the pond if they tried to dig one. Only a few said their homeplots were too small to accommodate a pond, and less than 10 percent reported that a lack of capital hindered their entry into this activity.

There is another factor, however, which did not come out in the survey answers, and that is the lack of feed. The one commercial fish pond is located near the school, and the school latrine is built over the pond. Villagers have said that this is the only place in the village which has access to this large a source of feeding material, and therefore the only location where a large number of fish can be raised. To purchase an equivalent amount of food would create credit or capital outlay problems, and villagers therefore do not attempt it. There are a few ponds set up by groups of households working together, but these do not reach a commercial level and are maintained for home use only. Thus, although lack of water emerges as the single most important limiting factor, feeding presents a further problem, and lack of sufficient feeding material keeps most ponds from achieving a commercial scale of operation.

For those who find themselves able to raise some fish the government at one time offered an opportunity to grow *tilapia*, a fast-breeding fish imported from the Philippines. By reproducing itself rapidly, this species gave villages a chance to produce large quantities of fish in very short periods of time, and it was hoped that this would add to both income and food resources in the villages. Whatever the results may have been in other parts of Viet Nam, all those who once raised *tilapia* in Khanh Hau have ceased doing so. The reasons given for this are not convincing—the fish could not live in the brackish water of the dry season, they were struck by disease, they did not taste good. A more plausible reason is that villagers are afraid to raise the *tilapia*, perhaps because of recurrent rumors in all parts of Viet Nam that the *tilapia* were carriers of leprosy, tuberculosis, and other illnesses—rumors reportedly started by the Viet Cong. Whatever the real reason, all that can be said with certainty is that *tilapia* are not now raised in the village despite government encouragement.

In terms of size, farmers raising 2,000 or more fish per year are considered "large" operators, and those raising less than this are considered "small." There are no "large" operators under this definition in Khanh Hau, and only one who approaches the upper limits of the "small" category. This distinction is related to the market practices of the buyers, for "small" operators must take their fish to the markets to sell them, while the buyers regularly call on the "large" operators and bid on their stock.

One species of fish raised in the village from purchased stock is called *ca tra*, a variety of catfish. Fingerlings are grown near Chau Doc, along the Cambodian border, and brought to Tan An for sale in lots of 100 or 1,000. They grow at the rate of about one kilo per year, and reach full growth after two years, at which time they weigh slightly over two kilos. Most farmer, however, sell them after one year. The villagers say they must buy the fingerlings because the adult fish will not spawn in the small local fishponds Conditions near Chau Doc, believed to be specially suited to these fish, are not duplicated elsewhere in the delta region.

The farmer who plans to raise fish must dig a pond, the size of which varies with the number of fish he will handle. The pond is usually fed through a ditch connecting it with some large source of water such as the stream or canal. Sometimes, however, small ponds will depend entirely on rainfall. The ditches are filled in once the water has reached a level of around one and one-half meters, and the water sources and the fish ponds are not connected once the stock of fish has been added. Many of the ponds are fenced in with cactus-like plants or wire to keep buffalo and cattle from using them, but some are not. Latrines are built over most of the fish ponds, and this fills the double function of feeding the fish and disposing of sewage.

The villagers seem to be concerned about the disposal of sewage in the fish ponds, and on one occasion took action through the village council to force a man to move his fish pond because he had placed it too close to the canal. Water from the canal is used for drinking and cooking, and villagers are anxious to avoid its pollution. Although latrines are built over many ponds, none are built directly over canals or streams. People say also that they are reluctant to eat fish from the fish ponds until after the latrines have been removed for a month or more. They have no qualms about selling them, however, even if they would not eat them themselves, and reason that if people want to buy these fish they are willing to sell them what they want.

Once the basic installation of a pond, fencing, and a latrine has been completed, the actual work connected with raising fish is minimal. There is little loss of stock during the growing period due to disease or theft, and no special problems except those advanced as reasons for refusing to raise the *tilapia*. About one month before the fish are to be sold, or approximately one year after the finger-lings were purchased, the villager may begin to feed the fish on rice bran only, and the latrine will no longer be used. This is done to fatten the fish for market, as well as make them more attractive locally as food.

Barring natural catastrophes, which seem infrequent, the potential return from raising fish is very high. The *ca tra* have sold for VN$ 20 to VN$ 30 per kilo at a time when the fingerlings cost VN$ 1.5 each. Initial out-of-pocket expenses are not great when compared to the expected returns, as shown in Table 5.4, and many of these are non-recurring over a period of three or four years. Including a large item for the interest which would accrue from an alternative investment, total costs of raising 2,000 fish are VN$ 11,200. Expected proceeds from the sale of 1,500 fish (assuming some loss and/or home use) at a minimum wholesale price of VN$ 20 per kilo would be VN$ 30,000, or a net profit for one year of VN$ 18,000. This is a net return of more than one and one-half times the amount of the total investment and is a much more lucrative opportunity than any other economic activity in the village. If commercial feed were purchased throughout the entire period, however, the size of the net return would be reduced, as the out-of-pocket costs would approximately double.

In addition to the *ca tra*, villagers raise another species called *ca ro*. This is a much smaller fish, a variety of tench, reaching a length of only four or five inches after three months' growth. These two species comprise the kinds of fish raised from fingerlings which are purchased for that specific purpose. In addition, farmers raise fish which are caught live in the fields and streams and transferred to ponds or ditches where they are kept until they are ready to be used by the family. This is not fish raising for commercial purposed, for the most part, but simply a way of supplementing the family diet and keeping their catches fresh for a longer period of time.

Fishing—Fishing is an activity which goes on at all time of the year, though it is more productive during and after the rainy season than it is during the dry months. Fish, shell fish, and frogs are found in the paddies and the streams and canals, and all members of the family engage in trying to catch them. For the most parts however, this is an activity of children and young adults, conducted on an individual household basis. None of the streams surrounding the village are large enough to permit the use of the large permanently positioned nets that are sometimes used in other villages in the area. Instead, those engaged in fishing use one of four main techniques.

TABLE 5.4
Estimated Costs of Raising Fish, Khanh Hau Village, 1958

Category of cost	Amount
1. Digging pond, 40m x 3m x 1.5 m	VN$ 2,000
2. Fish stock, 2,000 finger lings at 1.5 each	3,000
3. Fence and latrine, construction	1,400
4. Bran for feed	600
5. Interest on investment, VN$ 700 for one year	4,200
Total	VN$ 11,200

One of these is a large wide-mouthed fish trap, usually in the shape of a funnel, designed so that the fish swim into, and finally through, a narrow neck that is fitted with pointed bamboo sticks. These permit fish to go through, but not to swim back out, and they remain trapped in a larger attached receptacle until removed. These traps are usually put in place in the main part of the stream or in breaches made in the bundings between fields. Sometimes men will push them along the stream bottom, or several men will line up, covering the width of the stream with their traps. As they walk up the stream bed together they scoop up all fish swimming in their direction.

Another type of trapping involves use of a hand trap, a conical device made from rattan which is wide at one end and has a small hole through which the trapper may insert his hand at the narrow end. Young boys wait until the tide in the stream is low, then lower themselves into the water and walk slowly along the edge. As they do so, they plunge the traps into the side of the stream bank just below the water line. Fish and frogs often hang along the edge of the stream because the current there is less strong, and also because they eat the grasses and herbs that grow on the bank. The trapper can feel vibration in the trap if a fish or frog is caught in it, and holding the trap securely against the bank, he reaches in and removes the catch. If frogs are caught, the trapper breaks their legs so that they cannot jump and escape and carries them with all the other catch in reed sacks tied to his waist.

A second major technique includes several types of net fishing. The size of the net varies, depending on the size of the fish being netted and the strength of the fisherman. Small children use nets the size of large handkerchiefs, the four corners of which are each tied to bamboo sticks in a manner that resembles an inverted parachute. This is nothing more than a miniature model of the large permanently positioned nets that are placed along large streams, but the children who use the small ones will drop several in a row along the banks of a stream or pond and pick them up in turn. When they think there may be fish in the net, they reach out with sticks and lift the nets by hooking the small net. The size of catch is obviously extremely small in these cases. Other net devices are more like butterfly nets, and are used to scoop fish out of the water. Finally, adult fishermen use long nets which can be thrown across a stream and periodically hauled in to the shore.

A third technique is to drain the water from a field or scoop it from a pond or ditch, then pick up the fish that are left high and dry in the process. Children do this on a small scale. They select a part of a paddy field that is not yet plowed, build a small dike around a portion of it, then scoop the water out of the area surrounded by the dike. Again, the size of the fish caught in this way is very small—about the size of small sardines or minnows—and a large amount of effort goes into accumulating a very small catch.

Finally, young men and boys fish with hooks and lines attached to bamboo poles, a method used mainly in fishing from rice fields. Hooks are sometimes baited, sometimes not. The fish caught in this way are a little larger than those taken in the draining process or with the small nets, but they are still fairly small. This way is also used to catch frogs, crabs, and turtles and in fact seems more successful for this than for catching fish.

All local activity relating to fish probably supplies about half the fish actually consumed by village households, but in only a few cases does it add even modest amounts of cash income to the family. Barring some major improvement in irrigation facilities, it seems unlikely that there can be substantial increase in the number of fish raised commercially, although the encouragement of neighborhood ponds, together with the provision of credit for the purchase of low cost food, could undoubtedly bring some improvement in the amount of fish which would then be available for home consumption.

Domestic Animal Production

An over-all view of animal husbandry—A brief review of the survey data provides some idea of the relative importance of animal production on a household basis, if not in terms of village aggregates. A summary of the situation with respect to poultry is given in Table 5.5, where it may be seen that nearly four-fifths of the households raise either chickens, ducks, or both. At first glance, this seems a substantial proportion, for it indicates that a large majority of the households are engaged in this activity to some extent. However, again there are significant differences between socio-economic classes, with lower class households less extensively involved in this secondary production than either middle or upper class households.

A much higher proportion of all households (77.0 percent) raise chickens than raise ducks (38.0 percent). Some of the reasons for this will be touched upon below, but essentially they relate to the availability of resources which are necessary in each case. The difference in the proportions between socio-economic classes is less pronounced in the case of raising chickens than it is for raising ducks, although the same pattern of less opportunity for lower class households than for others exists in both.

As a measure of the volume of these activities, approximately two-thirds of all households who raise ducks or chickens do so for home use only. Only about one-third in either case sell any portion of the poultry they raise. Surprisingly, a larger proportion of lower class households who who raise poultry sell some part of their production than do either middle or upperclass households engaged in this activity. However, not a single household in the sample reported that it sold either chicken or duck eggs.

Swine production shows a different kind of pattern, for

TABLE 5.5
Poultry Raising by Socio-Economic Class, Village of Khanh Hau, 1958

Status	Upper Class		Middle Class		Lower Class		All Classes	
	No.	%	No.	%	No.	%	No.	%
Chickens only	5	41.7	5	27.8	32	45.7	42	42.0
Ducks only	-	-	1	5.6	1	1.4	2	2.0
Chickens and ducks	6	50.0	9	50.0	20	28.6	35	35.0
Neither	1	8.3	3	16.7	17	24.3	21	21.0
Total	12	100.0	18	100.1	70	100.0	100	100.0

only two-fifths of the households raise pigs. Moreover, a much larger proportion of middle class households are involved in this than either upper or lower class households. In fact, the proportions who raise and do not raise pigs among middle class households are almost exactly the reverse of that for the sample as a whole. Two-thirds of all households who raise pigs produce only one pig annually. Only 10 percent raise as many as three or more. Furthermore, this is a pattern which seems to hold for all classes. Finally, unlike poultry, a vast majority (92.5 percent) of the swine raised are sold, mostly in nearby markets.

Ownership of buffalo and cattle is the least extensive of all, as their relative costliness would lead one to expect. As is shown in Table 5.6, around three-fifths of all households own no large animals, and only 5 percent own both cattle and buffalo. The differences in proportions of ownership do not appear great between socio-economic classes. This is also true if ownership of cattle and buffalo is measured separately. However, a smaller proportion of all households (18 percent) own buffalo than own cattle (27 percent). Because buffalo are kept mainly as draft animals in farm operations, most households who own buffalo own at least two of them, the number considered necessary for a working team. Only one household reported that it owned only one, but one-third owned three or four. No household in the sample owned more than four, but there are a few households in the village which do. The pattern of cattle ownership is a little different, for among households owning cattle nearly one-third had only one cow, and nearly three-quarters of them owned only one or two.

Animal husbandry, therefore, presents a mixed picture. The proportion of village households engaged in raising domestic fowl or animals differs, but in no case can it be said that there is extensive involvement or economic return in this area of secondary farm production.

Poultry raisings—Villagers show extreme interest in raising poultry, but for various reasons this type of activity has not been expanded very far beyond that which they use for home consumption only. The few who raise large flocks of ducks on a commercial scale let the flocks find food in the rice fields once they are a few weeks old. The ducks feed on

TABLE 5.6
Ownership of Cattle and Buffalo, by Socio-Economic Class,
Village of Khanh, 1958

Ownership	Upper Class		Middle Class		Lower Class		All Classes	
	No.	%	No.	%	No.	%	No.	%
Buffalo only	2	16.7	4	22.2	6	8.6	12	12.0
Cattle only	3	25.0	3	16.7	16	22.9	22	22.0
Buffalo and cattle	-	-	2	11.1	3	4.3	5	5.0
Neither	7	58.3	9	50.0	45	64.3	61	61.0
Total	12	100.0	18	100.0	70	100.1	100	100.0

bits of grain left in the fields after the harvest, but in going from place to place they are often herded through fields that have not been harvested, and owners of these fields sometimes complain that this practice injures the plants. The lack of good-sized swimming areas where the ducks can be kept, and the lack of space for foraging seem to be the main limitations to more extensive activity.

In the case of chicken raising, the limitations have been different. Chickens in the village have difficulty surviving because of the ravages of what the villagers refer to only as *toi*, or "pestilence." Typically, chickens are allowed to run loose without restriction, feeding upon anything that is available in the yard or house, including the paddy which is stored in bins inside the house. No particular effort is made to feed them or care for them, with the result that large numbers of them are thin, sick-looking, and afflicted with skin disorders. The maximum rate of egg production is estimated at 16 days continuous laying, which undoubtedly accounts for the fact that none of the villagers questioned in the sample reported they had eggs for sale as surplus beyond those kept for home use.

One attempt was made to introduce improved techniques and methods of raising poultry by a staff member of the Fundamental Education Center. New stock provided by the Ministry of Agriculture was given to fifteen families in the village, along with instructions on building shelters for them, feeding them, taking precautions to ensure a clean water supply, and assistance in giving the chickens inoculations against poultry diseases. The households were advised to feed the chickens on a diet of broken rice, paddy, vegetable leaves, grass, bran, egg shells, together with ground shrimp and small fish.

Despite all precautions, all the chickens provided for this test died within a short period of time, and the experiment has not been repeated. The specific cause is not known but is probably the same type of disease which affects other poultry in the village. Some villagers ascribe the pestilence to bad luck or regard it as a punishment by heaven for unspecified misdeeds; others accept it as a fact of life to which they must adjust. The failure of the experiment obviously fortifies these points of view to some extent.

As far as can be determined from conversations and from observation, the families selected to participate in the poultry experiment continue to use the new methods which were introduced, but are back to raising local stock instead of imported strains. Aside from these few, however, there does not seem to be any tendency for other households to adopt the new methods. As in the case of corn and tomatoes which were introduced from outside the village, people in Khanh Hau feel that non-local strains of poultry are not suited to the climate and, in general, do less well than local stock. Some farmers even claim that local stock is fifty percent more resistant to disease than outside poultry. However, those who continue to use the new methods with local stock report visible improvement over the results obtained by other villagers. For example, they say that egg production is nearly double, though still only one-third the rate achieved by the imported new strains, and that local chickens grow fatter and are stronger under the new diet and improved care.

Small kerosene burning incubators were also introduced at the same time, also provided by the Ministry of Agriculture, and while those who used them say they were at least as good as normal methods, they were not enough of an improvement to arouse interest on the part of other villagers. A large part of the problem seems to have been that the eggs used were not carefully selected, and a high proportion did not hatch. Those who used the incubators say that a large number of eggs are needed to make its use profitable, and that it is difficult to get enough eggs locally for this purpose. They prefer to buy day-old chicks in the Tan An market for 4 to 5 piasters, rather than buy eggs from the Ministry of Agriculture at 2 piasters each and take the trouble to hatch them, with the attendant risk that some proportion will be lost.

Swine production—The raising of pigs has been attended with problems very similar to those of poultry. Pigs are also highly susceptible to illness, which the villagers refer to by the same term, *toi*, that they use for the disease which strikes poultry. New strains of pigs were also introduced into the village at one time, through the Ministry of Agriculture, and given to several of the farmers, with the requirement that they repay the government with one or two pigs from the first litter. These, in turn, were to be given to still other villagers. Many of the new stock died, however, despite widespread inoculation, and the experiment does not seem to have spread very far beyond the relatively few households who first took part in it.

Reaction to this experiment is somewhat like that in the poultry experiment, although the villagers do not seem to feel that the new varieties are more susceptible to disease than local ones. Both seem to be affected to an equal degree, and inoculations are not always successful in either case. Moreover, the villagers believe the off-spring of new varieties and local varieties are an improvement over the local strains. They seem easier to fatten with the same kinds and amounts of food, the meat tastes better, and it is not "grainy" and therefore does not smell bad. Farmers do not find any change in fertility, and the size of the litters seems to be the same. People in the village attribute the size of litters, or in fact the ability to raise pigs at all, to what they call possession of a "hand" (*tay*) or the "lot" or "favor" of heaven (*phan*). This is analogous to the Western notion of a "green thumb" in gardening, and many villagers feel that this is the determining factor in successful animal husbandry. Without it, it is useless to expect good results, and many have therefore apparently abandoned attempts to raise animals. Despite some complaints that participation in the government's program cost them money, the over-all attitude of the villagers, as in the case of the poultry scheme, is that the experiment was a "good" thing, even though it failed to produce any substantial improvement.

Except for a few farmers who have been more than usually successful, most of those who raise pigs in the customary way do so without much special attention or care. They will buy one or two small piglets each year, raise them for six months or so, and them sell them in the village or i in nearby markets. Young piglets cost around VN$ 400, and after six months sell for approximately VN$ 2,000. Depending on the type of care provided during this period, the cost of feeding during the six-month interval is about VN$ 1,000. This means a return on the amount invested in the animal in the vicinity of 50 percent, provided of course that the animal survives. Most pigs are fed rice bran mixed with the pulp from banana trees and table scraps. They move freely through the house and yard, rooting for other food where they can find it. A few provide sties for their animals, but this is not a general practice.

The sickness which attacks pigs in recognized by a sudden loss of appetite in the animal. Inoculations, furnished through the Provincial Veterinary Service, are given by the village at a cost of 15 piasters a shot, and some villagers use this service. However, others admit that if they find a pig has become ill, they will try to sell it to a buyer or to a slaughter house—an interesting insight into the kind of meat which sometimes makes its way into local markets. They also say there is general failure to comply with the law that requires that the deaths of animals be reported. If a pig dies, for example, they simply sell or eat the meat themselves, and do not bother to report the death.

A few farmers, those who have the "hand" for it, do raise pigs on a larger scale and generally exercise greater care in doing so. For example, they feed a sow who has just produced a. litter a mixture of rice and rice bran, gradually reducing the amount of rice and increasing the amount of bran over a period of one month. This is more expensive than other methods, but they believe this diet will give the piglets a better quality skin (the skin hair will be smoother) and longer ears. These are considered desirable qualities in pigs, indicative of health and good quality meat. Litters are born in the fields, and the birth is carefully supervised to prevent damage to the piglets. For the first fifteen days, the piglets are kept in a small enclosure so that they will not be smothered by the sow, and at feeding times the piglets are carefully rotated so that all will receive enough milk. At the age of two months they are ready for sale. Sows are not bred until they are at least five months old, and then no more than twice a year.

Buffalo and cattle—As shown earlier, ownership of buffalo and cattle is not very widespread, even among the upper and middle class households. It would be erroneous to minimize their importance, but it is nevertheless true that a majority of the households in the village are not involved in raising these large animals. The reasons for this are not, as in the case of pigs and poultry, that there are difficulties in raising them, but rather involve considerations of finance and convenience. Government-furnished inoculations have apparently been successful in minimizing the spread of disease among buffalo and cattle, and villagers have not registered complaints on this score.

However, aside from plowing and harrowing at the beginning of the planting season, and possibly a second harrowing and rolling which takes place prior to planting a second crop, there is almost no way in which the buffalo are used productively. A few families still use buffalo in the threshing process, but the traditional method has been abandoned by most households. They are not used as beasts of burden, do not haul carts in this village, and are not used to draw water or for similar chores. For a large part of the year, therefore, they are a care for which there is no concurrent return in work performed. Some villagers have said that if you have children who can look after the buffalo, it is cheaper to own one, but if you must hire someone to tend them it is more economical to hire them when they are needed.

Cattle, too, are little used as beasts of burden, and are regarded as inferior to buffalo for farm work. Because the pasturage is so poor, they give no milk for home use or for sale. Fresh milk and other dairy products are not used by most Vietnamese rural families, so this is not considered an important loss. The main purpose in raising cattle, therefore is for sale as meat, and while some are slaughtered throughout the year at village festivals, most are sold outside the village. The one exception is an imported cow which is being kept in the village by the Veterinary Service. Much larger than the typical Vietnamese cow, it is being raised for its milk-giving qualities. To aid in this project, the farmer who takes care of it supplements the usual diet of straw and grass with rice bran mixed with water and a mixture of bananas and sugar cane.

Probably the biggest bar to more widespread ownership of large animals is the financial one. Full-grown buffalo and cattle sell for upwards of VN$ 4,000, and calves sell for half that amount. This represents a sizeable investment by village standards, and there are risks attendant which many are unwilling to undertake. Under a buffalo loan program begun in early 1956, some farmers were able to borrow up to VN$ 3,500 toward the purchase of buffalo imported from Thailand. Since that time, however, no new opportunities to borrow have been open to people in this village. The general opinion of the program seems to be that the opportunity was a welcome one, although they point out that Thailand buffalo are small and do not work as well as Vietnamese.

Convience seems to be another factor, particularly among the upper class households, who in most cases could afford to own buffalo. Instead they prefer to rent the plowing services from others and therefore avoid the necessity of investing in, and caring for, animals which have a limited usefulness to them. Households in this socio-economic group are not interested in the additional income which might derive from renting plowing and harrowing services to others. At the other end of the scale, lower and middle class households who own or rent small amounts of land benefit from owning buffalo because they avoid payment of the cash costs of renting plowing service, and can also add another source of income by renting service to others. However, for them the initial cost is the stumbling block. The infrequency of cattle raising can probably be explained in the same terms.

The large animals are usually kept in a separate shed at night, located near or adjoining the house on the home plot. They are provided with shelter, straw, and water, but during the day are allowed to roam along village streets and paths, over dried rice fields, or are picketed in one of the few pasture spots that are available. There they eat the grasses and herbs that grow along the bundings or near the home plots, and there is no restriction on their movements other than keeping them away from garden areas. Young boys usually accompany them during the day to move them from spot to spot, to keep them from causing crop damage, and to bring them home at night. No payment is made for grazing rights, and with virtually unlimited access to all parts of the fields the villagers do not feel they have a problem in obtaining adequate pasturage. They are aware that the feed available to their animals is poor and that their cattle are thin by outside standards, but they do not seem overly concerned by these facts.

Future Prospects for Secondary Farm Production

The foregoing description should give some impression of the present role played by secondary farm production in Khanh Hau, and also some of the factors which seem to have been responsible for it. In a sense, there are few surprises, for the basic problem is the familiar one of poor resources or inadequate knowledge of how to make better use of mediocre ones. The most promising area for improvement is in the raising of poultry and pigs, but experience has shown that hasty experimentation does not always work, and the prevalence of disease in both cases poses a critical problem that requires sound technical assistance and advice. Superstition and folklore are also important blocks to change here, but obviously successful examples will go far in breaking these down. An increase in vegetable and fruit cultivation is inhibited by more fundamental difficulties—lack of water, lack of proper soils, and lack of financing to some extent. While some improvement can undoubtedly be made, this is not an area of great promise. Finally, buffalo and cattle, currently raised by a minority of villagers, could also be increased, although the area is not ideal for it, and there are financial problems associated with initial investment. Obtaining food is also a consideration, particularly if the number of animals increases substantially and the present pasturage facilities become overtaxed. A lack of access to water prevents more villagers from pursuing fish culture, and this is not always remediable by the efforts of the villagers themselves.

All in all, prospects for increasing farm income through increased secondary production are not bright. Although marginal improvements could be made in all areas, they hold little promise of substantial gains in village living standards. As was the case with rice production, we have further evidence of the basic incapacity of the village to support its growing population from its agricultural activities alone.

6

THE MARKETING PROCESS

The Sale of the Annual Rice Crop

The culmination of the effort and waiting that go into the production of rice paddy is in the sale of the harvest, and over two-thirds of the village crop is sold for cash. In most respects the marketing process is a simple one, but the market structure has been changing in recent years, possibly less in the area of Khanh Hau than elsewhere. It would be best to describe the market for rice from the farmer through all intermediate stages to retail and export, but this information was not readily available. The portion of the market process described here offers only the limited view as villagers tend to see it.

Since Khanh Hau produces paddy that matures at different rates, there is no single time when the farmers are seeking to sell. Instead, paddy flows onto the market over a period of months starting with the first harvests in September and continuing into the following February and March. Not only do the crops mature at different times, but the willingness to sell will vary with individual farmers. Some evidence of the pattern is provided by replies given in the survey, and which are shown in Table 6.1. They indicate that for village farmers as a whole, around one-fourth do not have enough paddy in a normal year to sell as a cash crop. Of those who do, the timing of the sale tends to fall into one of three main patterns. As might be expected, the patterns differ between the socio-economic classes, but in some ways the results of the survey are surprising.

A large proportion of farmers in the lower class (41.0 percent) do not raise enough paddy to sell any for cash, since the members of this group, by definition, have the smallest holdings of all. Selling the crop immediately after harvest implies a certain inability to delay marketing very long, a pressure to obtain cash, and one would expect to find that the lower income groups would fall heavily into this category

TABLE 6.1
Timing of Paddy Sales, by Socio-Economic Class, Village of Khanh Hau

Time of sale	Upper class	Middle class	Lower class	All classes
Immediately after harvest	36.4%	17.6%	17.9%	20.9%
Some immediately after harvest, some later	27.3	70.6	7.7	26.9
Throughout the year as cash is needed	9.1	5.9	30.8	20.9
When price is highest	18.2	5.9	2.6	6.1
Do not have enough to sell	9. 1	-	41.0	25. 4
Total	100. 1	100. 1	100. 1	100. 1

as well. This does not seem to be the case; in fact, over one-third of the upper class farmers replied that they also sold their paddy immediately after harvest. It may be that many upperclass farmers were pressed and therefore sold their crop as soon as possible. On the other hand, this may have been the time when they preferred to sell, and does not imply eagerness to get cash in all cases. The majority (54.6 percent) of the upper class households, however, sell their crop at various times after the harvest. A substantial proportion of middle class households sell some paddy immediately, but hold some for later sale. A large share of lower class farmers sell paddy throughout the year as their need for cash arises.

The probable explanation for these findings, assuming the responses to the question are fairly reliable, is that many farmers, but particularly those among the lower class, do not have enough paddy to constitute a genuine cash crop. All farmers supply their own rice needs from their crop-sometimes by keeping part of their harvest, but sometimes by selling their crop and buying paddy of lower quality and price for home needs. Immediate sale also provides the cash for repayment of debts and payment of rents. This would be represented by nearly one-half (47.8 percent) who sell part or all of their harvest immediately. Lower class households who have enough paddy to sell probably do not have very much, and their pattern therefore is frequently to keep paddy instead of converting it into cash, selling small amounts throughout the year as cash need arise. The temptation to spend cash is probably very great—therefore, the preference for holding less liquid assets. Only the upper class households showed any sizeable proportion (18.2 percent) who marketed essentially on the basis of price considerations, but the small size of the sample may have colored this result to some extent.

There are no central markets in the vicinity of Khanh Hau, where farmers and buyers can gather to arrange the sale of the paddy. Instead, buying and selling is on an individual basis and probably, on balance, works to the advantage of the buyers. At least three-fourths of those who sell paddy do so to rice merchants who either come from the village of Khanh Hau or from neighboring villages of similar size. These merchants are all Vietnamese, and all are also farmers on a full-time basis Villagers say that this has always been true, and that Chinese have never been important buyers of local paddy. In former times, Vietnamese worked as agents for Chinese, but now they work for their own account. Only 10 percent of the households sell directly to buyers from Cholon, still the center of the rice trade in Viet Nam, but a significant proportion of these are upperclass families who have larger amounts to sell and are therefore of greater interest to the Cholon merchants than the small volume producers. For example, none of the lower class households sell directly to Cholon buyers.[1]

The first contact leading to a sale of paddy may come from either the merchant or the farmer, depending on the needs in each case. A farmer anxious to sell some of his paddy seeks out one or more merchants, gets price quotations, and closes the sale at the best price he finds. Merchants who want paddy canvass farmers' homes, making offers and picking up what they can. In general, merchants will be seeking paddy at times when the price spread between

Saigon and the countryside is relatively high, but at other times it is the farmer who looks for a buyer.

Easy generalizations about the "price of paddy" are likely to be misleading, because in any case it is a function of many factors. In the first place, Viet Nam grows a great number of different varieties of rice, each distinguished from the other by taste, texture, and similar characteristics, and valued in different ways by the consuming public. Different parts of the country are suited to produce different varieties, and an experienced rice merchant can take a handful of paddy and tell where in Viet Nam it was grown. Among the varieties there is a further distinction between one of three grades, the grades in this case being fixed by the size and shape of the grain. Finally, there is the matter of the quality of the paddy, which is related to how well it has been winnowed, how well it has been dried, and what proportions of bran and broken rice can be expected to come from it. This is further complicated by the fact that the government had fixed a range of VN$ 40-60 to be paid for paddy of average quality in 1958-59, although the price of high and low quality rice was not subject to control. There is also the matter of transportation cost, which will tend to exert a depressing effect on paddy prices as one moves from Saigon to more distant producing areas.

The sources of price information open to the farmer are limited and haphazard, so he must bargain more or less blindly. There are no radio reports of Saigon prices, nor is there any price information available through the newspapers or government agencies. Instead, the farmer tries to judge the probable price he can get for his paddy from what he knows of prices paid to his neighbors or relatives, from scattered reports brought back to the village by other farmers, or from written reports from relatives who may live in Saigon. The farmer will start by asking what he considers to be a high price, given what information he has. If that is accepted, the word will be passed and other farmers will start out by asking even higher prices. If the original asking price is refused, and if he really wants to sell, he will he will have to reduce it until it is accepted. Thus, by crude maneuvering, the seller attempts to find the market price and make the best bargain he can find.

The buyers however, have access to much better information than the sellers, with the result that by moving quickly they can take full advantage of the imperfection in market knowledge on the selling side of the market. Merchants tend to gather daily at certain rice mills in the larger towns. There they come in contact with other merchants and with buyers from Cholon and discuss prices and market forecasts. These meetings tend to fulfill the function of a real commodity market, although they are not actually organized as such. Merchants also make trips to Cholon itself, and there learn at first hand the developments taking place in the main market. These contacts are much more frequent, and much more productive of sound information, than the farmers are able to achieve. For example, buyers will probably learn of a slight upward shift in the price of rice a day or two before this information is very widespread in the village, and by moving quickly can buy paddy from farmers at the old price. Once the farmers learn of the change, by noting the increased buying or from outside sources, those who can do so will hold out for the higher price which they then know can be paid, and the initial advantage to the buyer will have gone.

The volume of business which a merchant does in any one year is limited largely by his capital. The village merchants, who are the most frequent buyers in Khanh Hau, tend to be small operators with an annual turnover of no more than a few thousand *gia*. Some of them are so hampered by lack of capital that they buy from farmers on partial credit, promising payment of the balance when they have resold the paddy. This means they may offer slightly higher prices, which would reduce their profit on the operation and hamper their attempts to accumulate capital. Most merchants do not have a special place of business, but store the paddy they have purchased in rice mills until they are ready to sell it again. When they feel the price is at a desirable figure, they have the rice milled and then sell to one of the dealers from Cholon who tour the rice mills buying milled rice for shipment to Cholon. It is in the course of these contacts that the merchants come to know the movement of prices in the larger markets.

Another alternative is that the local merchant may

mill paddy into rice and take it directly to Cholon to trade on his own account. Once there, he takes samples of rice to various wholesalers, receives offers from them, and finally selects the one to whom he will sell. The government is also a buyer of rice, and sales here are also based on bids made when samples of the rice are shown. Although some merchants in Khanh Hau do sell directly to Cholon in this way, this is not a common practice. Most of them are too small and too unfamiliar with market practices in the large city to attempt any business activity beyond the Tan An area.

The merchant must transport paddy from the house of the seller to the mill where it will be stored until resold. The value of the bran extracted during the milling process will approximately cover the costs of transporting from the village to the nearby mills. The broken rice obtained is bagged and sold in Tan An, and is never shipped to Cholon. The whole milled rice, bagged in 100 kilo sacks, is now shipped primarily by truck, although some still moves by water through the network of rivers and canals. Transportation costs by truck (Tan An to Saigon-Cholon) in 1958 were VN$ 10 per 100 kilos, in addition to the taxes levied on the shipment in Tan An before it left for Cholon. Over and above the cost of milling the rice, offset by selling the bran, the markup on whole milled rice between Tan An and Cholon was in the vicinity of VN$ 43 to VN$ 48 per 100 kilos which included transportation cost, bagging, taxes, and a profit of from VN$ 5 to VN$ 10 for the merchant.

It should be emphasized, however, that this estimate of the price spread between the two cities is by no means firmly established. There are no published data which give actual prices paid and received, so this picture of the pricing is built from the descriptions provided by Khanh Hau and Tan An rice merchants. Their stories contradicted one another at some points, but the above represents a consensus of what they said. As a rule, merchants were very reluctant to give specific information on things such as prices, amounts handled per year, or share of the market, and so important detail is lacking. All merchants, however, complained that one of the things which acted to increase the price of milled rice in Saigon was the frequent inspection of shipments made by customs check points along the way. To avoid delay or penalty paymentss customs officers were offered, and accepted, bribes of varying amounts. The effects of this practice would, of course, be multiplied the farther a shipment had to travel, for this would mean an increased number of checkpoints to pass through.

As general practice, merchants prefer to keep a portion of their holdings in the form of milled rice to be ready to sell immediately should an attractive offer suddenly come along. On the other hand, if they can afford to do so they will keep another portion in the mills in paddy form so that they can place it on the market during the third or fourth lunar month, at a time when prices have usually advanced somewhat.

The rice merchants thus gather the paddy, transport it to the larger local mills, convert it into milled rice, and send it into the Cholon market as price conditions there make this most advantageous to them. Since they are in close contact with the Cholon market, they have a distinctly favorable position relative to the farmers, who are not only shut off from accurate and timely market information, but in many cases are under pressure to sell at least a portion of their paddy as soon as it is harvested. The price control program, which puts a floor as well as a ceiling on the price farmers receive for their average quality paddy, may provide some protection to the farmers. However, even with the change in the structure of the rice market in recent years, which offers greater competition on the buying side than before, it seems probable that, as the villagers believe, the price control program is more helpful to the consumers in the cities than it is to them.

The Rice Merchant

As noted earlier, the rice merchants with whom the villagers deal most frequently come from the same or a neighboring village, are Vietnamese, and usually are farmers themselves. Only the larger farmers in Khanh Hau deal with merchants coming from Cholon, and even these tend more and more to be Vietnamese rather than Chinese. Some of the village merchants learned the elements of the business from fathers or relatives, but a majority of them did not come from what could be termed mercantile families. Some of the merchants operate rice mills, in addition to farming and dealing in rice, but this is not true of all merchants or of all mill operators. In terms of socio-economic class, they tend to come from the middle and upper class, with more probably from the latter than the former. Only one of them can be classed as a "substantial" merchant, but even he could not be said to exercise an undue influence over paddy sales in the village. In short, the role of the rice merchant is one which is essentially secondary to other occupations, and people who engage in it are indistinguishable from their neighbors by virtue of wealth or social position.

Entry into the ranks of merchants is open to all who can provide adequate financing and a fair amount of skill and/or courage. Because of the intricacies of the trade, and the many pitfalls which can trap the beginner, the number of people engaged in this occupation changes from year to year. In one year as many as twenty to thirty may be in business, but this may drop to ten or less the following year. Success in this area depends not only on awareness of current prices and costs, but also on a thorough knowledge of rice itself. Lack of experience can lead to overestimation of the amount of milled rice and underestimation of the amount of broken rice, as well as miscalculation of the amounts of bran which will result from a given batch of paddy. On a large scale, this could be disastrous. For this reason, some rice mill operators refrain from acting as merchants, because they feel they do not have the experience to know fully what success in the field requires.

A number of recent failures are attributed, by the villagers, to the government's refusal to permit rice exports in 1957-58. In their view, several of the merchants had bought paddy at high prices and had milled and stored it in anticipation of even higher prices. The closing down of exports brought a subsequent drop in domestic prices, with the result that the merchants were forced to liquidate their stocks at a loss. This version is somewhat inaccurate, for although exports in 1957 were limited, Viet Nam still exported 183,871.8 metric rons of rice. The government's program of limitation may have had some depressing effect, but not a serious one. There seemed to be general agreement however, that the number of merchants had decreased from 1957 to 1958, and this was because most of them suffered severe losses for some reason in the prior year. Though this may reflect other factors, it still seems reasonable to add the hazard of changes in government policy to the other normal risks which the merchant faces.

The village rice merchants are of interest as a group because, like the rice mill operators, they represent the emergence of an entrepreneurial class in the village. In a few cases, of course, mill operator and merchant are the same person, but aside from that, the merchants and mill operators are both groups of men motivated by the desire to buy cheap and sell dear and are willing to risk savings and borrowings in the process. By and large, village society does not condemn them for trying to do so. No stigma attaches to the merchant as such, and although farmers bargain and haggle with him in selling their crops, the merchant does not seem hated or feared by them. Still, a number of factors weigh against commercial success and probably inhibit the rate at which entrepreneurial activity can grow.

A number of problems were brought out in discussion with merchants, all to the effect that Vietnamese are at a disadvantage as business men, particularly vis-a-vis the Chinese. The first of these was the pervasive lack of funds which limited the scale of Vietnamese business operations and the capacity to adopt new ideas. Closely linked to this was the belief that Vietnamese were distrustful of each other, a factor which made it difficult to maintain partnerships or to expand a business into one with numerous shares. Not only did this indicate a certain tendency toward instability in partnerships, but it also added to the difficulties in pooling funds and accumulating adequate supplies of capital. This same quality probably accounts for the apparent lack of collective action among rice merchants to fix prices or otherwise control the buying in the villages for their own advantage. Lack of experience is another factor, along with limited opportunities to acquire it. Vietnamese were also pictured as lacking organizational ability, as being unable to keep adequate records of their business dealings, and as less able to plan an operation carefully and carry it out.

Finally, these village merchants felt that Vietnamese frequently were not tactful in their business dealings and often failed to bestir themselves for the extra effort which might bring extra business. For some, a life of commercial trading is one which bothers the conscience. One villager, a devout Buddhist, was a merchant for a short time, but he gave it up because he felt he had to be a "teller of lies" in order to survive as a merchant. In his view, a necessary part of the occupation was to misinform farmers on the price of paddy in order to ensure a profit for himself. Rather than continue to do this, the man gave up his merchant activities to once again become a tenant farmer.

Despite these reported flaws or shortcomings in characteristics associated with business success, the most successful merchants have expanded their activities in volume and in area and show indications of being able to plan and organize business activities with skill. One of them, the son of a rice merchant, even draws on Vietnamese tradition to support his approach to life and has adopted as his motto a proverb which translates freely as, "The home of the truly big man is everywhere" (*Chi quan tu cuu chan nghiep, Dai truong phu tu ha gi gia*). With this outlook his interests have ranged from the Plaine des Jones as far north as Banmethuot. After suffering a severe loss in an accident which destroyed a truck and its cargo, he has borrowed money to begin again, this time by opening a rice mill.

On balance, the prospects for increased entrepreneurial activity seem good. The characteristics noted, if true, will provide drawbacks, but the increased opportunities, the greater competition which will be possible as a result of the growth of local rice mills, and the lack of strong cultural bars to the occupation of merchant-entrepreneur appear to be the more dominant influences at the present time.

7

THE ORGANIZATION OF HUMAN EFFORT

General Observations

It is a paradox that while specialization or the division of labor is important to any understanding of the high productivity found in industrialized societies of the West, the kind of specialization which takes place in peasant and primitive societies is often responsible for a "roundabout-ness" in production and distribution that detracts from the efficient use of resources. The question to consider therefore is not that of "specialization" versus "non-specialization, " but whether or not a society is organized in such a way as to contribute to increased productivity of human effort. It is important to examine the types of specialization found in Khanh Hau in this context, in addition to any purely descriptive value the topic may have.

Turning first to specialization by general type of primary activity, the most important single occupation in a rural community such as Khanh Hau is, of course, that of farming. Upwards of two-thirds of the heads of households regard this as their main occupation.[1] The only other primary occupation to claim a sizeable number of heads of households is that of laborer, from one-fifth to one-fourth. All other occupations, however important in other terms, are proportionately small.

For many household heads one occupation is not enough, and they supplement their incomes by secondary and tertiary activities of several kinds, in addition to relying on the labor imcome of spouses and children. The key role of farming also shows up here, for about two-fifths of the replies list farm labor as a secondary occupation. This is followed in importance by non-farm labor, included in about one-fourth of the replies, and then by a series of infrequently mentioned activities such as rice merchant, storekeeper, artisan, custodian, practitioner of traditional medicine, cook, musician, and so on, no one of which is numerically or proportionately significant.

About one-third (35 percent of the sample) of the households are supported by the income of one member, while the majority rely on the income of two or more members. A small percentage (6 percent of the sample) are households supported by children or other relatives and in which no member actually works for income. Significant differences exist between socio-economic classes, with a much larger proportion of the upper class households supported by a single member than in lower class households, where several people usually work for income. Middle class households fall between these two extremes.

Wives are gainfully employed in nearly one-third of all households. About half of the working wives in lower class households hold more than one income-earning job, but for the most part this really means two gainful occupations. The range of occupations for women is narrow, even more so than for men. Weaving and sewing register the largest number of participants, followed closely by farm labor. Only a very few work as domestic help, and the proportion engaged in petty commerce of one kind or another probably does not exceed 10 percent of all wives in the village.

Less than one-third of all households have sons and daughters over 12 years of age gainfully employed, but over half the households indicated that they either had no children or the children were not yet 12 years of age. Where the question was applicable, however, there was a distinct tendency for young people in upper class households not to be gainfully employed outside the home. Conversely, a majority of young people in both middle and lower class households had some gainful employment. The range of occupations followed that of the parents in terms of both the kinds of jobs performed and their relative importance.

This, in capsule form, gives some idea of who works in the village, the kinds of occupations, and the degree of diversification. On this kind of sample basis the minor occupations do not stand out clearly, for they constitute such a very small proportion of the total village activity,[2] but this nevertheless reflects accurately the relative degree of occupational specialization. It shows that in an agricultural village such as Khanh Hau the bulk of the working population is engaged in farming either as farmers or as farm laborers, and that there is relatively little division of labor in the sense of numerous different occupations followed by substantial numbers of people. Moreover, with a few exceptions, non-farm occupations are practiced in conjunction with something else, usually farming or farm labor. Thus, a carpenter may also farm, and a custodian may also work as a farm laborer.

Specialization within broad occupational categories is not carried very far either, other than for a tendency to make some division of tasks between men, women, and children (see Table 7.1). Most farmers and farm laborers are able to perform all the activities associated with raising rice and secondary crops and customarily do so. Even non-farm labor consists of such things as digging ditches and ponds, mounding the floors of houses, and repairing the thatch on roofs and walls, much of which is identical to normal farm activity in terms of the skills required. This simply indicates that the level of technical proficiency involved in the major village occupations (e.g., farmer, carpenter, storekeeper, etc.) is so low that those practising any one of these can usually perform any of the separate activities connected with it. If a farmer hires others to do the plowing or assist in the planting it may reflect a number of things, financial and status factors among them, but rarely a lack of ability to perform the same task himself. Even the specialization of work within occupations between men, women, and children overlaps to some extent, and does not seem to follow any set of-hard and fast rules. If any pattern is discernible, it is that the men do the key work in farming and all types of artisanry, while the women do all the other tasks. This does not seem functionally related to any feeling that the key jobs require strength which only men have, for women perform many tasks that involve heavy manual labor, but tradition seems to have reserved certain activities to the men, and this pattern is continued because there is nothing in the society generating pressures to alter it.

Gourou has reported a pattern of specialization in villages of the Tonkin Delta in the 1930's that is substantially different from anything found in Khanh Hau. In that northern delta area there was not only specialization in different home

TABLE 7.1
Work Specialization in Khanh Hau

Type of Work	Persons Performing the Work		
	Men	Women	Children
Replanting		X	
Weeding	X	X	
Reaping harvest	X	X	
Carrying paddy to mill		X	
Carrying water	X	X	
Collecting fuel		X	X
Fishing	X	X	X
Carrying paddy from field		X	
Buffalo tending		X	X
Gardening	X	X	
Cooking	X (some)	X	
Peddling	X (some)	X	
Carrying bricks, tiles		X	
Carrying sand		X	
Weaving		X	X (some)
Sewing by hand		X	
Sewing by machine	X	X	
Storekeeping	X	X	
Gleaning fields			X
Plowing	X		
Harrowing	X		
Seeding	X		
Uprooting	X		
Carrying seedlings	X		
Threshing	X	X (some)	
Irrigation	X		
Cutting fuel	X		
Scattering fertilizer	X		
Carpentry	X		
Roofing	X		
Carrying lumber	X		
Implement making	X		
Rice mill operation	X		

industries as between villages, but the manufacture of items was often broken down into component parts which were mad in different villages. There was also specialization by families, many of whom had carefully preserved handicraft skills and secrets over several generations.[3] Some of this specialization was due to the availability of raw materials nearby, but in many cases there seemed to be no such basis, and villages continued to engage in specialized production for which they had no natural or other advantage. Gourou believed the explanation lay in the perpetuation of routine tasks the secondary status of industry compared to agriculture, and the poverty of the artisan which precluded anything beyond very meager investment in industrial activity.[4] Whether this be sufficient explanation or not, Khanh Hau and its neighboring villages do not contain either the industry or the kinds and degrees of specialization described for Tonkin. The specialization found in Khanh Hau is rudimentary by comparison.

Agricultural Activity

Most villagers are, of course, familiar with farm work from childhood, and most of them can use the few simple tools and techniques which are associated with it. Even some of those who have acquired a specific skill such as carpentry will work as farm laborers when there is a slack demand for their craft and a demand for labor. In other words, the heavy dependence on the land means that nearly everyone is familiar with farm work and engages in it to some extent. Probably two-thirds to three-fourths of the adult villagers work as hired laborers at some time during a normal year, and in addition, there is some exchange of labor between households on a reciprocal basis. Despite the importance of labor from outside the household, village institutions do not organize the labor force very extensively.

The most important type of formal organization used in agriculture is a labor contracting service. The labor contractor (*trum cay*) is appointed annually by the village council upon his own application for permission to act in this capacity. The position is not hereditary, although there is some tendency for sons to follow fathers in it, in principle the job is open to anyone approved by the council. Further, the labor contractor does not gain much prestige or financial advantage from his appointment, and those who hold it are usually of modest means and social standing. There are no fixed limits to the number of such labor organizations the village may have, but since there does not seem to be much competition to form them, the number rarely changes from year to year. Khanh Hau has had three such organizations for several years.

These labor groups stem from the need to have several workers (*con cay*) at one time for certain farm activities, e.g., the transplanting of young rice shoots and the harvesting of the crop. Each labor contractor has from 40 to 60 people, both men and women, working under his direction. The laborers approach a contractor of their choice at the beginning of the year, arid once having agreed to work under him they may not change to another during that same year. However, there is no compulsion to join a group, and members are not required to accept work made available to them. While the groups retain this voluntary character, in practice the laborers in any group tend to come from the same neighborhood and to stay in the same group from year to year.

When farmers need field labor they contact one of the labor contractors and indicate when and where they want help. The contractor, in turn, summons laborers in his group, divides them into working units of appropriate size, and dispatches them at the proper time. One of the rights granted to the contractor is that of using a traditional buffalo horn signal to call the workers to his house when he has work for them to do. The function of the contractor is to distribute the available work evenly among the laborers attached to him, and provide farmers with an adequate supply of labor at the time it is needed. He also exercises a certain amount of supervision, along with the farmer, to ensure that the work is done properly, for his reputation as a contractor rests to an important degree on the performance of those who work in his group.

Wage Structure

Laborers in these work groups receive wages that are

standardized throughout the village and are the same as those for laborers hired individually. There is no village institution with the formal responsibility for setting wages, although on occasion, the village council may settle wage disputes between laborers and employers. Otherwise, it is generally accepted that everyone pays pretty much the same for similar kinds of work. The labor contractors decide the wage rate they will pay for the coming year, and there have been some upward adjustments in the past years to offset increases in the level of prices. In 1958 the wage for common labor, farm and non-farm, was VN$ 30 per day plus two meals for men, and VN$ 20 per day plus two meals for women. Some special labor, not supplied through the labor groups, is paid at a higher rate, e.g., those operating the water wheel receive more, as do people skilled in thatching roofs. The rate most frequently quoted here is VN$ 40 per day plus meals. However, even ordinary wage rates may be raised if the farmer is pressed and wants a job done quickly—actually, this is a bonus incentive arrangement to stimulate extra effort.

The labor contractor received pay from two sources—the laborers and the employer. The laborers pay him at the rate of VN$ 15 for every thirty man-days of labor he gets for them; the employer pays him at the rate of VN$ 1 for each man-day of labor he supplies.[5] Although the workers are given meals on the days they work, the contractor does not receive any food as compensation. All work is paid for at the completion of the job by the employer himself, not through the contractor.

Counting meals, the wage rate of unskilled farm labor does not compare unfavorably with the daily wage rate received by unskilled labor in Saigon industry. However, the work in the village is much less steady, and only a very small proportion of village laborers have more than six months of regular employment. Over half the laborers report they have four months' work or less in any year. There is relatively little to do during the months of the dry season when the farm work is finished for the year. This is the time when new bundings are built, new houses go up, fish ponds are dugs and similar activities take place. Much of this, of course, is done by the farmers themselves, for only the more well-to-do can afford to hire labor for these tasks.

Outside of the work arranged through the labor groups, all employment is on a direct employer-laborer basis. Someone hiring labor will seek out the person he wants and offer him work for a particular day or days. The laborers do not look for work themselves and apparently never go from house to house asking for employment, even though they have not had work for some time. In practice, farmers tend to hire a certain few men whose work they prefer, and while they rarely retain them for long periods of time, the farmers do try to reserve their time in advance. If the man they want is busy, they will get someone else. Most jobs require only a few days work at a time, so laborers shift employers frequently during the busy months. The young, conscientious, and able laborers are in greater demand than the old, the weak, and the careless.

The refusal to look actively for work is limited to employment in the village, and villagers do try to find jobs in towns such as Tan An and My Tho during the slack season. A few are successfuls but most are not. Those most likely to find work in towns are the ones with special skills, and several village residents work there regularly as carpenters, masons, bus drivers, and other specialists. There is a general feeling among unskilled laborers that town jobs are really not open to them because people in the towns keep the unskilled labor opportunities for local friends and relations. This is probably true, for none of these towns have much activity requiring common labor, and it would be natural for townspeople to exclude outsiders under the circumstances. The point is that the villagers are anxious to work if there is any opportunity to do so, and their refusal to canvass for jobs in the village does not extend to non-village work. As a guess, this reticence would seem to involve recognition that jobs within the village are limited, and the least embarrassing solution is to let the employers contact the people they want as job opportunities arise.

The more well-to-do farmers hire outside labor because they can afford it and because it is prestigious to avoid manual labor. At the other end of the socio-economic scale, the poorest households also hire outside workers, since they themselves lack buffalo and the major farm implements and must hire the labor which comes along with the capital equipment. Except for this, however, the poorest households tend to rely on labor exchange with others who are similarly situated, generally on a neighborhood basis. Even though many neighborhood clusters are made up of interrelated households, there is no clear indication that relatives are preferred in these exchanges. This also holds true in hiring labor, for over two-thirds of those in the sample hiring labor replied that they made no special effort to give work to relatives.

In summary, the organization of farm work is, on the whole, fairly casual. The only formal labor institution in the village is the organization of workers under the direction of labor contractors, and this covers only a portion of the total use of farm labor. Individual arrangements between employer and laborer are equally prevalent. Wages are not formally fixed but tend to be standard throughout the village, subject to some individual bargaining in special cases. There is also some labor exchange among poor households, but this cannot cover all labor needs, and even the poorest farmers must sometimes hire labor from outside the household.

Non-Agricultural Economic Activity

General—The heavy reliance on the soil which relegates non-agricultural activities to a minor role in village life does not mean that the latter are all unimportant, for they do function in response to a variety of needs. The people engaged in these non-farm activities do not fall into easily distinguishable classifications. Many, but not all, follow a long-standing family occupation, but since village society does not have well-defined institutions which allocate people into various occupations—there are no equivalents of occupational castes, guilds, or religious sanctions for or against certain kinds of work, for example—there is some mobility into and out of all occupations. All activities are compatible with farming; some of the less important non-farm occupations, such as weaving and petty commerce, are essentially sources of supplementary income for the wives of farm households. The factors which determine entry into non-farm activities therefore tend to vary somewhat with each case and are not functionally related to village institutions as such. It is unfortunate that there are few signs that these activities will develop much beyond their present secondary status.

Storekeeping—There are stores located in various parts of the village, but unlike some villages in the area there is nothing which could properly be termed a shopping or market center. The largest number of stores is found in the Ap Dinh-Ap Moi residence area, which is also the main population concentration in the village. Here there are a half-dozen business that are big enough to be classed as stores and at least that many more that are really only stands selling a limited number of articles. With so few, it is difficult to describe their location in terms of any pattern, but the most probable explanation is that they tend to cluster where people gather. For example, three of them are located near the school and the village *dinh* and council house, which is the most frequently visited part of the village, and these also tend to be the largest stores. The others, all much smaller, are strung out, on or near the main village street and toward the other end of the village. The neighboring village of Tan Huong, located just across the stream that divides it from Khanh Hau, does have a market area, and another collection of five or six stores is located there, obviously to catch the business of housewives going to the market for their daily food purchases.

Only two of the storekeepers in Khanh Hau itself are of Chinese origin, and both of these have had training and experience in preparing herb remedies and compounding traditional Chinese prescriptions. All other storekeepers are Vietnamese, all were born in the village, and all are married to someone from the village or related to a village family. Thus the stereotype of the Chinese or the outsider controlling village commerce does not hold true in Khanh Hau or, from limited observation, in the other villages nearby.

Most of the storekeepers had some previous experience in the same type of work prior to the time they established their present places of business. The Chinese, for example, went through an apprenticeship period in Chinese drug shops before striking out on their own—one of them began as an apprentice in Tan An. One Vietnamese learned the rudiments of the business from his father, who was also a storekeeper.

He added to this experience later by operating a charcoal business in Cholon, but this went bankrupt during the war years. The women storekeepers, of whom there are four, had either prior experience as an assistant in the store of another or started as a peddler or petty merchant in the market place. The women have thus tended to move into this occupation by gradual stages, often as expansions of their petty trading, and most of them come from farm rather than commercial families,, Some stores are run by wives of farmer husbands, and while the husband may take some active part in running the store, the chief responsibility for it rests with the wife. None of the Khanh Hau stores are large enough to require paid assistants or apprentices. Wives and husbands share the duties, which consist mainly of one of them being in the store while the other is away, and although older children may help out from time to time there is literally no opportunity for those outside the nuclear family to gain experience in this occupation. All stores are run by a nuclear family unit, and there is no participation by other members of the extended family. There is also no sign of extended family specialization, which means that a nuclear family operating a store is usually the only part of the extended family to do so.

The term "store" as used here refers to businesses selling a wide variety of general merchandise. In physical terms, the business area is usually the front part of a building that has living quarters for the storekeeper and his family either at the rear or attached at one side. Stores are located in all house types—thatch, frame, and brick—but all have the same feature of combining living and working space in the same or adjacent buildings. As you enter the store proper, the goods for sale are in full display on shelves and tables, and customers are free to examine them and select what they want. Occasionally there is a crude counter in the store where the cash box and some of the more commonly purchased items are kept together.

The inventories of goods on hand vary from store to store in terms of the range of things offered, and the size of the inventory reflects the storekeeper's access to capital or to credit. They prefer to stock a large variety rather than concentrate heavily on a few items, with the result that most of the stores duplicate one another's offerings. With the exception of one Chinese store that specializes largely in medicines, there is no tendency among the others to specialize in particular lines. A typical general store, therefore, will carry a selection of goods such as these—metal kitchen-ware, chinaware, crude kitchen pottery, water jars, writing materials and school supplies, chop sticks, canned milk, tea, limited amounts of canned food, wines and brandies, beer, soft drinks, joss, votive paper, candles, lamps, kerosene, textiles, some ready-made clothing, mosquito netting, hats, haberdashery, drug items, flashlights, wooden clogs and rubber sandals, fish traps, mats, baskets, shoulder boards, sickles, knives, rope, glassware, patent medicines, tobacco and cigarettes, betel leaves and areca nut, lime, spices, sauces, small cakes, candies, and limited amounts of fresh fruits and vegetables and dried fish. This is not intended to be an exhaustive list, nor do all the stores carry all of the above items. However, it provides some idea of the range and kind of things which can be purchased locally without leaving the village for the larger market towns. When asked what things they would like to add to their stocks, given the extra capital to do so, most storekeepers could not think of any item particularly in demand which they did not already have. A few who did not stock textiles replied they would do so if they could. One wanted to add bicycles, bicycle accessories, sewing machines, and fertilizer, none of which were sold in the village stores because, with the exception of fertilizer, they are all relatively expensive and turn over slowly in a rural community.

The competitive area extends beyond the boundaries of the village because large market towns are easily reached by cheap and frequent bus service. Thus prices in the large towns of Tan An and My Tho, and in the smaller but important market centers of Tan Hiep and Tan Huong, provide the competitive parameters for the village stores. Most storekeepers make a practice of checking retail prices in at least one of these places two or three times a week, usually when they go for their own inventory needs, but pricing practices are erratic, and price competition does not appear to be very vigorous. Some of them say they would not reduce a price to meet a lower one in stores in other towns until they could find a supplier who would also sell at a reduced rate. Not until they had worked off the old inventory at the higher price would they cut to a new lower level. Mark-ups tend to be high on low-priced things (e.g., 25 percent on cheap kitchen pottery) and lower on high-priced goods (e.g., clothing, handbags, luxury goods). A certain amount of bargaining may take place between customers and storekeepers on some of the more expensive things, but on standard items that are purchased frequently there is one fixed price for all. On the whole, therefore, bargaining in the stores is minimal. Barter is also very limited and rarely takes place between storekeepers and customers. What little barter there is involves neighbors and friends in the exchange of farm produce. The price structure in village stores is thus one of rough correspondence with prices in towns and villages nearby but subject to some price lag as the result of indifference, lack of full knowledge, or unwillingness to cut old profit margins.

Village storekeepers tend to feel that their business depends largely on their location, the variety of goods they stock, their ability to extend credit to customers, and the personality of the storekeeper himself. Prices cannot be too far out of line, but villagers do not "shop around" when patronizing village stores, and once they have selected a place they continue to deal with it almost exclusively. This opinion gains some support from the events of the last few years. The most recent store to come to Khanh Hau was opened by a Chinese in 1953. It is located directly across from the school and carries the largest selection of goods of any store in the village; in addition, the storekeeper is a practitioner and dispenser of Chinese medicine. Three older stores, all located in the same vicinity, report their sales in recent years have fallen off by one-fourth to one-third their former level. Some of this is due to poor harvests, but a major part of it must be ascribed to the appearance of the new competitor who came from outside the village. His locational advantage and his sale of medicines have attracted customers initially, and many of them have continued to concentrate their purchasing there. Since his prices are no lower than the other stores, and he does not extend credit widely, the explanation must rest on the factors indicated.

There is a distinct seasonal pattern in the sales of all stores. After the harvest, and particularly if it has been a good one, villagers tend to buy the more expensive things they need but cannot afford at other times of the year. The lunar new year is another special time for buying, and the demand for cloth and for children's clothes becomes specially heavy at that time. On the first and the fifteenth of each lunar month there is a spurt in the purchase of candles and joss for the ceremonies which celebrate those days. The most steady business, through the entire year, is for such things as sauces, kerosene, tobacco, candy, cakes and cookies, writing materials, tea, and the ingredients for chewing betel. Turnover of the rest of the stock is very slow, except for the pattern already noted.

All of the local storekeepers have started their present businesses themselves; none of them inherited his store or purchased it as a going concern. All of them have faced a problem of insufficient capital, and all have borrowed money to buy and maintain stocks. For borrowing, they rely on open-book credit from supplying merchants or organize or participate in a mutual aid society (*hoi*). Both methods are popular, but most storekeepers express a preference for the open-book credit if they can obtain it. Although they profess to pay no interest on such borrowing, and say that prices are not raised in such cases, there is probably some advance in the prices at which their purchases from suppliers are recorded. At times they extend partial credit on purchases, usually one-third of the purchase price. On some goods, textiles and pottery, for example, no credit is given at all. Thus, far from being financially strong, important factors in the village economy, village storekeepers are in fact heavily indebted to others and operating marginal enterprises that have developed relatively little.

The tempo of life in a village store is a slow and lazy one. The quiet that prevails most of the day is broken from time to time by the arrival of a child to buy two piasters worth of *nuoc mam*, or a farmer who has come to gossip and drink tea or wine, or a housewife stopping in to buy a bit of soap or some areca nut. The goods on the shelves are covered with dust of several months' accumulation; drippings from the jars of fish sauce bring flies to swarm in the warm sunshine that comes through the open doorway. A good day may see VN$300 of total sales; a poor one, and there are many, will bring VN$ 50 or less. In such a setting, the typical village storekeeper appears to be an unimaginative purveyor of a fairly standardized range of consumer items. He displays neither awareness of possibilities for expanding business by making the store a more attractive or economical place in which to buy, nor interest in directing customers' attention to special prices to attract sales. Storekeeping, to him, is simply a process of stocking a line of goods and waiting for people to walk in and buy them. It is true that lack of capital and the poverty of most people in the village set limits to what can be done, but there is a pervasive lack of drive or enterprise among the storekeepers and a failure to fully exploit the opportunities that do exist. None, for example, have made efforts to expand into wholesale rice buying, farm credit, rice milling, or transport, although there are no bars, other than financing and resourcefulness, to keep them from doing so. Future prosperity, from their standpoint, is tied almost exclusively to hopes for good rice crops and an opportunity to get more capital in order to widen the variety of their offerings. The prospects for finding a nucleus of risk-taking entrepreneurs among this group to spark economic development at the local level are therefore dim indeed.

Rice mill operations—Recent changes in the patterns under which rice is milled are extremely important, not only because of immediate effects on village life and village market opportunities, but also because of their implications for economic development in general. The milling operation is the single most technologically advanced and largest scaled process with which villagers have contact, and the mill owner-operators, as a group, are among the most enterprising in the society.

The past few years have witnessed a revolutionary change in the institutional setting for milling rice. Until about eight years ago, most of the rice that was milled commercially was taken to the large rice mills of Cholon, then and now a predominantly Chinese community. The commercial network of buyers and wholesalers gathered paddy from the countryside and shipped it, as paddy, to the Cholon mills. There it was converted to polished rice in one of the few large-scale mills, after which it was redistributed throughout the country through the wholesaling and retailing parts of the distribution system. Much of this entire process—the buying, shipping, milling, redistributing—was in the hands of Chinese business firms, although Vietnamese were active in some phases of it.

There were very few rice mills located outside Cholon. Farmers polished rice for home use in hand-operated grindstones which each family kept for this purpose. Polished rice available in the markets of the larger towns came from Cholon, and very little of it was milled locally. The heavy concentration on the buying side of the market worked to the disadvantage of the farmer selling his paddy. Farmers still complain that in those days the buyers could effectively prevent them from finding out the actual price of rice because the market was closely controlled. Price information was available only to those in the rice business, and since they tended to work cooperatively they could keep the farmer ignorant of any bargaining advantage he might have really had.

The important change of the last six or eight years has been the substantial growth in the number of local rice mills. In the vicinity of Khanh Hau, as an example, small rice mills have sprung up in all the neighboring villages, large mills have gone up in the town of Tan An, and Khanh Hau itself has two rice mills within its administrative boundaries. This development is significant in several ways. For one thing, because of the increase in the number of mills and their location near the source of paddy, polished rice is now supplied under more competitive conditions than before. For another, this effectively removes the concentration on the buying side of the paddy market, since paddy no longer goes only to Cholon. Local mills and local buyers now provide a more competitive market for the farmers' paddy than before. The spread of the important milling process to the countryside should therefore both increase the prices received by farmers for their paddy and reduce somewhat the price paid by retailers, other things being equal.

The villager in Khanh Hau has a choice of eleven mills in the immediate area—five of them in Khanh Hau itself and the neighboring village of Tan Huong, and six of them in Tan An. With the exception of one mill in Tan Huong, all of them are owned and operated by Vietnamese. The two mills actually located in Khanh Hau are owned by families that have been residents of the village for several generations, and one of the mills in Tan Huong is owned by a resident of Khanh Hau who comes from an old and important village family. Although all of the families engaged in milling have owned and operated farm land, and in some cases still do, all have also acted as rice merchants or landlords' agents and have had some entrepreneurial experience. This is more or less to be expected, because it requires large savings or a substantial amount of collateral to finance an investment the size of even a small rice mill, and large landowners or merchants would be the only ones likely to have these prerequisites. In addition, these types of background are more apt to provide the kind of experience needed to become a successful mill operator.

The entry of Vietnamese into the marketing and milling of rice, which has proceeded rapidly during the past ten years, is due to a number of developments. No data are available to permit an examination of the process in detail, but those engaged in the rice business in its various phases tend to advance similar explanations. They cite the fact that some Vietnamese managed to acquire funds for investment during the war years and for the first time found themselves in a position to start a business of their own. Many of them had gained some knowledge of machinery or marketing by working for Chinese or French firms and had begun to feel confident that they could work without supervision and for their own account. In addition, educational opportunities had broadened and literacy was rising. There was relaxation of the control which the Chinese and French are said to have had over the importation and sale of milling machinery, and it became available to anyone who could afford to pay for it. Finally, the decree which closed eleven selected occupations to foreigners, and which fell most heavily on those who retained Chinese citizenship, created opportunities for Vietnamese to get a foothold in the rice business. This did not take effect, however, until the general trend was already well-established.[6] All this does not provide a very solid basis for understanding the reasons why opportunities for Vietnamese began to widen at the particular time they did, but it seems obvious that there must have been some combination of accumulated experience and financial capacity to invest which occurred at about the same time.

The two mills located within the administrative boundaries of Khanh Hau are quite small, and both cater to the needs of villagers who mill small quantities of paddy at a time for home consumption. Superior to the old hand-milling process, the small mills nevertheless give poor polish to the rice, and rice that is intended for export or sale in larger towns is taken to the larger mills, either in Tan An or in larger neighboring Tan Huong. Where rice for home use is the sole concern, the villagers go to the mill that is most convenient to their homes, and it is this market which the two small mills, one in Ap Dinh and one in Ap Cau, tend to serve. This pattern was clearly brought out in the survey when people were asked where they milled their rice. All those in Ap Dinh reported they used the mill in Ap Dinh; all those in Ap Moi went to Ap Cau or Tan Huong.

The mill in Ap Dinh, the more thriving of the two, is typical of this highly localized operation. It is owned by a family that has built two other rice mills in distant villages and is currently operated by one of the brothers of the family. Built in 1952 at a cost of VN$ 250, 000, it contains a combination of new and second-hand machinery housed in a frame building with a metal roof. It is centrally located in the hamlet and is adjacent to a stream, so that paddy and rice can be transported by boat if desired. This latter is an important factor in the location of any rice mill, and all mills in the area are placed near a stream or river.

Inside the mill there is a single polishing machine, powered by a gasoline motor placed outside and in the rear. An array of sorters, sifters, and screens constructed of wood are run by conveyor belt from the same engine. These were all either made in Cholon or built on the premises by specialists who come from Cholon. The mill owner has one assistant, and together they are responsible for the entire operation, including minor repairs and maintenance of the engine and milling machinery.

Villagers who have come to have their paddy milled into polished rice line up inside the entrance in the order of their arrival. The amount of paddy brought by each is weighed and measured, recorded, and passed to the miller's assistant, who starts the different batches through the milling process at time intervals which keep the customers' paddy separated.

The paddy passes from the hopper into a separating machine which removes straw and bits of foreign matter, after which it is taken by conveyor to the top of the room where it begins a slow descent through various sifters and polishers. The result is a large proportion of the polished white rice, a smaller proportion of broken grains, and a quantity of rice bran, all of which belong to the owner of the paddy if he pays the highest milling price. The paddy husks are also saved, but these belong to the miller who sells them for fuel and fertilizer at a price of one piaster for a large sack. The proportions for paddy of average quality in the village are such that 100 *gia* of paddy (1900 kilos) will produce 1100 kilos of milled rice, plus 140 kilos of broken rice, plus 60 kilos of No. 1 bran and 120 kilos of white bran. Better quality paddy yields more milled rice and No. 1 bran, and therefore less broken rice and white bran. The lowest grades of paddy will do just the opposite.

The mill charges villagers VN$ 1.50 to VN$ 2.20 per *gia* for the milling service, the lower charge applying if the farmer does not want the bran. Since paddy is less likely to spoil than milled rice, people mill only enough to meet family needs for a week or ten days. The usual milling order, therefore, is a very small one. Moreover, there is no day or part of the week which is set aside for rice milling, so the demand for milling service is spread fairly evenly throughout the week. There is some seasonal pattern to the business, with the heaviest demand in the months of December through March, at the time of the harvest. This slackens somewhat in April and May, and demand after this is substantially less because some of the villagers will have exhausted their supplies of paddy and begun to buy milled rice in the markets. The seasonal pattern for the big mills in Tan An and elsewhere is more pronounced. As in the village, the heavy demand comes at harvest time, but from that part of the crop which is being sold for cash and prepared for shipment to Saigon and other large towns. The small local mills, being more tied to the tempo of small-scale home consumption, find the seasonal shifts less extreme.

Short of examining the accounts of the mill, one cannot get an exact picture of cost and price relationships, but from conversations and general observation it is possible to make a few speculative comments. First of all, it seems most plausible that the small local mill is little affected by the direct competition of the larger number of mills in the vicinity. Villagers go to the nearest mill with small quantities of paddy at a time. Any small differences in the milling fee would be more than offset by the cost and inconvenience of transporting rice and paddy a longer distance. While nearby mills thus exercise a limiting influence on prices, the local mill operator in Ap Dinh still has leeway in the charge he makes and could probably, for example, double the milling fee without substantial loss of customers.[7] This would not be true for the mill located in Ap Cau, for it is in a cluster of three other mills, and prices are uniform in all of them.

Given this freedom from immediate competition, the mill owner in Ap Dinh nevertheless appears to fix his prices to correspond with the other mills and at a mark-up that is about 50 percent above what he figures to be his unit costs. These are based on a rough calculation of the cost of labor, fuel, lubrication, spare parts and repairs, taxes, and license fees spread over an anticipated annual volume of milling. The mill owner makes no provision for depreciation, interest on his investment in the mill, or salary for his own services. What remains after paying immediate out-of-pocket expenses is regarded as return to the owner.

Since the machinery is largely second-hand, the mill has frequent breakdowns , and the owner must make frequent repairs and replacements of broken or worn-out parts. Minor difficulties can be handled on the spot, but a major breakdown, perhaps requiring a new part, necessitates the attention of a technician from Cholon. Since the only people able to make major repairs are in Cholon, the cost of repairs is higher the greater the distance of the mill from Cholon. Still, the owner had no plans to buy new machinery because he found the present arrangement, even with the many repairs, fully satisfactory. He found that costs, particularly fuel costs, tend to go up over time, which he felt could usually be traced to the need for some repair, and that costs generally drop back to former levels once it has been made. The mill owner thus conducts his business with reference essentially to the net return after paying out-of-pocket expenses, and without any particular program to replace equipment that has become worn out or obsolete. Since the mill runs fairly steadily through much of the year, idle capacity is not a critical problem, and the owner does not feel impelled to increase the efficiency of operation beyond present levels.

Instead of expanding or improving the mill in Khanh Hau, the family which owns the mill in Ap Dinh has chosen to expand the number of mills it owns and to place them in other villages. Actually, these new mills are located over 200 kilometers apart, one south of the Mekong and the other in a relatively unsettled area that is being opened for development. This willingness to move into new areas, and sometimes into different lines of business, is a characteristic of many of the new mill owners and operators. Of those in or near the village, approximately half also act as rice merchants on their own account, buying paddy and holding it for later milling and sale when prices have improved. One owner, a resident of Khanh Hau whose mill was in neighboring Tan Huong, bought paddy for his own account in a resettlement area over 100 kilometers distant from his mill. His reasons for doing so were to utilize the mill's capacity more fully, since the poor harvest in the Khanh Hau area did not provide enough rice to do so through customer demand alone. The others do not follow this practice—the mill in Ap Dinh, for example, does not have much storage space, and the mill owner does not buy for his own account or store paddy for other merchants—but some of them have invested in transport enterprises or have acquired an interest in other types of business. All of the owners in the area are also farmers, and all of them actively cultivate their lands. None of them are reported to lend money in the village for farming or any other purpose, although all of them are in a position to do so.

The liquid capital of mill owners is limited, for much is tied up in the mills. The owner of the mill in Ap Dinh reported that the latest mill he built cost VN$ 350,000, of which he was able to raise VN$ 250,000 from his own funds. The additional VN$ 100,000 was borrowed from relatives at a monthly interest rate of 3 percent. He expected to be able to repay this loan within six months out of income from the new mill. The wooden parts of the milling machinery were actually constructed in Khanh Hau by craftsmen brought from

Cholon and were shipped by water to the new site in the Plaine des Jones for assembly there.

To summarize impressions of this occupation, there is much that is encouraging in the way in which mill operators carry out their role. It is true that the operation of the local mills is, in many respects, routine and inefficient, but the owner-operators as a group show much resourcefulness and a willingness to move into new areas of the countryside and into new lines of enterprise. There is undoubtedly a selective factor at work, for, with one exception, none of the local mill owners were engaged in that business ten years ago. Men who have seized an opportunity once before will probably be quick to do so again.

Implement making and carpentry—The trades of implement maker and carpenter are the two most important occupations within the craft category, from the standpoint of both the number of persons involved in them and their contribution to village economic activity. In this connection it should be pointed out that, like all other activities—rice milling, marketing, and farming, to name the most important—the practice of these trades is not confined to the village, but cuts across administrative boundaries throughout a wide area. In Khanh Hau itself there are no more than three or four implement makers, but possibly twenty-five to thirty carpenters who make their living substantially from these occupations. Villagers in Khanh Hau can and do draw upon craftsmen from outside, and Khanh Hau artisans are called to work in other villages. Both crafts call for skill and experience of an order not possessed by the ordinary village inhabitant, and while not especially lucrative, they provide most of these artisans with a standard of living that is high by comparison with most village farmers. In turn, villagers rely on them to provide the tools needed in farming and to build their houses and furniture. The men who now perform these essential tasks are also in a position to play an important part in introducing innovation and change.

Although many of these artisans follow the craft of their fathers, entry into these occupations is not entirely determined by nuclear family relationships. All craftsmen go through a period of apprenticeship, and this is sometimes arranged for the sons of friends or distant relatives. Fathers undertake to train their own sons if it is decided they will follow the same occupation, but it is not inevitable that they will. For example, one carpenter in Khanh Hau did not train his own son in carpentry because the boy seemed to lack the necessary skill. Instead, he took as an apprentice a nephew who later worked with him in full partnership as a journeyman.

A distinction is made between implement making and carpentry, and the two kinds of activity are kept quite separate. Carpenters will repair some farm implements but rarely try to make them, because they claim they do not have the required skills. Conversely, implement makers do not build houses or make furniture for the same reason. This alleged lack of skill is somewhat difficult to understand, for neither the implements nor the houses and furniture are very complex, and a man skilled in the use of tools should have little difficulty in copying the work that others have done. Nevertheless, the specialization tends to persist.

Both carpenters and implement makers work on the basis of special orders and do not produce for speculative sale. In many cases, the customer furnishes the materials, and the artisan supplies only the labor. If the customer requests it, the craftsman will provide the necessary materials, but the quality will depend on the amount the customer wants to spend. In any event, all items are built to the specifications of the customer, with some possible alteration at the suggestion of the builder. The wood used in implements and other items must be brought in from outside the village, for there is no wood available from local supplies. Most artisans have favorite suppliers from whom they obtain the best quality woods, and some of these are quite distant. One implement maker, for example, goes as far as Cholon and Bien Hoa for his wood and even orders it a year in advance of use to ensure proper seasoning. If the customer is less particular and if the amount required is small, the wood will be purchased from a small lumber dealer in Khanh Hau or Tan An, but they, in turn, must bring it from elsewhere. Wood is usually available only in a limited number of large sizes, and all cutting to the sizes needed must be done by hand.

The typical artisan owns a set of simple tools, many of foreign manufacture, valued at from VN$ 1,000 to VN$ 2,000. It usually includes saws of various sizes, a hatchet, chisels, plane, drills (to be used with a bow), a square, a metal ruler, a plumb line, pliers, and a hammer. Only the metal parts of the tools are purchased; the wooden handles are made by the owner. Costs of replacement, largely to provide new blades for chisels, planes, and saws, may run from VN$ 500 to VN$ 600 annually.

Both types of craftsmen price their services in basically the same way, on an estimate of the labor time involved in the job. The cost of materials, if purchased, is extra. Implement makers know the amount of time needed to make the different farm tools and quote standard prices accordingly. The pricing of carpenters' services to build a house is slightly different, since houses are less standardized. Customers rarely solicit competitive bids from several carpenters, but instead the more general practice is to approach a carpenter whose reputation is known and agree on a price for the job. This is usually based on the carpenter's estimate of the time that will be involved, modified by a certain amount of bargaining before agreement is reached. The going wage rate for skilled workmen of this kind is not fixed in any way, i.e., there is no guild or association which sets the wage rate, but the most commonly quoted figures were from VN$ 50 to VN$ 60 per day. Although there is a wide area over which there is competition between the craftsmen of several villages, it is not a bidding or price competition. Instead, the artisan tries to attract customers through a reputation for good workmanship. Relatives and satisfied customers tell others of his skill, and, in effect, a decision to hire is made before any price negotiations take place. Thus craftsmen are more concerned with the quality of output than with shading the price of services. In the case of house construction, another element affects the choice of a carpenter. House construction is begun only on certain propitious days according to the lunar calendar, and if the carpenter of a customer's choice is otherwise engaged on that day, the customer will hire another carpenter. It is preferable to start construction on the proper day rather than delay because a particular workman is not available. There is also some tendency to hire relatives in preference to others, but it is difficult to estimate the importance of this in terms of the allocation of orders.

There is some indication that these craftsmen are willing

to adopt innovations, although on the surface, much of what they do, as well as their way of doing it, remains traditional and unchanged. Implement makers, for example, have influenced the change in types of plow and the adoption of the threshing sledge. One man also proudly displayed a partially completed water wheel on which the axle was set in imported ball bearings, an addition which greatly reduces the physical work of pedalling the wheel. While its adoption is not at all widespread, it nevertheless represents a very recent attempt at innovation. Several of these artisans expressed interest in learning similar kinds of change and improvement, but there was little evidence that they actively experiment to develop new ideas on their own.

In the case of carpenters, examples of successful innovation are more difficult to find, either in their work methods or the design of the things they make. For example, in the construction of the frame for a house of wood or thatch, a very large proportion of the time spent on it goes into planing the wood and assembling the frame itself. Each piece is cut to fit exactly into the others to make the frame solid and durable. The pieces are tested and reshaped until, like an intricate wooden puzzle, the fit is perfect. Screws and nails are seldom used, but wooden pegs are driven into the fitted joints. Carpenters say that they realize this time-consuming assembly of house frames is not very efficient, but they fear that more extensive use of nails or other changes in method would increase the cost of the house by more than the savings in labor time could reduce it. Like the implement makers, they express an eagerness to learn new methods, but with the condition that the final cost of the product not be increased through their adoption. If one can believe statements such as these, craftsmen do not seem concerned that innovation may result in some loss in work time or subscribe to any "lump of work" view. Rather, they tend to believe that a change which can bring a reduction in total costs to customers will lead to an increase in the quantity of their services demanded by the community as a whole.

Most of these skilled workmen do some farming or gardening in addition to their main occupation. There is a certain amount of seasonal change in the demand for their services—both houses and farm implements are usually built during the dry season—but there is enough demand throughout the year so that there is never the complete slack that occurs in farming. Moreover, what seasonal drop in demand does occur comes during the normal growing season, so that between some farming and their main occupation most artisans remain fully employed through much of the year.

As a group these craftsmen turn out good quality, unimaginative, and basically simple work. They show little inclination to experiment and tinker and little artistic talent or awareness. Ready to accept change and not particularly resistant to new ideas, they nevertheless do not seem to be a promising source for initiating change. By knowledge and experience they are the group most likely to shift easily to the use and repair of engines and machines, but thus far they have had little opportunity to become familiar with either. In short, they constitute a pool of limited skills, potentially valuable as an aid in implimenting economic development, but unlikely to stimulate it.

Weaving—Weaving is a marginal activity in Khanh Hau, with probably no more than 15 percent of all households weaving for income and, perhaps, an equal additional number weaving for home use only. Moreover, not only is the extra income very small for those households who engage in it, but the workmanship and artistic quality of their products is extremely limited.

Weaving for income is carried on by very poor families, many of them households headed by a widow, and is restricted to utilitarian items such as bed mats, rice baskets, and bolsters. No one works with bamboo or rattan, and the more elaborate woven goods that are seen in the village are all made elsewhere[8] and sold to villagers in the stores or nearby towns. Residents of Khanh Hau explain the undeveloped status of weaving by the lack of village sources of weaving materials. Reeds do not grow in the village and must be bought in Tan An or other markets, which in turn import them from the Plaine des Jones area to the west. The bamboo grown in the village is also unsuitable for handicraft work.

Women produce woven goods on special order only, and when they have orders in hand they buy the reeds necessary to make them. Lacking working capital, most feel they cannot afford to produce for general sale, and there is no "cottage industry" in the village, with middle men to organize the activity, advance credit or materials, and ultimately collect finished products for general speculative sale.

Reeds are purchased in bundles of standard size, the prices of which vary according to the length of the reeds. These are soaked in water for about thirty minutes, then pounded with a heavy mallet and allowed to dry. The process is repeated three or four times, after which the reeds are soft and pliable enough to be handled easily. The weaving itself is tedious and time-consuming. For example, a Large mat measuring approximately 7 feet by 6 feet would take three days to complete; two smaller mats measuring 3 feet by 1.5 feet could be finished in one day. Depending somewhat on the nature of the final product, the net return to the weaver is about VN$ 7 to VN$ 10 per day.

Because most of the things woven are for normal daily use, little attempt is made to improve their appearance by weaving intricate designs or colors into them.[9] Some women profess interest in learning new designs, and some offered to copy anything for which they could have a model, but this applied only to the simplest articles. By and large, the lack of village artistry in weaving, wood carving, house decoration, or clothing is striking. Lovely woven materials are made by Vietnamese from other parts of the country, but in this area the level of handicrafts has never been very advanced, and parents have little knowledge to pass on to their children.

Thus, prospects for handicraft development in the village are poor, at least in terms of building on the level of arts which already exists. People could probably be taught to weave, but there is little natural advantage in doing so. Further, the returns from this kind of work are currently so low that unless income expectations rise substantially, it is unlikely that weaving for income will increase much beyond present levels.

Petty commerce—In addition to the few stores in the village, inhabitants are served by numerous petty merchants, Largely women, ranging downward in scale of activities from those who keep small stocks of goods in a part of their houses to door-to-door peddlers and roadside vendors. As pointed out earlier, some of the women storekeepers got their start in these smaller-scale activities, but few ever expand beyond the very limited earlier stage.

The lack of a central village market in Khanh Hau has created opportunities for some villagers to go to the larger market towns and bring back items of daily food consumption which can be resold to village residents who do not go to the market themselves. Peddlers selling fresh fruit and vegetables, fish (live and carried in kerosene tins of water), and fish sauces pass along the village paths, stopping at houses to display and sell their wares. Buyer and seller bargain over the price of these items, and on occasion the seller may move on to the next house if the price is not agreeable. Prices for goods sold in this way tend to be fairly close to the prices charged in the markets, and the profit on each sale is quite small. Prices charged by the peddlers cannot exceed market prices by too wide a margin; otherwise the villagers themselves would begin to go directly to the markets. The peddlers therefore provide a convenience, but the closeness of the markets limits the price villagers will pay for it.

Refreshments in the village are also provided by mobile vendors. Canopied, bicycle-powered stands selling ices, beer, and soft drinks move slowly along the main street of Ap Dinh or station themselves near the school at recess and at the end of classes. Most of their business is with children, to whom they sell a confection of shaved ice saturated with flavored syrup. They also sell small pieces of ice used to chill food or drinks, but no one uses ice for refrigeration. This type of vendor is always a man, and there are two from outside the village who regularly call in the village with their mobile stands. They attend all large gatherings, such as village ceremonies, soccer matches, and other occasions. The vendors buy their ice, beer, and soft drinks in Tan An or Tan Huong; the syrups are mixed at home from sugar, water, and artificial coloring.

Another very small-scale business is conducted by several elderly women who set up small food stands near the school during the months when it is in session. These women have amsmall stock of dried fish, sheets of manioc which they cook over portable charcoal braziers, glutinous rice wrapped in banana leaves, and loaves of french bread and relishes which they sell as sandwiches. Pupils buy these as snacks at recess, for children either bring their own lunches or return home to eat at noon. Laborers on the way to and from the fields and other passersby also buy a snack occasionally, but total sales by each peddler cannot exceed VN$ 10 or VN$ 15 a day.

The common denominator of these petty merchants is that, with the exception of the mobile refreshment stands, all are women, and all operate with minute capital investments and very small sales volume. What they sell is limited both by the amount they can invest in saleable goods and by what they can carry on their shoulder boards. Almost no commercial skill or knowledge is necessary, although a skillful bargainer can probably do better on door-to-door sales of foods than one who is content to conclude sales quickly. The work itself is less tedious and time-consuming than weaving or farm labor, for most peddling is done in the morning, and the day's supplies are sold out by noon. This means it is really a part-time activity and can be carried on in conjunction with other occupations. Petty commerce of this kind fills a useful function in the village, but it is nevertheless a marginal activity with little potential for carry-over or development beyond its present low level.

Other occupations—For the sake of completeness it is necessary to mention briefly the several people who are engaged in other specialities. For example, there are two masons in the village, and a few people have had experience as laborers in brickyards. There is also a retired railway employee and three or four bus drivers. Perhaps as many as half a dozen people have had some instruction in, or knowledge about, traditional Vietnamese medicine and herb remedies; one man acts as a first aid practitioner, giving inoculations and administering simple treatments. The members of the village council carry on regular correspondence and maintain records and accounts, and at least one resident male has become a government civil servant. There are barbers, tailors (men and women), priests for Cao Dai and Buddhist temples, teachers in the village school (who come from outside the village), janitors, geomancers, and musicians. Some of these are full-time occupations, but some, like priests, geomancers, and musicians, are employed in these capacities only on ceremonial occasions. The medical practitioners, both Western and traditional, are farmers by primary occupation. With the possible exception of the government-assigned teachers, bus drivers, and the several tailors and seamstresses, these numerically unimportant occupations do not call for highly developed skills. Those who do manage to acquire a high degree of mechanical, commercial, clerical, or professional skill generally leave the village.

Summary

The organization of human effort in Khanh Hau is carried out in uncomplicated ways and with few formal institutions to assist in it. There is specialization, and it separates certain primary and secondary occupations, but it is not a rigid or restrictive specialization of labor and does not hamper occupational or social mobility. It also adds little to productivity, although villagers do depend on specialists to perform certain jobs or functions, and most of them could not duplicate exactly all the goods and services which they now consume out of village production as a whole. This reflects simply that the level of technology in village production is so low that it would not be difficult for any farmer to provide himself with reasonably good substitutes for the things he now acquires from village specialists. Were he to do so, it is unlikely that the production of rice and other farm items would decline, for complete household self-sufficiency would not result in too wide a dispersal of activity or in a substantial decrease in levels of technical skill or artisanry. We therefore find some specialization in existence, some familiarity with it, even some dependence on the convenience or capital-saving it contributes, but this is not a society in which specialization is well advanced or particularly important. What is true for individual households within the village seems equally true for whole villages in the delta region, and there is little of the village specialization found in central and northern Viet Nam.

The failure of specialization to contribute more to productivity than it has is probably due to ignorance of advanced technology in production which requires extensive division of labor and not to ignorance of specialization itself or of the benefits which might accrue. There is no evidence that villagers would oppose specialization, assuming they were assured an adequate income through specialization in ways now unknown to them, but it is unlikely to progress much farther unless clear advantages can be found in it. At present all indications are that such change must be brought from outside the village.

8

PRODUCTIVITY IN AGRICULTURE

To the economist, with his particular point of view and interest, a study of village life is important largely for the light it may shed on the organization of production and, therefore, on the underlying reasons which explain the range and amount of goods and services which are available to the villagers themselves. This is because the discipline of economics has traditionally been concerned-with "economizing, " with making the most of resources which are assumed scarce everywhere relative to human wants—even in wealthy societies. Within this frame of reference the problem of development becomes a matter of identifying the available resources and examining the manner in which they are employed to determine (a) whether or not more could be produced by some shift in the factor proportions, and (b) to what extent new techniques, new capital equipment, or new ideas can be easily acquired and adopted with productive advantage to the society.[1] Enough has been said at this point of the manner in which economic activity in the village is organized and conducted to permit some analysis of it from the standpoint of productivity.

Productivity of the Land

Turning first to productivity, as measured by the yields per unit of land area (hectare), it is possible to get some crude approximation of the ability of the village to provide for its needs from utilization of this important resource. Lacking accurate measurement of yields in the village, but using the assumed average of 120 *gia* per hectare cited earlier, we have an estimate of 2,280 kilos of paddy per hectare as a measure of the average productivity of village rice land.[2] This puts the village at a substantial advantage compared to the average for all Viet Nam in 1959, reported as 1,450 kilos per hectare.[3] It is also better than the averages for Thailand, the Philippines, Indonesia, India, Burma, and Brazil, and more comparable to the 1957 average for mainland China of 2,670 kilos per hectare. However, it is still well below the 5,100 kilos per hectare produced in Italy, the 4,810 kilos per hectare produced in Japan, or even the 3,430 kilos per hectare produced in the U.S. in 1955.[4] What can be done to alter this picture, recognizing that it is already more favorable than the yield performance believed to be typical for Viet Nam?

The first possibility is to use the land for alonger period each year, since it is currently unproductive for half or more of any twelve-month period. This, of course, is because the seasonal rains provide adequate moisture for crop production only part of each year. Irrigation therefore suggests itself as an alternative to this limitation on the productivity of the land imposed by nature, but it is an alternative which requires more real investment than the village itself can raise, because local streams and creeks are affected by the tidal action of the sea and turn salty or brackish during the dry months. Further, reliable underground sources of fresh water lie at depths of 400 feet or more. American technicians state that irrigation wells are not feasible in the region, and certainly irrigation projects that would tap the distant year-round sources of fresh water are beyond the reach of individual farmers or even groups of villages. Certain areas of the village could be converted from one-crop to two-crop land by building canals which extend existing streams, but irrigation by this means can be carried on only during the normal rainy season when the streams are fresh. Major expansion of production possibilities beyond the present two-crop limitations imposed by rainfall conditions must therefore be ruled out as far as local initiative is concerned.

Granting the difficulties in increasing productivity of the land by lengthening the time it can be used, are there ways of increasing productivity within a growing season of the current length? On the face of it, it would seem that there would be, given the productivity achievements in rice culture attained elsewhere in the world. On the other hand, there are several reasons why rapid increase in productivity is unlikely, in addition to the inability to lengthen the growing season.

In some types of agriculture, the relative abundance of land makes it possible to employ extensive methods of cultivation with farm machinery of advanced design. Productivity in such cases, whether measured as output per unit of land area or output per unit of labor, is usually quite high. Rice cultivation does not fall within this category, however, for some of the highest yields per unit of land area in the world have been recorded in areas, such as Japan, where the typical size of farm holding is small and the methods used are labor-intensive, not extensive. Therefore, the fact that the average owner of rice land in Khanh Hau has 4.7 hectares, or that the average tenant holding is 2.4 hectares, or even that the average size of holding distributed under the land reform program is only 1.6 hectares, does not by itself give cause for alarm. Doubts over future increases in land productivity arise from other sources and must be approached through more devious paths.

If there is any effect on the productivity of the land because of the size of typical farmsteads, it is an indirect one through the squeeze felt by the farmer attempting to support a large household on the income (in money and in kind) from a small plot of land. Reference has already been made to the use of chemical fertilizers by the villagers and to the great enthusiasm with which they are now employed. Use is conditioned partly by financial considerations and partly by the experience over the years with amounts, timing, and kinds that are most effective. However, since there has been no careful, informed study of the fertilizer requirements for high yields in the village, and certainly no attempt to educate the farmers on the proper kinds and amounts to use on individual fields, it seems highly probable that their use could be made much more effective than it has been in the past; this would be one of the most promising methods of increasing the productivity of the land.

Leaving aside the question of getting accurate technical information to farmers in the village—something which would have to come from initiative and resources outside the village itself and which is currently largely unavailable—the major limiting factor affecting the use of chemical fertilizer is the financial ability to buy adequate amounts of it. Data from the village do not permit any exact statement, since no attempt was made to measure average gross or net household incomes, but family budget data strongly suggest that the present low standard of living leaves little surplus for the purchase of additional fertilizer, even though this may result in more production later in the year. The high incidence of indebtedness also attests to this state of affairs, although the main debt problem is finding someone willing to lend rather than the size of the debts typically owed. In short, assuming (as seems reasonable) that altering the factor proportions to increase the amount of capital going into the productive mix (here, chiefly chemical fertilizer) could increase the output per hectare, the typical farm in Khanh Hau, tenant or owner-operated, is "too small" to do this, in the sense that nothing is left from each year's crop to provide the funds for such additional capital investment. Even if the farmers knew the proper amounts and kinds of fertilizers to obtain, which is currently not the case, they are precluded from obtaining more chemical fertilizer at present by a lack of lending sources, rather than by any unwillingness on their part to add to their indebtedness.

Nor does there seem to be much opportunity to increase the productivity of the land by adding crops other than rice. Here we encounter the same problem that prevents more extensive double cropping of rice, i.e., lack of water, but there is a further limitation in the kinds of soil which are found in Khanh Hau. This was discussed in the description of secondary crops, and it was noted there that second crops of vegetables, generally succeeding a single rice crop, have been limited to the small area of the village where sandy soil has permitted this type of diversification. Technical means may exist which make it possible to use black clay soil for crops other than rice within the normal growing season, but these are currently unknown to the villagers. Growing additional crops of vegetables, without reducing the size of rice production, would require additional inputs of labor and the further employment of existing capital goods, but this could be done without difficulty. The major limiting factors appear to be the pattern of rainfall, the lack of irrigation opportunities, and the unsuitability of the soil for dry cultivation techniques.

Productivity of Labor

There remains to be considered the problem of labor's productivity in the village, although any generalizations on

this topic are also hazardous. For example, observation of cultivation techniques leaves one with the impression that additional
labor alone would result in small increases in production, if any
at all. Rice fields do not seem to suffer from lack of care. In the
jargon, one would expect the marginal physical productivity of
labor (unaccompanied by technical aids such as more fertilizer,
insecticides, and the like) to be very small, perhaps approaching
zero. This observation may be an incorrect one, for in some high-
yield rice-producing areas, such as Japan, the amount of direct
labor expended on the annual crop is much higher than that found
in Khanh Hau. One estimate for Japan (1949) placed the labor input
at 870 man-hours for the average acre of rice. This would be at least
three times the labor input typical for Khanh Hau, and as indicated
earlier the yields in Japan on the average were about twice those in
Khanh Hau. On the basis of this kind of evidence it would appear
that devoting more time to rice cultivation would produce results,
although what specific activity would be most fruitful in this respect
is not clear without careful study by technicians familiar with the
different techniques. Clearly, the differential yields between Japan
and Khanh Hau can be due to many different factors, but it is also
true that the cultivation of rice in Japan is much more "intensive,"
in the sense of heavy application of the plentiful factor of labor to
the relatively scarce factor of land, than it is in Khanh Hau. Therefore, lacking either the means to increase the use of more advanced
capital equipment (including irrigation and chemical fertilizers)
or to increase the average size of the farmstead (thus assuming no
major emigration of population from the village), more intensive
cultivation presents one of the most promising, though in no way
a certain, means of increasing total product in the village.

How much more intensive application of labor is possible under
existing circumstances? There are at least six months of the year
during which the large majority of employable labor in the village
does not work except sporadically on largely maintenance tasks.
This time, of course, does not coincide with the growing season for
rice or any other crop, so to this extent it does not represent underemployment or unemployment during the peak needs for labor. However, if we take as a measure of the available labor force all the men

from 17 through 44 years of age, and all the women from the ages of 17 through 22, the village would have 623 persons in the work force.[5]

Assuming a peak growing season for the main rice crop of 96 working days during four lunar months, this would mean an available labor input of 59,808 man-days in the village. Assuming further a total labor requirement of 55,554 man-days for the crop,[6] there would still be an excess of over 4,000 man-days of labor that would not be utilized. In other words, if the workforce in the village were fully employed (six days a week) during the peak of the growing season, there would be more man-days of labor available than are currently used on the rice crop, as closely as this can be determined. In fact, this kind of comparison indicates that peak labor needs do not exceed about five-and-one-half days a week for each member of the work force.

This gives some measure of the degree of underemployment during the time of maximum labor needs, and it indicates that while underemployment is not serious, it probably does exist. This corresponds with the impressions of village life gained during the height of the rice growing season, at which time most households were fairly busy on their own land or as hired or exchange labor on the land of others, but not completely so. What this means is that there is no limitation imposed by the size or availability of the work force in the village which precludes additional labor inputs on the main rice crop. Providing there is knowledge available on how additional labor can be productively employed, labor inputs could be substantially increased without adding to the present work force from the ranks of the young, the old, or the women who have been assumed to remain at home.

Tenancy and Productivity

As far as can be determined, the conditions of tenancy as such do not constitute a major obstacle to increased productivity. For example, most rent contracts are in terms of fixed amounts per crop year, which permits tenants the full benefit from increased productivity, at least during the life of the contract. Permanent increases in annual yields, however, would ultimately lead to increases in the fixed amount rents. Even private (secret) rent agreements based on percentages of actual yields permit the tenant some benefit from increased production, although less than if he pays only stipulated amounts.

Sharecropping has never been practiced in this area. The typical landlord in Khanh Hau and neighboring villages has been content to collect his rents and has shown little interest in making improvements which could increase the productivity of his land or in providing assistance to his tenants. Landlords have never been important sources of credit to tenants, and they do not provide tools, draft animals, seed, or other supplies. Over time, most tenants have therefore acquired the few simple tools they need. Moreover, they may expect some reimbursement for any improvements made on the land if the land is taken back by the owner. This failure of landlords to promote increased productivity constitutes a negative productivity effect inherent in tenancy relationships at the present time, but the opposite side of the coin is that tenants are not deeply in debt to their landlords or dependent on them for the tools of production and are not discouraged from undertaking improvements on their own initiative. Landlord-tenant relationships are not accompanied by the crushing indebtedness or complete dependency which, in some countries, keep the tenant in a state of virtual serfdom and rob him of any hope of escaping his situation. Most tenants are in debt to some degree (to neighbors, relatives, the government, and friends, but not to landlords), but this is equally true of small landowners. Indebtedness in this village appears more related to the difficulties encountered in meeting living and operating expenses out of the income from small holdings than it is to tenancy status as such.

In short, most rents are fixed charges held in check to some degree by agrarian reform provisions. The power of landlords has been significantly weakened, tenure is moderately secure, and tenants are not dependent on landlords for credit, tools, or other production needs. Other than the fact that an important share of tenants' gross income must be paid in rents, thereby reducing the amount potentially available for aids to increased productivity, there appear to be no important limitations to productivity increases that would not apply to small landowners to an equal degree.

Land Reform and Productivity

It would be presumptuous to judge the entire Land reform program on the basis of what has happened in one village, for there is considerable variation in local problems of redistribution. Nevertheless, a qualified assessment can be made for that part of the delta which lies north of the Mekong River, for the experience of this village is probably typical of this region.

One of the first things to recognize is the political necessity of a land reform program of some kind. In the southern part of Viet Nam, particularly, absentee and large-scale landownership had become a focal point for political unrest and discontent. The Viet Minh promised to redistribute the large holdings, and regardless of the sincerity or economic viability of that promise, the new Republic of Viet Nam had to come through with a comparable program of its own to gain the support of the peasantry and offset the land appetite whetted by the expectation of land under the Viet Minh. This is in addition to the desire to accomplish land reform on its own merits, which was undoubtedly present to some degree.

Given this necessity, concern centers on the way in which the reform is being carried out and its probable effects. Khanh Hau was fortunate in that land records were not destroyed, and there was no problem of identifying plots for redistribution. Administratively, therefore, there were few important complications. Even so, the program did not assume tangible proportions at the village level until nearly two years after Ordinance No. 57 had been promulgated and more than six months after the necessary identification and application work had been completed at the local and provincial levels. This slowness had both good and bad effects. For one thing, it probably meant a more careful job, but it also caused some Loss in political impact. This was compounded by the fact that only about one-quarter of the households in the village benefited directly from the reform. The general impression one gets is that most villagers think the land reform took an inordinately long time to complete and that even then it did not do too much good.

Political considerations aside, evaluations of the economic effects of the land reform might proceed from estimates of probable changes, if any, in factor proportions. In the case of land, the short-term prospects are for no change at all. This is because the land redistribution simply transferred ownership rights to tenants on the land they had been operating as tenants. It did not involve reorganization or consolidation of land holdings in anyway, and, as Chart 3.3 shows, it had relatively little effect in equalizing the size of land holdings. In fact, the new owners created by the program are, on the average, smaller in terms of size of holding than either the average village resident landowners or the average village tenant farmers. Over time, inheritance should lead to smaller holdings per household, but this will be a relatively slow process. For the present, land reform does not seem to be bringing any significant change in the amount of land utilized per farming unit, i.e., per household.

There is also little likelihood that the land redistribution will be accompanied by changes in farming methods which will alter productivity in one direction or another. The large landlord in this village has never operated his lands for his own account, a condition which seems to apply in neighboring villages as well. Instead, he has been content to rent out his land in the relatively small plots typical of all tenancies in the village and even to permit sub-leasing in some cases. Agrarian reform therefore should not bring immediate changes in methods of cultivation, because the same people, utilizing the same plots of land and employing the same methods, will operate the land as owners instead of tenants. Large landlords in fliis area have shown no interest in advanced agricultural techniques and have not been identifiable as the source of technical innovations. Their elimination therefore cannot be construed as loss of a source of stimulation of efficiency in production.

On the other hand, it is equally unlikely that agrarian reform as such will lead to the adoption of new methods and increased productivity, for reasons already discus sed.

The change from tenant status to small landowner should eventually result in increased income as rental payments are eliminated, assuming other things remain equal, but this will be delayed for six years until the six annual installments on the land have been paid. Prices received for paddy vary from year to year and according to the grade and variety of the paddy. Farmers also switch from one variety of paddy to another from one year to the next. But, assuming paddy of average varieties, valued at prices prevailing in 1958-59,[7] the real burden of the annual installments would range from about 750 kilos of paddy for the poorest land to about 950 kilos for the best land. This would be slightly higher than rents paid by tenants on the poorest quality land but less than the rent on the best land, because the latter was more undervalued in the redistribution. Rents formerly paid on such land reflected actual productivity and therefore were probably higher for good land than the annual installments will be. Any general increase in the price received for paddy would, of course, further reduce the real burden for all the new landowners. It is also unlikely that the eventual elimination of rental payments will be offset by tax liabilities, assuming present tax rates of VN$ 98 per hectare for the best quality land remain in effect. Due to its concern over possible adverse political repercussions, the government has evidenced little enthusiasm for increasing the yield from land taxes much beyond this level. Thus, with the possible exception of those receiving the poorest grades of land, and whose real burden of payments may be greater than their former rents, the transfer of ownership appears to entail no net new burden in the initial stages. When payment in full has been made, net farm income per household should therefore increase by the full amount of former rents, again assuming other things are equal.

In view of the limitations to changes in factor proportions already noted, the productivity effects of the land redistribution would seem to rest largely on how the farm households utilize this anticipated increase in income. As pointed out earlier, the most promising possibilities in the short run include increased and more knowledgeable use of chemical fertilizers and, to a lesser extent, the introduction of new seeds and more intensive labor application, all developments which would be greatly helped by wider dissemination of technical information. However, the marginal propensity to consume among these farm households is probably very high, and much of the increased income probably will be consumed instead of being applied to measures which increase productivity. Further, little or no savings and widespread indebtedness seem characteristic of the households which held small amounts of land before the land redistribution, and there is this experience to support expectations that the same pattern will be true for the newly created landowners.

A final word may be said with respect to the possible side effects within the village. The lack of significant economic activity other than farming means dependence on the export of over half the total paddy crop in order to purchase the fruit, vegetables, meat, and fish that are not produced in adequate amounts, as well as a large variety of manufactured consumer goods and handicraft items. Even locally made wooden farm implements are purchased in neighboring villages as frequently as they are bought in Khanh Hau itself. Projecting past experience into the near future, the possibility of stimulating side effects in local handicrafts and industry does not appear very great, for the shift from tenancy to ownership as a result of agrarian reform will probably increase imports from outside the village rather than increase the demand for goods and services produced from village resources.

All of these considerations point up a basic dilemma of this land reform—although it is politically necessary, it is probably economically ineffective. It tends to perpetuate the marginal small landowner, delays the adjustment to more productive industrial activities by creating new ties to the land, and holds out a promise of substantial economic improvement which it probably will not keep.

9

VILLAGE EXPENDITURE AND THE STANDARD OF LIVING

The Size of Typical Household Expenditures

A record of the regular expenditure made by typical village households provides important insights into their economic position in two ways—it shows how people spend their income and therefore what constitutes the elements of their standard of living, and it also offers a means of estimating their income by approaching this from the expenditure side. Twenty households were asked to keep detailed daily records of their expenditures over an eight-week period during the months of October-December 1958, and it is these records which provide the bulk of the material for the description which follows.[1]

Expenditures can be considered from many standpoints, and for the individual household the total outlay per week or other time period is probably the most useful way to think of them. Average household expenditures over an eight-week period are shown in Table 9.1 for each of the three socio-economic classes, and these indicate that total expenditures ranged from as low as VN$ 376.1 per week for the lower class to VN$ 743.9 for the upper class. Converting these into U.S. dollar equivalents, lower class households spent an average of US$ 5.36 per week, as against US$ 10.63 per week by upper class households.[2] On an annual basis, lower class households spent VN$ 19,557 for regular purchases of food and non-food items, or US$ 249.40. However, this does not all represent actual cash outlay, for in most cases all the rice and about half the fish, vegetable, and fruit purchases recorded were supplied by the villagers from their own farms and gardens. Thus, average weekly cash outlays for lower class families were VN$ 279.5, or US$ 3.99, and comparable average annual expenditures were VN$ 14,536 and US$ 207.66.[3]

Average household expenditures per time period increase from the lower to the upper socio-economic level, and this increase takes place in both major categories of regular

TABLE 9.1
Average Weekly Household Expenditures
on Food and Non-Food Items Regularly Purchased,
Village of Khanh Hau, October-December 1958

	Weekly Expenditure (VN$)		
Socio-economic class	Food	Non-food	Total
Upper	423.1	320.8	743.9
Middle	274.4	157.3	431.7
Lower	241.4	134.7	376.1

Source: Family budget records.

expenditure. The differences are most marked between the middle class and the upper class, for expenditures by the latter are over 70 percent higher than those of the former. By contrast, middle class household expenditures exceed lower class spending by only 15 percent. The gap between the lower class and the upper class is, of course, the greatest, and upper class weekly expenses are about double those of lower class households. Middle and lower class households also tend to spend approximately the same percentage on food, i.e., 63.6 percent and 64.2 percent of their regular expenditures, respectively, and this was higher than the 56.9 percent spent on food by upper class households.

Average weekly expenditures over time are shown in Figure 9.1 and, as would be expected, the spending by lower class families shows the least variation from week to week. The eight-week period over which records were kept began in October, just before the first harvest, and continued into December. This presumably would show if village household spending changed very greatly as a result of the harvest, since stocks of food and money would be at their lowest just prior to harvest.

The data, however, do not indicate any great increase at the time the harvest came in, which was about the second and third weeks. Lower and middle class households increased expenditures slightly at that time, but upper class household spending shows a steady downward trend until the eighth week,

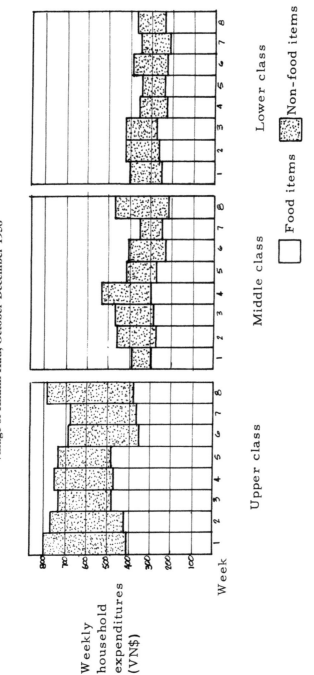

Figure 9.1

Average Weekly Household Expenditures, by Socio-Economic Class, on Food and Non-Food Items Regularly Purchased,
Village of Khanh Hau, October–December 1958

at which time it did increase. Unfortunately, these patterns cannot be used as a guide to normal behavior, because the harvest in
Khanh Hau in 1958-59 was a very poor one. Failure to increase
spending by large amounts may have been due to the realization
that the harvest would be poor and that spending had to be curbed
if households were to husband their resources until the following
year. It is also possible that spending tends to be relatively stable
at all times throughout the year, but the fact of a poor harvest in the
year studied casts considerable doubt on this interpretation.

Food expenditures by middle class families tended to go down
over the eight-week period, but those by upper class families varied the most. Food expenditures by lower class families remained
relatively stable throughout. The variation in the upper class may
reflect the smallness of the sample size for that class, but the stability of food spending by the lower class suggests that this may
be close to the minimum expenditure for food needs which would
include the main staples of diet, but with few extras.

Whereas household expenditure is the most useful measure of
the levels maintained by the spending unit as a whole, per capita
estimates of expenditures on regularly purchased items may give
a better picture of the living standards of individuals. It is important in this case because upper and middle class families tend to
be larger than lower class families, both in this sample and in the
village as a whole, and the apparent differences in expenditures by
mid¬dle and lower class households on a spending unit basis tend
to disappear when converted to a per capita basis.

The per capita expenditures on food and non-food items regularly purchased were computed on a daily, rather than a weekly,
basis, and the summary tabulation is presented in Table 9.2.[4] As
shown there, per capita expenditures by middle and lower class
families were about the same. In fact, per capita expenditure
by lower class households on all items slightly exceeded that of
middle class households. Also, upper class per capita expenditure
exceeds that of the other classes by less than does expenditure by
households. In this case, it is only 40 to 50 percent greater than the
two lower classes. Once again, per capita expenditures on food are
proportionately larger for middle and lower class individuals

TABLE 9.2
Average Daily Per Capita Expenditures on Food and Non-Food Items Regularly
Purchased, Village of Khanh Hau, October-December 1958

Socio-economic class	Daily Expenditures (VN$)		
	Food	Non-food	Total
Upper	9. 0	6. 8	15. 8
Middle	6.6	3.7	10.3
Lower	6.7	4.4	11. 1

Source: Family budget records

(64.1 percent and 60.4 percent, respectively) than for upper class persons (57.0 percent).

On an annual basis, the lowest per capita expenditures, those for the middle class, total VN$ 3,760, or US$ 53.71. Cash outlay per year, however, again assuming that 40 percent of the food expenditures are furnished in kind, is only VN$ 2,795, or US$ 39.94. For the highest group, the upper class, annual per capita expenditures were VN$ 5,767, or the equivalent of US$ 82.39, while annual per capita cash expenditures were VN$ 4,453, or US$ 63.61.

Per capita spending over time is illustrated in Figure 9.2, and the patterns which emerge there contain much the same characteristics as the weekly household expenditures, i.e., some tendency for spending to decline in the later weeks, stability of food expenditures by the lower class, and slight increases in spending the first two weeks of the total period. The similarity in the level of per capita spending by middle and lower classes is shown in the fact that for two weeks—the third and fourth—per capita spending by middle class households exceeded that of the lower class, while in other weeks—the fifth, sixth, and eighth—the two were almost the same.

It was also possible to compile the average weekly per capita expenditures on the major food items and in this way determine how food spending varied as between the different socio-economic classes. This distribution is given in Table 9.3. According to these data, the proportion of total food

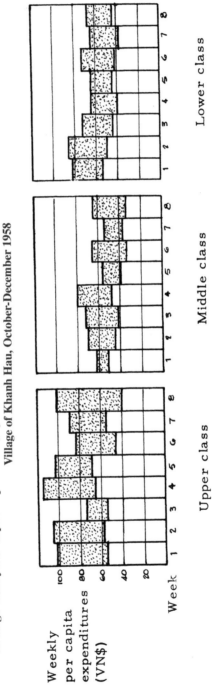

FIGURE 9.2

Average Weekly Per Capita Expenditures, by Socio-Economic Class, on Food and Non-Food Items Regularly Purchased, Village of Khanh Hau, October-December 1958

TABLE 9.3

Average Weekly Per Capita Expenditures on Major Food Items, by Socio-Economic Class,
Village of Khanh Hau, October-December 1958

Type of expenditure	Upper Class		Middle Class		Lower Class	
	VN$	%	VN$	%	VN$	%
Rice	12.6	20.0	16.1	34.8	18.9	40.3
Meat and eggs	16.1	25.6	7.7	16.7	10.5	22.4
Fish	8.4	13.3	6.3	13.6	6.3	13.4
Fish sauce	2.8	4.4	2.8	6.1	2.8	6.0
Other sauces	1.4	2.2	1.4	3.0	1.4	3.0
Vegetables	3.5	5.6	2.8	6.1	2.1	4.5
Fruit	3.5	5.6	1.4	3.0	1.4	3.0
Other food items	14.7	23.3	7.7	16.7	3.5	7.5
Total	63.0	100.0	46.2	100.0	46.9	100.1

Source: Family budget records

expenditure devoted to rice, per capita, is twice as high in lower class households as in upper class households, although actual per capita consumption is only half again as much. Middle class households also seem to consume more rice per capita than do upper class households, and by almost the same margin as the lower class. Consumption of such things as fish, fish sauce, other sauces, vegetables, and fruits are quite similar for all classes, although upper class households seem to use proportionally fewer sauces, and, both proportionally and absolutely, slightly more fruit and vegetables. One interesting point to emerge from these comparisons is the finding that lower class per capita expenditures on meat and eggs exceed those by middle class households, again in terms of both the proportion of total food spending and also the absolute amount. This is hard to account for in any way other than that middle class households are larger than lower class households, and that their equal or larger household consumption of meat and eggs results in a lower per capita consumption in comparison. The final item of "other food items" is quite large in upper class households but very small in lower class houses. This would include such things as sugar, flour, bread, tea, canned milk, delicacies, and special foods. Their relative absence from the diet of lower class families, together with the stability of the level of food spending of this group, tends to further support the earlier observation that these villagers live fairly close to a simple basic diet that includes few frills or minor luxuries and is probably deficient in food value. Since no attempt was made in this study to measure the food value of the typical diet, this latter point cannot be stated as an established fact. However, considering the kinds and amounts of food which the villagers said they eat regularly, it seems unlikely that they are receiving an adequate supply of those elements of diet which build and protect good health.

In addition to these food and non-food items which are purchased more or less regularly throughout the year, villagers were asked to give estimates of the amounts spent on 17 special kinds of expenditures during the previous year. These were expenditures not included in the family budget records and, as far as could be determined, covered all really important household expenditure that remained beyond those in the family budget records. Some, in fact, turned out to be quite unimportant. These expenditures will be discussed in some detail later on, but at this point only their relative size will be considered, as taken from Table 9.4.

For the 18 families who gave replies, the average annual special expenditure ranged from VN$ 8,574 for lower class families to VN$ 21,410 for the upper class. Middle class households reported an average of VN$ 10,190 spent on these special items per year. The respective amounts for lower, middle, and upper class households, in equivalent figures, were US$ 122.49, US$ 145.57, and US$ 305.86.

Converting the data to per capita estimates, special expenditures ran from VN$ 1,461 for the lower class to VN$ 1,717 for the middle class and VN$ 3,374 for the upper class, equivalent to US$ 20.87, US$ 24.53, and US$ 48.20, respectively. Unlike the per capita figures for items regularly purchased, the lower class spending is below that for the middle class. However, the spread between lower and upper class is again a large one, with the former less than half the latter. This suggests that if these socio-economic divisions are meaningful, middle class and lower class households fare about the same with respect to the per capita consumption of items which are purchased regularly and which constitute the necessary purchases for the members, but that middle class families can be distinguished as being somewhat better off in terms of the consumption of things which go beyond the necessities. Upper class household members are clearly better off with respect to both kinds of purchases.

By adding these household and per capita annual special expenditures to the annual estimates of items purchased regularly, as taken from family budget records, it is possible to derive a set of annual household and per capita expenditures for the different socio-economic classes, exclusive of the costs of farm operation (see Table 9.5). These annual estimates should be a close approximation of the total consumption expenditures made by villagers in the respective classes.[5] For the lower and middle classes, these consumption estimates are probably good approximations of net income per household or per capita.

The element of savings has been omitted from these estimates. Villagers were not asked directly to estimate their

TABLE 9.4
Special Annual Expenditures, by Families and Socio-Economic Classes,
Village of Khanh Hau, 1958

Category of expenditure	Upper Class				Middle Class				
	#1	#5	#8	#2	#6	#7	#10	#12	#21
Household goods	-	-	70	3,000	-	300	-	-	700
Major repairs	15,000	6,000	-	7,000	-	100	-	1,650	1,000
Medical care	3,000	1,500	1,500	500	5,000	3,000	300	2,000	1,000
Taxes	400	550	-	39	30	252	30	-	200
Interest payments	1,500	2,000	500	100	-	400	300	-	7,200
Tet celebration	2,200	1,500	2,000	600	1,000	700	1,000	1,000	2,000
Mid-Autumn Festival	-	100	-	-	-	-	-	-	-
Family aniversaries	200	3,800	4,000	-	100	100	180	2,400	2,800
Village ceremonies:									
Cau An	300	400	400	300	50	50	200	300	300
Ha Dien	100	80	100	50	20	-	50	30	50
Xa Toi	70	30	100	10	10	30	50	20	100
Thuong Dien	100	70	-	-	20	-	50	20	50
Gifts	2,200	5,000	2,000	2,000	2,000	1,200	1,500	1,000	800
Pagoda contributions	-	900	60	-	-	-	1,000	500	-
Homeplot rent	19	30	200	-	80	-	250	50	-
Clothing	-	3,000	3,250	-	1,000	2,000	-	-	-
Total	25,089	24,960	14,180	13,599	9,310	8,132	4,910	8,970	16,200

TABLE 9.4 (cont.)

Category of expenditure	Lower Class								
	#9	#11	#13	#14	#15	#16	#17	#18	#19
Household goods	5,000	2,000	2,200	100	-	-	-	4,600	-
Major repairs	3,000	4,000	300	2,000	-	-	-	4,300	-
Medical care	4,000	300	1,500	1,000	2,500	1,500	1,200	1,000	-
Taxes	-	-	-	-	-	79	-	-	-
Interest payments	-	400	450	100	-	-	500	3,200	100
Tet celebration	3,000	600	800	200	1,500	900	1,000	1,000	400
Mid-Autumn Festival	-	-	-	-	50	-	-	30	-
Family aniversaries	-	450	800	1,000	800	50	1,000	1,200	200
Village ceremonies:									
Cau An	50	50	100	30	100	30	100	50	200
Ha Dien	50	-	30	-	-	30	-	-	100
Xa Toi	-	30	10	20	50	25	-	30	-
Thuong Dien	50	-	10	-	-	20	200	50	50
Gifts	1,000	500	500	1,000	1,000	1,000	1,500	1,000	1,000
Pagoda contributions	-	-	-	-	200	60	1,000	-	200
Homeplot rent	60	150	50	50	10	-	-	100	20
Clothing	4,000	-	-	-	-	-	500	-	500
Total	20,210	8,480	6,750	5,500	6,240	3,685	7,000	16,560	2,770

TABLE 9.5
Estimated Total Annual Expenditures, by Households and Per Capita,
Village of Khanh Hau, 1958

Socio-economic class	Total Value		Cash Outlay	
	VN$	US$[a]	VN$	US$[a]
Household expenditure				
Upper	60,093	858.47	51,293	732.76
Middle	32,638	466.26	26,931	384.73
Lower	28,131	401.87	23,110	330.14
Per capita expenditure				
Upper	9,141	130.59	7,827	111.81
Middle	5,477	78.24	4,513	64.47
Lower	5,513	78.76	4,535	64.79

a. Computed at a rate of exchange of VN$ 70 = US$1.

Source: Family budget records.

savings during the previous year, because it seemed unlikely that the answers would be reliable. For one thing, villagers were defensive on this subject and became vague when asked about accumulations of cash or other valuables. In addition, a question on annual savings would tend to be ambiguous from their standpoint. Thrift is not particularly valued as a virtue among these people, and few of them make conscious efforts to save for specific goals. Major purchases tend to be deferred until the current income at some time is large enough to enable the purchase to be made, and in this sense the "savings" and the expenditure occur in the same year.

For lower and middle class families, the volume of savings in any given year is probably negligible or non-existent. The best evidence for this is the high incidence of debt in these classes, which would be avoided at the high interest rates prevailing if savings were available. There is some debt at the upper class levels as well, but it is less prevalent there. Thus, it appears more likely that any saving that is done will be done by this Latter group. The amounts, however, will depend on factors which affect the size of the harvest, and these have varied greatly over the past three years in this village.

Taking all these things into account, the annual household and per capita expenditures by lower class households, and therefore a large majority of the households in the village, should also provide a good approximation of net income. Both savings and farm expenses are here assumed to be negligible. This would be the income situation most typical of the village. However, with upward adjustments to account for farm expense on farms of average size—around VN$ 4,000 to VN$ 5,000 per household per year—one could convert the expenditure by middle class households into an estimate of the gross income of farmers who have two to four hectares of land. This would be less representative of the income of most villagers, but it would provide one measure of the economic performance of farms of this size in the particular area.

Assuming these expenditures as approximations of income, with the qualifications mentioned above, the delta region of Viet Nam does not rank particularly high in per capita income by comparison with other underdeveloped countries in Asia and Latin America. For example, per capita expenditures by upper class households in Khanh Hau are lower than the per capita income of Japan and the Philippines, and middle class per capita expenditures are lower than per capita income in Egypt. In general, the villagers in Khanh Hau seem to be somewhat better off in per capita terms than residents of India and Pakistan, but below the countries noted above and Latin American countries such as Puerto Rico, Cuba, and British Guiana.[6] Comparisons of this kind are admittedly hazardous, from many standpoints, and not too much should be made of them. Nevertheless, they do provide a perspective of sorts, and on this basis this rural sector of Viet Nam is not providing well, even by the standards of countries somewhat similarly situated.

This is an unexpected conclusion to reach because, to an outsider, it seems that people in Khanh Hau fare pretty well. No one appears to be starving, there are feasts and celebrations throughout the year, and many of the villagers look healthy and well clothed. Moreover, Vietnamese in Saigon intellectual and government circles generally will assert that the villages in the south are richer than those in central Viet Nam, and that life in the south is much easier because the villagers there can provide for their needs with much less effort. This may be true as a comparative statement, but it does not follow that the majority of the people in the south live well, or even that they currently have the means to attain a living standard as high as some other Asian countries. The lack of acute *misere*, the cleanliness of the people, the lovely setting of coconut palms and lush vegetation, and the picturesque thatch houses should not bar recognition that, as the family budget data suggest, actual living standards are lower than may at first sight appear and that a substantial majority of the village lives at or near subsistence levels.

It is possible that the family budget records have understated actual consumption and that some of the items of diet which are supplied directly in kind were not fully recorded. Some consumption in kind was included in the records, but some may have been overlooked. Trying to assess this possibility, the most probable items to be understated would be herbs and plants which grow wild and which are used in the diet, some fish which are caught by members of the household, and the amount of rice recorded which may possibly be less than that actually used. With the exception of rice, these are relatively minor items, and making allowance for some underreporting of them would not add substantially to the level of food expenditures.

In the category of non-food items, no attempt was made to estimate transportation or entertainment expenses, and major ceremonial expenses such as weddings and funerals were omitted. A number of other rather small, and usually infrequent, expenses were also not documented in detail, such as the purchase of lottery tickets, purchases of gold and other jewelry, horoscopes, and children's spending on sweets. Finally, it is possible that there was some understatement of the amounts spent on the special annual expenditures, since these were recollections for which there were no supporting records. However, considering the size and nature of these omissions and possible understatements, it is unlikely that total expenditures should be raised by very much to account for them. As an informed guess, the estimated annual per capita and household expenditures might be increased by 10 to 15 percent to account for under-reporting and omissions, but that it should be more than this is doubtful, particularly since the two years preceding this study had been poor ones, and small marginal expenditures were probably kept to a minimum.

Village Food Consumption

Patterns of expenditure expressed in terms of currency can show something about relative living standards and the changes which take place over time, but they fail to give a picture of what this means in quantities and varieties of things consumed. Casual observation indicates that living standards are extremely low by comparison with the West, but it would not tell in what basic respects they are deficient or to what extent they could affect productive effort. However, the family budget reports give enough detail of the daily purchases made by village households to begin to place together some idea of what village life is like.

In a rice village, the single most important item in the family diet is obviously rice. This is even indicated by the way in which Vietnamese speak of eating, which is literally to "eat rice" (*an com*), or of serving a meal, which is to "serve rice" (*don com*). Villagers generally believe that it is the rice which provides them with the food values they need for health and strength and that the main contribution of other food is to improve the taste of the meal. A major concern of each household is that it obtain enough rice to last until the next harvest, and a common way to express degrees of poverty is to state the number of months' supply of rice a family has on hand—thus, "that family is very poor and has only enough rice to last through the fifth lunar month."

In normal years, most of the tenants and landowners can supply their rice requirements from their own harvests. Laborers can supply at least a part of their needs in kind because harvest labor is paid in paddy. Only the few who receive cash wages, or, like store keepers, have their income almost entirely in cash, must buy most of their rice. In either case, whether purchased or supplied from their fields, rice represents about forty percent of the value of total food expenditures for a majority of villagers, and it is higher than that for the poorest inhabitants.

In terms of personal consumption, a typical adult villager will probably eat slightly less than one litre of uncooked milled rice (*gao*) per day (.8 or .9 litres), although this varies with the age of the person, the sex, the amount of physical labor being done, and even the season of the year. During the dry season when work is slack, many families will eat only two meals a day. During the growing season this increases to three meals. This may also be expressed as three to four bowls of rice at each meal for each adult, although admittedly this is a very imprecise way of describing rice consumption. A certain amount of glutinous rice (*com nep*) is also eaten, but this kind of rice is reserved for special occasions such as the first and fifteenth of each lunar month, death anniversaries of ancestors, and the new year. It is also presented as a sacrifice offering at village festivals and as gift offerings at weddings and funerals. Glutinous rice is usually more expensive than ordinary rice, although this was not true for 1958, the year in which family budget records were kept. Many farmers in the village have grown glutinous rice on a part of their cultivated land at different times, but most families in the sample bought what glutinous rice they used.

The amount of protein in a typical village diet is very small, for the principal sources of protein are expensive, and villagers do not appreciate the importance of this item in their diet. Their schedule of daily purchases shows that they tend to consume around two kilos of meat of all kinds (pork, beef, buffalo, chicken, or duck) per household per week. The poorest families buy meat very infrequently, and "frequently" in this case would mean two or three times a week at most.

The most common meat consumed in the village is pork, which is purchased from peddlers or at the markets in Tan Huong or Tan An. Beef appears on the tables of the wealthier families from time to time, but rarely in the poor homes, and buffalo is eaten even less than beef. Chicken and duck are used, but not as often as pork. This is somewhat surprising, since these fowl are raised in the village, and there is less of a problem of preservation than in the case of butchering hogs or beef that come from one's own stock. It is also surprising to find that eggs are used as infrequently as they are. Both chicken and duck eggs are used, but generally no more than five to ten eggs per household per week. This does not seem to vary between income or occupation groups, although duck eggs are cheaper than chicken eggs and are bought more often. The eggs which are consumed come from nearby markets or from a farmer's own poultry. Very few of the eggs which are bought come from households within the village itself. There is some tendency for chicken to appear most often in the budgets around the beginning and middle of the lunar month.

In addition to these standard meats, villagers eat dog and cat very infrequently and also rabbit, frog, and paddy rat, but not often enough for any of these to be considered as regular diet items. The paddy rats that are used are caught in the fields, but the villagers say that they are hard to find and catch and are therefore rarely eaten.

The week-in, week-out consumption of rrreat therefore tends to be minimal, perhaps no more than one-half kilo per person per week. This estimate should be increased, however, by taking into account the fact that meats are served at feasts of all kinds. Considering the many opportunities village adults have to attend both private and village feasts in the course of a year and that such meals consist almost exclusively of meat dishes in various forms, weekly per capita meat consumption may actually be as much as twice the amount indicated. Expenditures for meat would also include some purchase of lard (*mo*) for cooking, since record keepers failed to distinguish between the two. Peanut oil (*dau dau phung*) is much less commonly used, except for those Cao Dai and Buddhist families who regularly observe meatless fast days and substitute peanut oil for lard in cooking on these days.

Another important source of protein in the diet is fish and shrimp, and most families tend to consume about as much fish as meat in the course of a normal week. Since fish is much less expensive, it is relatively more important in the budgets of the poor families. Fish consumption is divided almost equally between fresh fish (*ca tuoi*), dried fish (*kho ca*), and salted fish (*ca muoi*). Dried or salted fish appears almost daily on the budgets of all families, but fresh fish does not.

There is a fairly large market for fresh fish in Tan An,

and villagers buy fish there or from peddlers who bring it from there. The villagers also take advantage of the rainy season when fish can be caught in the streams and rice fields.[7] Since fish appears so regularly in the daily meals, it is not surprising to find that it is rarely served at feasts, except as the final dish of the meal. The reason for its steady use in ordinary household meals is clearly its low cost (VN$ 20-30 per kilo, as compared with the cheapest meat, pork, which costs VN$ 35-40 per kilo) or elimination of the cash outlay entirely when villagers can catch their own.

The Vietnamese have developed a wide variety of sauces which add flavor to the meals at relatively little expense, the most famous of which is *nuoc mam*—a sauce that is distilled from small fish. Village families use this in over half their meals. The second most popular is soy sauce (*tuong*), used regularly in all households and also on occasions when religious observance requires a meatless cuisine and bars the use of sauces derived from fish and shrimp. In addition to these two most common sauces, villagers also use *mam kho, mam mui, mam loc, mam song, mam nem,* and *mam chung,* all made from fish or shrimp. These vary in price, and their use depends on the economic status of the consumer or his need for something special and unusual. The latter three in particular are quite expensive and are used only rarely.

Typical family consumption of sauces of all kinds tends to be from two-and-one-half to three litres per week, or around one-half litre per person per week, and this is true for all income or occupation groups. Like rice, and because of its relation to rice in the meal, it is an indispensable daily item. Most people in the village buy a grade of *nuoc mam* slightly higher than the lowest grade, which sells for VN$ 22 or 23 a *tin*—an earthenware pot containing from 2.9 to 3.0 litres. In recent years, many families have been unable to buy their *nuoc mam* by the *tin* and instead buy it on a day-to-day basis in small quantities costing only a few piastres at a time. This does not add greatly to the total cost, but it does reflect a shortage of cash and a tendency to dole it out on daily purchases that are kept as small as possible. Since there is little assurance that there will be work (and therefore cash income) from one day to the next, people are reluctant to use a large share of the cash on hand for a single purchase, even when it is as important to them as *nuoc mam.*

Many have thought that the high consumption of fish and shrimp sauces by Vietnamese supplies protein to a diet that is, by and large, lacking in it. From the evidence of these family budgets it seems true that typical families do use large quantities of sauce, certainly from the standpoint of the Western observer who generally uses little or none. However, it seems doubtful that the sauces provide much food value, because the distillation process must remove a great deal of it.[8]

Vegetables constitute the third most important item of regular daily consumption after rice and sauces. Usually served in some cooked form, they appear mainly in soups and in side dishes to be eaten with rice. The most commonly used include bindweed (*rau muong*), cabbage (*rau cai*), lettuce (*rau song*), white turnip (*cai be trang*), turnip (*cu cai*), tomatoes (*ca chua*), manioc (*khoai tu*), sweet potatoes (*khoai mo*), "green leaf vegetable" (*dua cai*), cucumber (*muop*), gourd (*bau*), bamboo sprouts (*mang*), a vegetable like bindweed (*rau ngo*), and a kind of cucumber (*dau bap*). White potatoes (*khoai tay*) are rarely used but do appear from time to time.

Consumption by weight is fairly high, and a majority of households use from eleven to fifteen kilos of vegetables a week. Vegetables are cheap, and most kinds sell for only two or three piastres a kilo in the village or in nearby markets. A villager's ability to supply the needs of his family from his own garden will vary, depending upon the location and size of his home plot and the amount of rainfall during the growing season. Even so, a substantial portion of all vegetables consumed is grown locally. There is some very small-scale selling activity within the village, but it is not well organized and does not constitute an important part of all purchases of vegetables by villagers. The vegetable markets in towns such as Tan An are well supplied throughout the year from the area near the Mekong River, and people who must buy their vegetables use these markets rather than rely on other village producers.

In addition to vegetables grown in gardens or purchased in the markets, villagers supplement the vegetable content of their diet with herbs and plants which grow in the fields and around ponds, and gathering greens of this kind is a regular activity of women and children. Not significant items in the diet, most of them are used to provide flavoring for soups and other dishes, and many are considered to have medicinal properties of a generally beneficial sort, i.e., something is "good for the liver," or "good for the lungs."

Although fruit is readily available in the markets, and to a lesser extent in the village itself, the village households consume less fruit, by weight, than vegetables. The most commonly used are bananas (*chuoi*), papaya (*dudu*), which grow in the village, and pineapple (*thorn*). Coconuts (*dua*) are eaten, but generally on special occasions such as when guests arrive at the house to pay a social call. Other fruits that appear regularly, but in smaller amounts, are lemons (*chanh*) and guava (*oi*). Children buy small lengths of sugar cane (*mia*) to chew on the way to and from school or between meals.

As in the case of vegetables, villagers supply a portion of their needs from their own gardens, but they also buy varying proportions in the markets. Fruit trees are grown in all parts of the village, but less extensively than vegetables. Typical family consumption of fruit ranges from one to five kilos per week, and the prices paid range from two to six piastres per kilo. Fruit is usually served after a meal as a dessert or between meals as a snack.

These represent the main items that appear in the regular diet of village households, but a number of other things are commonly used in small quantities or under special circumstances. For example, the villagers use salt at the rate of about one kilo every two weeks, and poor families buy it in small quantities at one piastre a time. They also use a variety of spices—pepper (*hot tieu*), red peppers (*ot*), onion (*hanh*), and garlic (*toi*)—at a rate of one or two piastres worth a day. White sugar is a luxury, found only in the homes of the wealthier landowners, but tablets of brown sugar are used in most village households. Some families use French bread, which they buy in portions of a long loaf, with meals or as between-meal snacks for the children. Families with new-born children buy canned evaporated milk, and this is true for families at all economic levels, but others use it very rarely, if at all. Tea is drunk at all meals and is served at all hours during the day. A visitor in any home is immediately offered tea, though it is often very weak. Village stores sell small packages of tea for two to five piastres, and the typical family will consume about 150 grams of tea weekly. Some of the poorest people in the village brew a drink called *binh linh* from the seeds of a plant grown locally. It has a taste vaguely like tea and is supposed to be an aid to general health. Peanuts are considered a luxury and appear only on special occasions. Finally, cookies, small cakes, and sweets are available in all the village stores, but their use is limited to special occasions, when guests call, or as treats for children. As would be expected, small tenants, small landowners, and laborers do not buy them very frequently.

Putting this information together into a picture of the "typical" or "usual" standard of living in terms of daily diet, an adult will eat three times a day during the crop season, each meal built around the staple rice. The twelve or so bowls of rice a day will be eaten with *nuoc mam* or soy sauce and will be accompanied by a vegetable soup or quick fried vegetables and by either dried or fresh fish. The fish and vegetables will also be cooked and eaten with one of the several sauces. At least one of the meals will be followed by some fruit, and tea will be drunk at all times during the day. At least once every two weeks, on the average, the head of the household will attend a village or family celebration where the main meal will consist of meat dishes. His wife will also have opportunities to eat out, but to a somewhat lesser extent. Children seem to eat smaller quantities and to have less variety, and for many the diet is largely one of rice, sauce, and fruit.

Consumption of Non-Food Items

In addition to their daily food needs, village households tend to buy some non-food items on a regular basis, most of them purchased in the village stores. These are all things which can be bought in small units for small amounts of cash outlay and all are more or less necessary in the sense that they provide a bare minimum of amenities beyond subsistence. Taken as a group of expenditures, they illustrate the paucity of material goods in the lives of the villagers and the limitations to effective demand for goods in the rural areas.

The large amount of attention given to the cult of the ancestors does not lead to as large expenditures on things such as incense sticks (*huong*), votive paper (*ma*), or candles (*den cay*) as might be supposed. Devout Buddhist or Cao Dai families use candles in religious rites, but other families seemingly use them much less. The use of votive paper seems to be declining, and while incense sticks are widely used, constituting a steady item of expenditure, the amount runs only to eight or ten piastres a week for most families.

Some families use charcoal for cooking purposes, and those who do spend about four piastres a day at village stores. However, fuel is not a major problem, and poor families can either gather firewood locally or use rice husks or rice straw. Some villagers use coconut husks for fuel, and a few well-to-do households have special stoves with a stoker attachment which feeds rice husks into the flames. Rice husks belong to the miller after the rice has been polished but could be bought for one piastre a large sack. Very few villagers use matches, and most seem to have cheap mechanical cigarette lighters which they fill with gasoline. Almost every home buys some kerosene (*dau hoi*) for lighting, at a minimum to maintain a continual light in the small lamp placed at the altar of the ancestors. It is common practice to buy kerosene one litre at a time, and only a few buy it in the five-gallon tins. Less than half the village families seem able to afford gasoline pressure lamps.

The family budget records show irregular purchases of traditional Vietnamese medicines and home remedies, bought from local Chinese drug merchants in small packages costing ten to twenty piastres each. These include such things as mint oil, laxative pills, and barks, herbs, and leaves for relief of coughs, headache, stomach trouble, and other ills. Storekeepers say that the use of traditional medicines has been declining for some years, and while villagers continue to buy them to some extent they have also begun to use Western medicines in increasing amounts. These are dispensed through a local male nurse, who also gives inoculations, or through drug stores in Tan An and My Tho. The most common pattern is to rely on the Vietnamese and Chinese remedies for minor illness or where the ailment is rather general in nature. In more serious cases, villagers tend to seek Western medical care. Often families will "hedge" and take both traditional and Western medicine for an ailment, and although they generally accept Western medicine as the more effective of the two, they are not convinced it will always work. By taking both, they seem to count on improving the chance of cure.

Soap (*xa bong*) is an item of regular purchase, but in small quantities only. Rough laundry soap manufactured in Viet Nam is the only kind used to any extent, and this is purchased once every two weeks in portions of one-quarter kilo or more. Village stores also have toothpaste and toilet soap in stock, but none of the family budgets showed any purchase of these during the eight-week period of the budget check.

Areca nut (*cau*), betel leaf (*trau*), and tobacco (*thuoc re*) are important items of regular consumption, appearing in the expenditures of almost every family. The cost of these runs from VN$ 30 to 60 per week for most of the families—in a few cases even more. To "chew betel, " slices of areca nut are placed in the mouth along with betel leaf wrapped around a small quantity of lime, and the combination is chewed for some time but not swallowed. Some rub tobacco over the teeth and gums during the chewing to vary the taste. The use of betel, though widespread in the village, is largely limited to adults over thirty years of age. Younger people do not seem to have acquired the habit very extensively. Men of all ages smoke cigarettes, which they roll themselves from the strong black tobacco grown in Viet Nam and Laos. Some of the older women will smoke cigarettes on occasion, but this is not very common. There is very little pipe smoking by anyone. Manufactured cigarettes (*thuoc hut*) are sold in all village stores, but they are expensive for villagers (VN$ 8-15 per package) and are bought mainly to serve guests at ceremonies and feasts, not for daily use.

Some families spend money on beer (*la-ve*) and soft drinks (*nuoc ngot*), but this is less important in the budget than the amount spent for rice wine (*ruou de*), usually referred to by the French-derived word *choum-choum*. The use of wine varies, of course, from family to family, but at one extreme wine is an important sacrificial offering in village and family ceremonies, and there is usually a minimum purchase of one small wine pitcher (*si*) at the first and the fifteenth of the lunar month at a cost of six piastres for a pitcher. On the other hand, some villagers, even though quite poor, spend from four to six piastres a day, several days each week, for rice wine which they purchase by the pitcher or by the individual drink in village stores. It is difficult to place any quantitative estimate on the extent of drinking in the village, but, aside from ceremonial use, there is probably relatively little heavy drinking by villagers on a regular basis. There is a good deal of drinking at feasts, but even there participation in drinking bouts is not universal. One of the stereotyped versions of village life is that of desperately poor farmers drinking up an important part of their income in riotous village feasts where large quantities of rice wine are served. Observations and the evidence of the family budgets does not bear this out, and although rice wine accounts for a larger share of the typical budget than beer or soft drinks, drinking does not constitute a serious social or economic problem in the village, with the exception of a very few cases.

Some other scattered items appeared in the family budgets under non-food expenditures, but they are non-recurring and irregular for the most part. For example, things woven from reeds or rattan, such as baskets, fish traps, and conical hats, are not made in the village homes to any extent but must be purchased in the market. The same is true for pottery, rice bowls, and kitchen utensils. A few families recorded the purchase of rubber sandals (*giep*) or wooden clogs (*guoc*) for which they paid from VN$ 8 to 15 a pair. Families with children in school bought paper notebooks, pens, and pencils, but only one family who had a son in secondary school purchased textbooks. Newspapers are not delivered regularly to the village, and while some of the more well-to-do buy papers occasionally, it is not a regular purchase item. For the most part, villagers do not acquire books, although the records included an entry for the purchase of some prayer-books and religious texts.

Looking back over these major items of non-food consumption by village families, they seem few in number and relatively meager in the contribution they make to material well-being. The more important ones include altar effects used in carrying out the cult of the ancestors, medicines, tobacco and the ingredients necessary for chewing betel, rice wine, beer, soft drinks, small quantities of laundry soap, and kerosene for lighting. But these and other items noted do not make a complete account of living standards in real terms, for there are also other important and infrequent purchases during the year. To obtain some estimate of what these major items are, and how much is spent for them, it was necessary to rely on the ability of villagers to recall their previous year's expenditures. This is unsatisfactory in many respects, but it does provide some indication of the relative importance of the different kinds of expenses.

Special Expenditures

The first thing that stands out in these special expenditures, shown in Table 9.4, is the large spread in the amounts reported. This partly reflects the basic economic status of each household and its size, but more importantly it is due to large outlays which some of the families had in the particular year on which they were questioned. Within the different socio-economic classes there is a fair degree of consistency with respect to certain kinds of normal expenditures, primarily such things as ceremonials, gifts, medical care, homeplot rentals, and taxes. Outside of these, expenditures vary according to the particular problems facing individual families, and this seems to account for the large differences in most cases.

The importance of ceremonies and feasts is shown in the large amounts reportedly spent on the chief village occasions and for presents given to others at weddings and funerals. On the average around one-third of all non-regular expenditures are made for these purposes, although it may range as high as one-half or as low as one-fifth. With the exception of those who act as heads of the extended family, and who have primary responsibility for celebrating the cult of the ancestors, most families make their largest outlays in celebration of the lunar new year (*Tet*). These run about VN$ 2,000 for upper class households and around VN$ 1,000 for others. This would include some purchase of clothing for the children in the family, a traditional *Tet* expenditure amounting to perhaps VN$ 50-100 per child. Most of the rest goes for food, particularly meat, for use in family feasts and for sweets and candy to offer visitors. A small proportion is spent on *Tet* decorations, on altar effects, and on firecrackers.

Even the poorest families will have a few firecrackers at Tet, but not in quantities which could be called extravagant.

In addition to *Tet*, there are four main community celebrations to which villagers give money. The most important of these is the *Cau An* ("Request for Peace," or the Festival of the Village Guardian Spirit). Members of the Council of Notables are under obligation to make larger contributions than others in the village. Upper class householders in the sample gave at least VN$ 300, and one gave VN$ 400 on this occasion. Others tend to give less, although the amount varies with the circumstances. For example, larger than usual contributions were made by one young man who paid for his father and his brothers and by two older men who were highly motivated by strong religious beliefs to give generously. The other celebrations—*Ha Dien* (Descent to the Fields), *Xa Toi* (Release of the Evil Spirits), and *Thuong Dien* (Closing of the Fields)—are not as heavily supported. Donations at these times were about one-third of those for the *Cau An*, and once again there was a tendency for landowners and village notables to give more than tenant-laborers. Only three families among those asked spent any money for the *Ram Thang Tarn* (Middle Autumn Festival); essentially a Chinese festival largely given over to children, but widely celebrated in North and Central Viet Nam, it is clearly not important in this southern rural area.

Some of the households make their largest expenditures for a series of family feasts and celebrations—principally the death anniversaries (*Cung Com*) and the ceremonial cleaning of family graves (*tao mo*). These are usually land owners or those who have the use of family land (*huong hoa*) and who therefore are in a better position to assume the expense of the feasts which are given on these occasions. Four among the middle and upper class householders reported expenses of between VN$ 2,400 and VN$ 4,000 for these purposes, but the others spent amounts which varied from nothing at all to VN$ 200. These latter have no responsibility to give feasts or contribute to the feasts given by other relatives because their position in the family does not require it. Sometimes, however, they may give relatively small amounts to the family member actually holding the feasts. For example, the family reporting the largest total expenditures during the year spent only VN$ 200 for anniversaries and grave cleaning. This was because the head of this household did not have family cult responsibilities, and although fairly well-to-do by village standards, he did not feel obligated to make large contributions to the family celebrations. The villagers say that the amounts spent on family celebrations change from year to year depending on the size of the harvest and the general economic condition of the person responsible. While important, the size of these expenditures should not be considered as fixed.

Gifts for weddings and funerals comprise an important and regular expense, in most cases amounting to more than is spent at *Tet* or for family anniversaries. They are considered a burdensome expense, but one that is not easily avoided. The upper class householders probably tend to spend more for gifts than other classes. Totals of VN$ 2,000 to VN$ 5,000 were reported for the former, while the latter ranged from VN$ 500 to VN$ 2,000. There is also some variation in the size of gift totals due to the age of the head of household. New households spend less than those established for a longer time. The latter have a wider circle of acquaintances and therefore are invited to attend the functions more often. In a sense, these gifts represent savings for future occasions of the same kind because reciprocity requires return gifts in the future. This does not work out evenly in all cases, and there is no strict accounting of the size and origins of gifts. Returns therefore do not always match outlays, but it is still valid to regard these partly, at least, as a type of savings rather than pure expense.

In addition to the expense of family ceremonies and community celebrations, some families make contributions to local temples. The largest of these are made by Cao Dai adherents who seem, on the whole, to be extremely conscientious in their religious observances. One household, headed by an elderly man of strong religious beliefs, made a VN$ 500 contribution to the Buddhist temple, but the rest of the group made quite small contributions if they made any at all. These examples are consistent with the observation that the religious or spiritual life of the village centers largely in the family and community cults rather than in organized religious sects, and further, that older people are the chief supporters of organized religion. Although individual households may give active support to local temples, by and large organized religions do not constitute an important drain on household finances. This is also true for geomancers and sorcerers. Most families said that they used them and had their horoscopes read during the year, but the amounts spent on this were very small, and, with one exception, respondents would not even give an estimate. This is hard to evaluate in light of the fact that they itemized very small payments in other categories. However, even if they were slightly evasive in this case, it does not seem likely that this expense is great.

Aside from the amounts spent for ceremonies and fes¬tivals, the most important expenditure for typical families was reportedly for medical care. The socio-economic status of the household probably is less important here than the extent and seriousness of the illness, and there is also probably some double counting, because the annual estimate would include the recurring small purchases of medicine, some of which were reported in the daily budget records. Still, the size of the annual medical expense is largely influenced by major illness, and none occurred in these families during the eight-week record-keeping period. Except for families with some very important sickness, typical annual expenditures ran between VN$ 1,000 and VN$ 2,000 in all classes. One poor tenant had VN$ 5,000 in medical expenses during the year. The bulk of all medical cost is for medicines and not for the services of practitioners.

As indicated earlier, there is a growing tendency to use Western medicines along with, or in preference to, traditional medicine in serious cases, and these must be purchased. The hospital in Tan An gives free medicine only when the patient is hospitalized. Some of the families reported payments for x-rays, which are obtainable only in Saigon. However, this was restricted to better educated and more well-to-do households who appreciate the advantage of proper diagnosis of illness and have the means to obtain it. Inoculations can be obtained from the village nurse, but he is not affiliated with the government health service, and villagers must pay for these at a rate of twelve to fifteen piastres for a single shot.

The one medical service that villagers pay for as such, and which is incurred by all economic levels, is that of midwives. The fee for midwives' services is VN$ 100; confinement is in the patient's home. There is some support in the village for plans to build a maternity center. The Fundamental Education Center has sought to encourage the village to build one as a "self-help" project, but progress toward it has been slow. The family reporting the largest medical expenses for the year, VN$ 5,000, complained that this large amount was due to the inefficiency and poor care given by one of the local midwives. As a result of her ineptitude, the mother became quite ill, and a large sum of money had to be spent for drugs and medicines for her recovery. Without knowing the details of the case, it is impossible to say to what extent the midwife was at fault, for conditions in any tenant's thatch-roofed house are far from sanitary, and the opportunities for infection are great. What is interesting is the causal connection which this family has drawn.

Another important outlay is the cost of major repairs on the houses. About one-third of those questioned reported large expenses for such things as replacing the roof or walls or replacing the support columns. The size of these expenses varies both with the amount replaced and the quality of the materials used. In some cases an entire roof must be replaced; in others, only a section is re-roofed. Where minor expenses were reported, the repairs consisted of patching or very minor replacements of portions of the house. The bulk of the costs in this category was for materials, which in the case of thatch roofs and walls are purchased from other villagers. Repairs of this kind become necessary every four years, as a rule, although higher quality materials will last for a slightly longer period. Support columns for the house last much longer and, depending on the quality of the wood, should not require replacement for at least twenty years.

The purchase of household furnishings and equipment appeared as an important expense in the response of a few families. This would be typical for young families who are beginning to acquire household goods over the first few years of marriage, but it also included a number of purchases of replacement goods and repairs on household equipment. One family purchased a battery radio at a cost of VN$ 4,000 for the radio and battery. Other common items were bicycle repairs, replacement of glass fronts in cabinets, and purchases of new tables and chairs, wardrobes, and kitchen equipment.

The responses also give a picture of how the burden of interest on debt affects a cross section of village inhabitants. All classes reported interest payments during the year, ranging from VN$ 100 to VN$ 7,200. The largest amount represented interest on a six-months' loan of VN$ 24,000 at the going rate of five percent per month. The money was borrowed to purchase rice land. The largest interest payment by a lower class household, VN$ 3,200 for the year, also represented a rate of five percent per month, and was the interest due for eight months on an original loan of VN$ 8,000. Over two-thirds of those questioned answered that they had debts on which they had paid interest in the previous year.

In addition to one loan for the purchase of new land, the reasons for going into debt were primarily to obtain funds for farm operations—to buy fertilizer, to hire labor for transplanting, or similar needs. Those fortunate enough to obtain a government loan for such purposes, at an annual interest rate of twelve percent, reported the relatively low interest payments which are shown. This was true generally for the tenants in the group. One family had to borrow to meet the expense of medical care, but this was an interest-free loan made by relatives. None of the households in the group reported that they had loaned money during the previous year.

Taxes and homeplot rents do not seem to be particularly important annual expenses from the evidence of this small sample. This, too, corresponds with general observations and with comments picked up from time to time in other contexts. Villagers do not complain about taxes and if questioned will usually reply that the tax system is "fair." No landowners in this group own much rice land, and their tax liability is not very high. One of them acquired his land in the agrarian reform program. Since this land was not actually received until 1958, it was not listed on the tax rolls as of the time of the interview, and the owner did not pay any taxes during the previous year. Three tenants who reported tax payments paid either a tax on buffalo or a tax on their homeplot. Those reporting no taxes for the previous year either own nothing that is currently taxable or were delinquent in tax payments.

The rental of homeplots is nominal and for the most

part amounts to less than VN$ 100 per year. Some landowners do not own the Land on which their houses are built, while some farm tenants do own their own homeplots. The former situation is likely to be true where the landowner has acquired his land in fairly recent times, and the latter where the home-plot is all that remains of family holdings that once may have included rice land. Altogether, neither the tax on, nor the rental of, homeplots is very high in the village. Since the tenancy of homeplots seems quite secure, villagers do not buy them and are content to build their houses on them.

Responses to the categories of "clothing" and "other expenses" (not inserted in Table 9.4) were not too satisfactory. Several indicated that they had made fairly large outlays for clothing, but in other cases this was mixed with an estimate of all other non-regular expenses. Some families apparently made no clothing purchases at all for adult members, and clothing for children was included under the *Tet* estimate. Clothing needs are not very great in the village. A few dress garments are kept for special occasions, but since they are seldom used they are not replaced very frequently. Daily clothing consists of black cotton shirts and trousers for both men and women, and these are literally worn until they are rags. Until that time, they are patched and mended to extend the useful life as long as possible, and therefore the purchase of new clothing is to some extent deferrable.

Failure to obtain many examples of "other" expenditures can probably be interpreted as an indication that there are no really major expenses not already listed. The possible exceptions to this would be the years in which a family had a wedding or a funeral, and this would mean expense to the extent that gifts received failed to cover the cost of the ceremonies. Since these households had kept daily records of food and non-food expenditures, it was not necessary to get an estimate of the kinds of miscellaneous expenses which would have been included in those budget reports. Some of the people who were questioned reported that their expenditures for 1958 were less than normal and that this was due to the bad crop years which had plagued the village for the two previous seasons. While it is impossible to be absolutely certain, the cooperative attitude of those who participated in these budget reports, plus the knowledge of village life obtained from other

sources, gives some assurance that the list of major expendi¬tures
is reasonably complete.

Consumer Prestige Durables

In addition to the special purchases made during the year, the
ownership pattern for prestige durables provides another insight into
living standards. An inventory of consumer goods of this kind, com-
piled from replies given in the sample survey, is presented in Table
9.6. Distinctions between socio-economic classes, evidenced by
various types of conspicuous consumption, emerge very clearly.

This particular list of consumer durables was drawn up from
advance observations of consumer habits. It includes all of the
things families tend to buy as soon as they can afford to do so and
consists of the things which denote both prestige and some material achievement. Some of these, of course, are functional, and
their possession may be considered necessary to an extent, for they
may provide utility or comfort. In this category would be a sewing
machine, pressure lamp, wardrobe, bicycle, motor bike, and table
and chairs. The rest of the list, however, falls more clearly into the
class of luxury or ornamental goods.

For the village as a whole, only two items—brass altar fixtures
and wardrobes—are owned by at least half of all the households.
All other durables are found less commonly than this. If ownership is divided by socio-economic class, all but three of the goods
listed are owned by at least half of all upper class households. The
comparable figure for the middle class is that all but six of the
goods are owned by at least half of these households. However,
ownership by lower class households is significantly lower than
either of these, for there is not a single good on the list which is
owned by as many as half of them. In fact, with the exception of a
wardrobe, fewer than one-third of the lower class households own
any of these prestige durables. In the case of three items, no lower
class household in the sample owned them at all.

The significance of some of these things may not be immediately apparent, and a few words of explanation may
therefore be helpful. For example, family photographs are
highly valued because they are a means of keeping alive the
memory of family members in a society where the family cult is

TABLE 9.6

Ownership of Prestige Durables, by Socio-Economic Class, Village of Khanh Hau, 1958

Item	Upper Class No.	Upper Class %	Middle Class No.	Middle Class %	Lower Class No.	Lower Class %	All Classes No.	All Classes %
Sewing machine	2	16.7	8	44.4	4	5.7	14	14.0
Pressure lamp	11	91.7	12	66.7	15	21.4	38	38.0
Photographs	11	91.7	12	66.7	18	25.7	41	41.0
Brass altar fixtures	11	91.7	15	83.3	23	32.9	49	49.0
Armchairs and center table	12	100.0	13	72.2	14	20.0	39	39.0
Potted plants	6	50.0	6	33.3	3	4.3	15	15.0
Chinese character fresco	8	66.7	9	50.0	22	31.4	39	39.0
Wardrobe	11	91.7	16	88.9	31	44.3	58	58.0
Wristwatch	6	50.0	3	16.7	-	-	9	9.0
Wall clock	10	83.3	9	50.0	8	11.4	27	27.0
Marble table	6	50.0	6	33.3	3	4.3	15	15.0
Bicycle	10	83.3	9	50.0	11	15.7	30	30.0
Scooter or motor bike	4	33.3	1	5.6	-	-	5	5.0
Glass front cabinet	9	75.0	13	72.2	18	25.7	40	40.0
Radio	2	16.7	1	5.6	-	-	3	3.0

extremely important. Brass altar fixtures, which adorn the family altar, are more handsome than those made of wood and therefore add honor and respect to the practice of the cult. The same is true of the frescoes of Chinese characters which are used to decorate the altar area. These contain mottos, proverbs, wishes, and greetings which also serve to add prestige to the family and the celebration of its cult. The arm chairs and table, placed in the area before the main family altar, are reserved as a place of honor for the reception of important guests. These pieces of furniture are of wood, but there is added prestige if the table top is of marble, or if the chairs and table are inlaid with mother-of-pearl. The same is true of wardrobes, for although these provide storage space for clothing and important documents, they can also be decorated with inlay or constructed of fine, highly polished woods, thus adding a touch of beauty and luxury. A glass front cabinet is also valued as a place to display family china and family relics or souvenirs. Wall clocks are largely ornamental and a prestige symbol in a society where promptness is unnecessary and rare. These clocks are very plain, without elaborate design, and many of them are not in working condition. One household owned three of them, hung on the wall in a single row, all showing a slightly different time of day. Potted plants, set in the courtyard of the house, serve as the ornamental shrubbery, and well-to-do homes have several of them on display.

In terms of demand, then, these items represent the kinds of things which would be purchased if incomes increased, though there would, of course, be increased demand for other things as well. But if a family wanted to increase its prestige and add goods which would honor its house, as well as providing some modicum of utility, the chances are they would buy selections from this group. These are, in effect, the equivalent of the television set, the new car, the well-kept lawn and garden, and the wall-to-wall carpeting of suburban America.

10

CREDIT AND SAVINGS IN A
RURAL COMMUNITY

Credit Problems and Credit Facilities

Debt size and incidence—Although a large share of the vigor of Western industrial economies derives from the extensive use of credit of all kinds, debt in rural areas has long been considered a major factor in retarding development. This is due to the particular forms which agrarian debt takes in many parts of the world and to the fact that credit is frequently difficult to obtain or available only at rates of interest considered extremely high by Western standards. Credit conditions in Khanh Hau reflect many of the familiar characteristics of rural debt in underdeveloped areas, but in some respects they differ from them and also from some impressions that are commonly held of the situation in Viet Nam itself.

To judge from data obtained in the sample survey, approximately two-thirds of the village households have debts of some kind, while about one-third are free of debt. These findings are shown in Table 10.1. The variation in debt incidence between socio-economic classes is also given there, but the significant differences between the groups seem to be largely between the upper class households and all other village households. While only one-quarter of the former group indicate they have acquired debts, the percentages for the two latter groups are roughly similar, e. g. , upwards of two-thirds. The relative freedom from debt shown for the upper class households is more or less expected, especially since, as will be developed later, it is this group which supplies an important share of the credit for the rest of the village. In the case of the lower class households, the more than one-quarter who report they have no debts are not necessarily in this situation by choice. Those who own no land have difficulties in obtaining credit, because they have nothing to mortgage or use as collateral. This emerges slightly in the data given in Table 10.2, where debt incidence is tabulated by land tenure status, and where a smaller percentage of landless

TABLE 10.1
Debt Incidence, by Socio-Economic Class, Village of Khanh Hau, 1958

Debt status	Upper Class		Middle Class		Lower Class		Total	
	No.	%	No.	%	No.	%	No.	%
Have debts	3	25.0	12	66.7	50	71.4	65	65.0
Have no debts	9	75.0	6	33.3	20	28.6	35	35.0
Total	12	100.0	18	100.0	70	100.0	100	100.0

laborers report having debts than do tenants, although a larger percentage of the laborers have debts than do landowners. Finally, the above estimates probably understate the full extent of indebtedness by some amount because the survey question referred only to monetary debt. Small debts in kind are also incurred, often by families who have not assumed any monetary obligations.

A slight majority of the households who are indebted have total debts under VN$ 3,000, and over one-third owe less than VN$ 2,000. At the other end of the scale, over one-quarter have debts of VN$ 5,000 or more, and around 10

TABLE 10.2
Debt Incidence, by Land Tenure Status, Village of Khanh Hau, 1959

Debt status	Landowners		Tenants		Laborers[a]		Total	
	No.	%	No.	%	No.	%	No.	%
Have debts	10	45.5	35	76.1	20	62.5	65	65.0
Have no debts	12	54.5	11	23.9	12	37.5	35	35.0
Total	22	100.0	46	100.0	32	100.0	100	100.0

a. Includes all households which do not own or rent land.

TABLE 10.3
Debt Size, Village of Khanh Hau, 1958

Size of debt (VN$)	All Classes No.	%
Less than 1,000	10	15.4
1, 000 to 1,999	13	20.0
2,000 to 2,999	14	21.5
3, 000 to 3,999	8	12.3
4,000 to 4,999	2	3.1
5,000 to 5,999	9	13.8
6,000 to 6,999	1	1.5
7,000 to 7,999	1	1.5
8,000 to 8,999		
9,000 to 9,999		
10, 000 and over	7	10. 8
Total	65	99.9

percent have debts of over VN$ 10, 000. These estimates are all based on the same sample, a more detailed breakdown of which is shown in Table 10.3. Once again, these are probably understatements to some degree, not only because they would not include borrowings in kind, but also because the answers to the question on debt were often given in terms such as "two or three thousand," "four or five thousand," and so on. Even taking the high figure in such cases, they may still have included some understating.

From one point of view, the reported size of debts does not seem unduly large. For most households this probably represents less than 15 percent of gross annual income, which in Western societies would not be regarded as an unusual or unduly heavy obligation. In the village, however, this would be a less valid evaluation, for the gross income is low to begin with, and a margin for savings from which to repay debts does not exist in many cases. Difficulties in this respect are increased by the prevailing high interest rates.

Very large debts, i.e., over VN$ 10,000, are incurred

by all socio-economic classes, but, on the basis of an admittedly small number of cases, there are some grounds for assuming that they are, proportionately, more common among upper and middle class households than they are among lower class families. Sometimes they arise out of distress or emergency needs, but because security of some kind is generally required most non-land-owning lower class families are effectively excluded from sources of any credit, let alone large Loans. For upper and middle class households, a large debt may be acquired to buy more land or to invest in some business enterprise. For example, one upper class household in the sample contracted a large debt of VN$ 35,000 to purchase a motorcycle bus to transport goods and persons between towns along the main highway nearby. This was not unusual, and informal conversations (outisde the sample survey) produced examples of borrowings to buy rice mills, to obtain an interest in shops, and to purchase paddy and lumber for transport and speculative sale.

The single most important reason for borrowing (24 percent) reported in the sample was to buy food and other necessities, chiefly during the period between harvests. This was followed by borrowings to buy fertilizer, to pay medical expenses, to pay ceremonial expenses, and to cover other farming costs, in roughly that order. However, if borrowing to buy fertilizer is lumped with that for other farming expense, the combined category would be the reason most frequently given. Beyond these, which were advanced most often, there were several other scattered responses, including repayment of other debts, raising capital for business investment, meeting expenses incurred in pig raising, for house repairs, for education, and so on. Significantly, no household reported borrowing to pay taxes.

These replies related to the reasons given most frequently and not to the volume of loans under each category. Unfortunately, no attempt was made to match the reasons for the loans with the amount borrowed—the result of a decision to not press the respondents for that much detail in the answers. However, it seems very probable that borrowing to buy fertilizer is also the most important reason in money terms, and that together with the borrowing to meet other farm expenses it would comprise a substantial part of all village debt.

There are significant differences between the socio-economic classes with respect to the needs to borrow. Middle class households and lower class households both report that a relatively large proportion (18.5 and 28.1 percent, respectively) borrow to buy food and other necessities, but middle class households show a much larger percentage who borrow to buy fertilizer and to meet other farm expenses. In contrast, lower class households indicate proportionately more need to borrow for medical expenses and to pay for ceremonies than do middle class households. So few upper class households in the sample did any borrowing that the replies show no tendency to bunch at any one reason or group of reasons, but, interestingly, they contain no examples of borrowing to buy fertilizer or food and other necessities—the two reasons most frequently given by the other two socio-economic groups.

A final item in this initial view of debt conditions in the village, given in Table 10.4, shows that, on the whole, debt has been increasing in recent years. As asked, the question sought only a reaction by the villagers to the change in their debt position, and it was not concerned with specific time periods or specific amounts of debt. That slightly more than half (52.3 percent) should feel that their debts have increased was expected, given the poor harvests of the previous two years. It is surprising, however, to find that over half the lower class households believe their debts have either decreased or remained the same during the recent past. One is tempted to draw from this the conclusion that bad harvests are less likely to affect the debt position of lower class households than others, since their income, though low, derives to a greater extent from wage labor for others, and this goes on prior to the harvest and regardless of the ultimate size of the crop. Higher socio-economic class households may therefore be more susceptible to debt because bad harvests adversely affect their ability to meet the expenses of the following year. However, the data are not complete enough to document this, and it is offered only as a plausible, if unsubstantiated, hypothesis.

Types of farm and consumer debt—Despite the apparent precision in the survey replies to questions on debt and interest, debts actually take a variety of forms, and easy generalizations

TABLE 10.4
Change in Debt Status in Recent Years, by Socio-Economic Class,
Village of Khanh Hau, 1958

Debt status	Upper Class		Middle Class		Lower Class		Total	
	No.	%	No.	%	No.	%	No.	%
Increasing	2	66.67	8	66.67	24	48.0	34	52.3
Decreasing	1	33.33	2	66.67	9	18.0	12	18.5
Remained about the same	-	-	2	16.67	17	34.0	19	29.2
Total	3	100.00	12	100.01	50	100.0	65	100.0

are not possible. To a large extent, these different forms reflect varying credit needs and varying means by which to meet them. This does not mean that credit is widely available but does mean there is some choice in the manner in which it may be obtained.

It is sometimes held that before the war the large landlords in Viet Nam were an important source of agricultural credit for their tenants, and, since they benefited through increased productivity on their land in the form of higher rents, they made efforts to help their tenants achieve it, notably through loans. Since the war, according to this point of view, the break-up of large landholdings and the corresponding increase in the number of small landowners have eliminated a major source of credit from the agrarian scene. Although more people now own land, they no longer have access to the credit they need to work it efficiently.

As far as this particular village is concerned, this state of affairs apparently never existed. In general, landlords in the area were reluctant to extend agricultural credit to their tenants and did so only under unfavorable conditions to the tenants. For example, when loans were made, the date of repayment was set to fall due prior to the actual harvest of the crop so that the tenant could not meet his obligations. The landlord would then offer to buy the crop, as yet unharvested, at some fraction of its probable value—one-half to two-thirds.

The tenant thus lost part of the value of his crop, in addition to paying prevailing rates of interest during the life of the loan. Tenants could be forced into this unprofitable arrangement by their need for credit and their need for land. Landlords held out the threat to take back their land against those who protested too strenuously. Moreover, land rents were usually set in terms of a specified amount of rice at the end of the harvest. Since the rent would not vary with the size of the crop, the landlords had no interest in increasing the productivity of their tenants. Villages still tend to characterize the pre-war attitude of landlords as one of concern only for collecting their rents, not in aiding measures which might improve living conditions among the tenants.

It is impossible at this date to verify either of the above versions of the pre-war landlord-tenant credit relationships. However, it is clear that the power of the landlords has been curtailed as a result of the events of the war years and the subsequent moves toward agrarian reform. If they ever did much lending under the conditions ascribed to them, they do very little of it at the present time. The closest approach is the pre-purchase of crops, but without the tie-in with previous lending. This is a way of obtaining funds that is generally limited to conditions of extreme distress. A farmer thus pressed will seek a buyer to purchase his crop before it is harvested. The buyer having estimated the probable yield will pay the seller one-half its estimated value and will retain the total proceeds from the crop when it is finally harvested. The farmer, in such cases, generally loses half of his expected gross income from the crop, but there are risks to the buyer as well. If there is a bad harvest, due to insect damage or crop disease that takes place after the transaction, the buyer will also lose. Another variation of this is to pre-purchase specific amounts of paddy for delivery after the harvest. In this case a farmer will receive payment for a certain nunnber of *gia* of paddy at the beginning of the planting season, at a price which is generally 40 to 50 percent of the expected value of paddy at harvest. After the harvest, the farmer delivers the paddy to fulfill his contract. These types of "futures" transactions do not give rise to transferrable contracts, as far as can be determined.

As indicated earlier, borrowing to purchase fertilizer

is an important credit need, and credit arrangements have therefore developed to meet it specifically. When selling fertilizer on credit, merchants usually increase the price of the fertilizer in fixing the conditions of the transaction. As an example, a farmer wishing to buy three bags of chemical fertilizer which sell originally for VN$ 180 per bag will find that the sale price to him is set at VN$ 210 per bag. Interest for the period of the loan is calculated as 5 percent per month on the inflated total sale price of VN$ 630, rather than on the lower price of VN$ 540 which would be paid in a cash sale. This combination of an inflated price and a quoted interest rate means that the effective interest rate is higher than the quoted rate—in this example, provided by a farmer who had purchased his fertilizer under these conditions, it was doubled. In addition to arrangements of this kind, fertilizer is purchased directly with money borrowed from sources other than the merchants and under conditions described below in the discussion of credit availability. This is, of course, true of other kinds of purchases as well.

Storekeepers in the village and in neighboring market areas advance limited amounts of credit to their regular customers. As a rule they do not seem to lend money, but instead use open book credit for items taken from the store. The amounts individual storekeepers are willing to carry in this way will vary, but some have said that as many as one-third of their customers are indebted to them to some extent. One storekeeper denied that he gave any credit at all, but this seems improbable since offering credit is a ready way to attract a steady clientele. No interest is charged as such on open book credit in stores, but the amount of the debt is carried at somewhat higher prices than would be paid if the transactions were for cash.

The storekeepers, in turn, are all indebted to the wholesalers from whom they purchase their stocks of goods. They, too, obtain open book credit which they are committed to repay as rapidly as their turnover permits, and no date is set for repayment. Again, no quoted interest rates are fixed for the amount of the loan, but the prices are not subject to bargaining and are therefore higher than would otherwise apply.

Another form of consumer credit that is very common is to borrow rice at one time with the promise to repay after the harvest, and in kind, one-and-one-half to two times the amount borrowed. This is a form of loan that is used to cover the most basic food needs in a family that has not been able to set aside enough rice to last between the harvests. The effective rates on such loans, 100 percent per annum or more, are higher than most straight monetary loans made for small amounts and for similar purposes.

It is easier for those who have land to borrow money because the land can be pledged as a security, and land is the most acceptable type of collateral. In general, the landowner must pledge all of his land, even though the amount he wishes to borrow is only a small percentage of the total value of his land. The person holding the mortgage is usually willing to extend the loan indefinitely into the future, with the provision that any unpaid interest is added to the principal, and interest is then calculated on the annually compounded total of principal and unpaid interest. There have been very few instances in which a creditor has foreclosed a mortgage. Instead, it is more common practice for a debtor, finding his debt mounting because of his inability to meet interest payments, to sell some portion of his land and use these sales proceeds to pay his debts.

Villagers recounted several instances of large debts which had accumulated and forced the debtor to sell land as a means of meeting them. One account that was typical of these involved an original loan of VN$ 7,000 at an annual rate of interest of 30 percent, which is a typical long-term rate. At the end of the first year, the borrower could not pay either interest or principal, so the interest for the second year was calculated on a new total of VN$ 9,100. This unfortunately continued over a five-year period, at the end of which time the total debt, principal plus interest, was nearly VN$ 26,000. The interest due on this amount for the sixth year was actually greater than the amount of the original loan. To meet it, the borrower was forced to sell a portion of his land.

Mutual aid societies (hoi)—One special type of loan arrangement found in Viet Nam, and known as a *hoi*, is essentially a mutual aid society or *tontine*. Derived from a similar Chinese institution, the particular form a *hoi* takes varies from one part of Viet Nam to another. There is some variation even within a village, but the type used in Khanh Hau is like that found in Saigon and other parts of the Mekong delta region.

Actually, the *hoi* is almost as much a gambling game and social gathering as it is a mutual aid society. Over the limited period of the society's existence some of the members gain and some lose, with gains and losses depending partly on the skill with which the participants make their bids. The society is founded by one person who needs funds and who assumes responsibility for organization. He tries to find ten or twelve others who wish to participate, some of whom will also be anxious to borrow money. Neither the number of members nor the amount which the organizer gets from the society is fixed, but will depend to some extent on circumstances and the needs and resources of those interested in taking part. The *hoi* exists long enough for each member to receive funds once, after which it closes permanently.

To illustrate how the society works, Table 10.5 shows the process for a simplified example in which an organizer invites only four others to participate, each undertaking to pay the organizer VN$ 1,000 the first month, or a total of VN$ 4,000, which is the amount it is assumed the organizer wanted to borrow. The first meeting is a festive occasion, and the organizer gives the other participants a large dinner in appreciation for their willingness to take part. In the example, Mr. A is the organizer, and row 1, which is the first month, shows that each of the others pay VN$ 1,000 to Mr. A. Each cell in the table indicates payments; a blank cell indicates receipt. The amounts paid are totalled by columns, and after the first month the amounts Mr. A pays into the *hoi* are shown in the column under his name. Receipts are totalled by rows, and the amount that Mr. A receives is shown at the end of row 1, which contains the payments made by others to the recipient for that month, Mr. A.

At the beginning of the second month, all members of the *hoi* meet again at the organizer's home, but this time there is no feast. Refreshments are served, and all the participants except Mr. A, who has already received his loan "from the *hoi*, will bid for a chance to obtain money from it. Bids are marked secretly on pieces of paper, folded, and handed in for examination. A bid contains the amount of "interest" the bidder is willing to pay for the use of the funds of

TABLE 10.5
Operation of a Mutual Aid Society *(Hoi)*

Month	A	B	C	D	E	Total amount received
		Amount Paid by Each Member				
1	-	1,000	1,000	1,000	1,000	4,000
2	1,000	650	650	-	650	2,950
3	1,000	-	800	1,000	800	3,600
4	1,000	1,000	-	1,000	850	3,850
5	1,000	1,000	1,000	1,000	-	4,000
Total amount paid	4,000	3,650	3,450	4,000	3,300	

the *hoi*, and the member making the highest bid gets the loan for that month. Since the *hoi* is based on an original contribution of VN$ 1,000 per month, the "interest" bid is deducted from this amount to determine how much each of the others will pay the successful bidder in the month in which he wins the bid.

To give an example of how this works, assume that Mr. D is the successful bidder in the second month, and that he made the highest "interest" bid of VN$ 350. The other three bidders, Messrs. B, C, and E, each pay VN$ 650 to Mr. D (VN$ 1,000 minus the VN$ 350 bid), for total receipts by Mr. D of VN$ 2,950. Mr. A is committed to repayment at a rate of VN$ 1,000 each month after he receives his loan. All the others are similarly required to pay VN$ 1,000 each month after they receive their loans. Mr. D's receipts are shown at the end of row 2, the month in which he won them, and they total VN$ 2,950. His total payments appear at the bottom of the column headed by his name, and these will ultimately amount to VN$ 4,000.

In the third month, Mr. B wins with an "interest" bid of VN$ 200. He therefore receives VN$ 800 each (VN$ 1,000 minus VN$ 200) from Mr. C and Mr. E, neither of whom have won yet themselves, and VN$ 1,000 from Mr. A and Mr. D, who have already received funds from the *hoi*. His total receipts are shown at the end of row 3, the month in which he won, and his ultimate total payments are shown at the bottom of the column under his name. The play proceeds in this way, with only Mr. C and Mr. E bidding in the fourth month, when it is assumed that Mr. C wins the bid. The *hoi* comes to a conclusion with Mr. E receiving the final payments made by all other members in the fifth month, and without his having to make any further bid for them.

The net results to each of the participants are shown in Table 10.6. Mr. A receives an interest-free loan of VN$ 4,000 for his efforts to organize the *hoi*, while Messrs. B and D pay interest of VN$ 50 and VN$ 1,050 respectively for the amounts they received. Messrs. C and E actually gain from their participation and in effect receive interest for the amounts they' have paid in. The interest thus paid and received will depend on the course of the bidding over time, which, in turn, will depend on how badly the participants want money from the *hoi*. Those who need funds will make higher bids than those who do not, but since the bidding is secret they will not know how high to go in order to win the bid. Those gaining the bid early in the life of the society will wind up paying interest, but presumably they are also those who most want a loan. Those who do not need a loan will make low bids, and by holding back hope to get the bid only toward the end. At that time the chances increase that they will receive a positive net return for their participation.

The *hoi* thus performs several functions. It provides an occasion for a social gathering, it has elements of gambling that, like poker, depend to some extent on the ability to bluff, and it also is a source of loans for those who need them. While it is one of the more important sources of credit, there are some limitations on participation. For example, it is more common for merchants and women to take part than others, for these are more likely to have regular sources of income from storekeeping and petty commerce. Regular income is important, because the participants must be able to meet the monthly payments when they come due. The *hoi* thus has become a way to acquire capital for a stock of goods, liquidation of which will provide the monthly income with which to make repayments. The survey data indicate that around 15 percent of the number of loans made in the village take this form.

TABLE 10.6
Gains and Losses to Participants in a Mutual Aid Society *(Hoi)*

Participant	Total receipts (VN$)	Total payments (VN$)	Net gain or loss (VN$)
A	4,000	4,000	-
B	3,600	3,650	- 50
C	3,850	3,450	+ 400
D	2,950	4,000	- 1,050
E	4,000	3,300	+ 700
Total	18,400	18,400	-

The identity of creditors and availability of credit—An attempt to identify the main sources of credit in the village resulted in the listing shown in Table 10.7. This does not indicate their relative importance in terms of the volume of loans originating with them, but only in the number of instances that these sources were named by debtors.

According to these replies, the two most frequently used sources of credit are relatives and friends and neighbors outside the extended family. The government's loan program also emerges as an important credit source, followed closely by the *hoi*. Landlords and storekeepers, often considered the major creditors in rural communities, appear to be the least important of all. In the entire survey, not a single household reported they had borrowed money from a professional money lender.

From this information, and from numerous other conversations with the villagers, it seems clear that Chinese and Indian money lenders are not important elements in the credit structure of this area at the present time and, in fact, have never been very important. Loans have always been obtained from other Vietnamese and almost always from those resident in the village. Indian and Chinese money lenders do engage in lending activities in the larger towns, such as Tan An and My Tho, but these are limited to loans to tradesmen and small

TABLE 10.7
Major Credit Sources, Village of Khanh Hau, 1958

Creditor	No.	%
Relatives	34	35.8
Government	17	17.9
Hoi	14	14.7
Storekeepers	6	6.3
Landlords	4	4. 2
Other[a]	20	21.1
Total	95	100.0

a. Includes neighbors and friends outside the extended family.

businesses. Both lending groups tend to refrain from making agricultural loans, a preference which is reciprocated by the villagers who prefer to deal with other villagers and not with outsiders. This does not mean that there is no borrowing at all from professional moneylenders, but there are none resident in the village, and dealings with them are very infrequent and of limited importance to the total credit available—far less than the role commonly ascribed to them.

The great dependence on relatives and friends for loans, shown in over half the cases reported in the survey, probably reflects the stringent conditions attached to borrowing in straight business transactions. The reluctance of well-to-do landowners to lend money without large amounts of security has been touched upon earlier, but it can be emphasized again. In fact, most large landowners prefer not to lend to villagers, whether tenants or not, but instead will channel loanable funds into the larger towns for the use of the merchants, rice mill operators, and similar types of borrowers there. Villagers explain that this preference is due to the concern which the well-to-do feel over the safety of their funds. Such lenders do not want to bother with problems of collection, which they assume would be burdensome in cases where there is little or no collateral for the loan. Therefore, they lend where the credit risks are less, and despite the villagers' need for funds, they restrict lending to cases where there is, in their opinion, adequate security.

This means that direct business loans are usually available only to those who own land or who have a crop almost ready for harvest. It also partly explains why the price of fertilizer can advance to two or three times its original price at the time it is most needed. Farmers would be willing to borrow money early in the season in order to buy fertilizer when prices are still low, but money is simply not available to them at that time, particularly if they are tenants and have no land to pledge against the loan. Only when the crop is well advanced, and the creditor can see for himself that there will be means to make repayment, can the farmer borrow what he needs for fertilizer. By that time, however, increasing demand for it has led to sharp price increases in the local markets.

This refusal to offer credit, except under restrictive conditions, forces people to turn to relatives and friends for funds. The survey indicates that only people in the lower class, and then mainly the laborers, go to storekeepers for credit, but there do not appear to be other significant differences between the creditors of middle and lower class households. So few upper class households reported debts that no real comparison on these matters is possible. The same impression holds if the replies are tabulated by land tenure status. Except for a slightly higher percentage of laborers than tenants who rely on relatives, and a smaller percentage who obtain credit from friends, there is little difference between credit sources used by these two groups. In fact, if the number of times relatives and friends and neighbors are used as sources is combined, both tenants and laborers rely upon them in over 57 percent of all cases. This is perhaps the more realistic way to look at it, for the kinds of loans one gets from friends and neighbors or relatives are alike, in that there is less concern with collateral, although the interest structure is different.

It is very common for villagers to have more than one creditor, as shown by the survey finding that 72.3 percent of those with debts had multiple creditors. This seems to be due to limited willingness or ability to lend on the part of creditors, as well as a diversification of credit needs and therefore of the forms and sources of credit. There is no significant difference between socio-economic classes, and all classes of household show the same tendency to rely on more than one source of credit.

Interest rates—Generalizations about the structure of interest rates in the village must be made and accepted with caution, for the most striking thing about it is its diverse character. Furthermore, some forms of debt are such that the rate of interest is indeterminate for the most part, e. g., the *hoi* and certain kinds of loans in kind. It is possible to present a general impression of interest rates and how they may be related to size of loans, length of time, and identity of the creditor, but the foregoing qualifications to the completeness of this picture should be kept in mind throughout.

One of the first things to note in Table 10.8, which shows the spread of interest rates, is the rather high proportion of interest-free lending which takes place—approximately one-third of the loans reported.[1] The most common rate applied was 5 percent per month, which was found in less than one-third the cases. Another one-third fell within the range of one to four percent per month, and only slightly more than 10 percent of the reported loans were at rates in excess of 5 percent per month.

Villagers have said in interviews that interest rates change with the size of the loan. High rates of 10 percent per month would be set for small loans of VN$ 1,000 or less, 5 percent per month for loans of VN$ 1,000 to VN$ 10,000 and 2 to 3 percent per month for loans above that. The survey findings do not reveal such clear-cut distinctions. Although there is some tendency for the rates to be higher on small debts than on larger ones, the debt size at which the rate changes is not readily discernible. For one thing, the survey findings show that a large proportion of the small-size loans are made interest-free. In the sample, 45.9 percent of all loans under VN$ 3,000 were made without interest, and this leaves relatively few cases on which to base a generalization that is very impressive.

However, eliminating all interest-free loans, and including only the monetary loans for which interest rates are deter-minate, around two-thirds of all loans under VN$ 3,000

TABLE 10.8
Range of Interest Rates, Village of Khanh Hau, 1958

Interest rate (per month)	Reported Debts No.	%
Interest-free	19	33. 3
1 percent	6	10.7
2 percent		
3 percent	6	10.7
4 percent	3	5.4
5 percent	16	28.6
6 percent		
7 percent		
8 percent	5	8.9
9 percent		
10 percent	1	1.8
Total	56	100.0

bear rates of 5 percent per month or more, while 52.6 percent of all loans of VN$ 3,000 or over fall in the same rate bracket. The reverse of this, of course, is that while only one-third of the loans under VN$ 3,000 bore rates of interest of less than 5 percent, nearly half of those over VN$ 3,000 were at the lower rates. Thus there is some slight evidence to support the view that interest rates change with the size of the loan involved, although with rather wide variation.

The data were not complete enough to permit any investigation of the relationship between time and the rate of interest. In one sense, many loans become long-term loans because the borrower cannot repay. The Lender, often unwilling to foreclose on the collateral which has been put up, permits the debt to continue. Most loans that start out as long-term ones are also usually fairly large loans, with the result that long-term loans and large loans tend to be the same thing, and the observed tendency for interest rates to decrease with size can be ascribed to a combination of these two factors.

The identity of the creditor is also important when considering the structure of interest rates. Once again, the survey data are too thin to give a firm picture of the relationships in all cases, but they show, for example, that about half (53.6 percent) of loans made by relatives are without interest. They also show that interest rates can run the full gamut in this category, for two reported they paid 8 percent per month and one 10 percent per month on loans from relatives. This corresponds with other reports to the effect that although borrowing from relatives is an important source of credit and often is made without interest, this is not always true. Family ties sometimes are not strong enough to overcome the desire to obtain a return on goods or money loaned within the extended family.

Interest charges are more standard when borrowing from friends. Again, this is an important credit source and one which does not require the security that is necessary when the debt is between relative strangers. However, there were no cases where borrowing from friends or neighbors took place without some interest. Furthermore, the general pattern of interest rates in such cases is rather high, for over four-fifths of those borrowing from this source paid rates of 5 percent per month or more. These also tended to be smaller loans, for the most part, and riskier because of the lack of security in some cases, but the distinction between friends and relatives as sources of credit seems a significant one as far as interest rates are concerned.

So few cases were reported under each of the other sources that it is not possible to establish any clear findings. For what it may be worth, some reported interest-free loans from both storekeepers and landlords, but there were not enough instances to say how widespread this may be. Government loans were reported at the 1 percent per month which is fixed in the loan contracts, and no attempt was made to compute interest rates for participation in the *hoi*.

To generalize from these scattered observations and survey findings, the market for loans in the village is clearly not organized to a point where interest rates show a tendency to cluster around well-defined factors such as size of loan, length of time, degree of risk, and so on. Nor does there seem to be any traditional pattern which sets the conditions under which borrowing takes place within kin groups, within residence groups, or within the village as a whole. Except for the kinds of tendencies noted throughout the discussion of interest rates, it is probably true that the rate prevailing in any given situation depends mainly on the individual circumstances in each case.

Government credit—Three different governmental agricultural credit programs have come into the village since 1955. All sought to increase credit availability to farmers in the small landowner, small tenant category, but the most recent program, that of the National Agricultural Credit Office (NACO), has been the most efficient and the most far-reaching in its effectiveness. Established in 1957 by presidential decree, and supported by American aid funds, the first loans available through it were granted in the village in 1958.

Earlier programs included four-year loans for buffalo purchase, which were issued at the beginning of the year in 1956, and one-year agricultural loans which were granted in mid-year 1956. Under the first, 21 farmers were able to borrow VN$ 3,500 each, while under the second 36 farmers borrowed amounts ranging from VN$ 500 to VN$ 2,000, although over four-fifths of them received the latter figure. These 36 were the successful applicants out of a total of 100 who originally requested credit. In 1957, 100 villagers again applied for loans through the government's program, but none of them received funds in that year, presumably because of difficulties at administrative levels above the village.

In July 1958, the village received 100 application forms for credit under the newly established NACO program, and an additional 53 forms were subsequently obtained. These were passed out to the hamlet chiefs, who, in turn, passed them to the heads of the five-family groups in their hamlets. The NACO program required that recipients of the forms be actual residents of the village, working the land themselves as small landowners or tenants, and poor and in need of credit, but the village council made no attempt to determine the 100 neediest cases in the village. With the distribution of the application blanks a matter of discretion at the hamlet level, there obviously were opportunities for favoritism in handing them out. In fact, complaints on this score are commonly heard in the village. However, when the application forms were returned to the council it was possible to observe the applicants, and many of them were known to be among the poorest farmers in the village. Despite whatever degree of personal favoritism may have been involved, the credit program was reaching some of the farmers who needed funds most urgently.

Applications are processed through the village council, any member of which can certify that the information given is correct. The council does not pass on the merits of the case, only on the accuracy. Completed forms are sent to the NACO office in the district, where decisions on amounts to be granted are made. The maximum anyone can borrow is VN$ 3,000, available chiefly to farmers who are operating the larger pieces of land, and the minimum is VN$ 800 for farmers operating one hectare or less. The rate of interest is fixed at 1 percent per month. In 1958, 142 applicants actually received loans of from VN$ 1,000 to VN$ 3,000, distributed as shown in Table 10.9. The 11 rejections were for such reasons as: the applicants were either too young or too old (five cases), the forms had been improperly prepared (two cases), the applicant had not repaid his loan for 1956 (one case), the applicant had too much land (one case), and the applicants did not have a rent contract (two cases). The processing of applications at the district branch office was quite rapid, and payment was made by the NACO official within one month of the time the applications were forwarded. This was too late for use in meeting planting costs, but was still in time to help pay for chemical fertilizers.

Reaction to the government's credit program was favorable, and approximately one-quarter of the village households benefited from it. The villagers hoped that it would continue at least at the level of 1958, but the experience of 1956-57 has made them skeptical. There were some complaints over alleged favoritism, already mentioned, and some tendency to believe that the program did not help the small landowner as much as the small tenant, but there did not seem to be any evidence that this latter complaint is valid. The savings in interest were so impressive that there were no complaints that the interest rate was too high.

There was one further reaction to the government credit program that is not a complaint, but a suggestion for modification, and it was supported by a large cross-section of the village population. Specifically, it would replace agricultural loans of money with loans in fertilizer, which is the most

TABLE 10.9
Requests Received and NACO Loans Granted, Village of Khanh Hau, 1958

Amount	Requests Received		Loans Granted	
(VN$)	No.	%	No.	%
1,000	7	4.6	9	6.3
1,500	7	4.6	8	5.6
2,000	83	54.2	76	53.5
3,000	42	27.5	49	34.5
4,000	9	5.9	-	-
5,000	5	3. 3	-	-
Total	153	100. 1	142	99.9

important agricultural credit need. The suggestion was proposed at a village meeting at one time, enthusiastically accepted, and a recommendation to this effect was actually forwarded to the NACO district office. Two reasons were usually advanced in support of this change. One of them relates to the low income of many families and their need for cash to meet daily needs. Receipt of a large cash loan, particularly if it has been a bad year, places a. great temptation in the hands of poor households, with the result that some or all of the cash may go for long-delayed consumer purchases at the expense of farm needs. Loans of fertilizer would eliminate this type of temptation and would ensure that the loans were used as intended. The second reason reflects the dislike and distrust which most villagers hold for the merchants who sell fertilizer. Having watched them manipulate the stocks of fertilizer so that prices would be forced up in the past, the villagers fear that money loans play into the hands of the merchants. They feel that prices will be put up artificially because farmers will still have to obtain their fertilizer through the merchants and that much of the advantage of the loans will be dissipated in higher prices. Direct loans in fertilizer will by-pass the merchants, and they will not be able to reap any advantage from sales to the small landowners and tenants who are the beneficiaries of the loan program.

Something of this kind was actually carried out in the village through the National Revolutionary Movement (NEM) party in 1958 and with apparent success. The national party organization distributed fertilizer to the district party headquarters, and village party units arranged with the district for delivery to the village. Prices were fixed for Khanh Hau below the market prices in Tan An, and fertilizer was available to party members and non-members, but party members were eligible to buy on partial credit. Phosphate tricalcique was distributed to party members at one-third down in cash and ammonium sulphate at one-half in cash, with the balance in each case payable after the harvest. Farmers with poor grades of land were permitted to buy up to 10 bags of each kind, but the farmers with good land were limited to 7 bags of each per hectare. To become eligible for the credit, a farmer had only to join the local party unit, and this could be done at any time, even after the fertilizer had been delivered to the village. During the distribution period, party membership increased by fifty households.

In this one year, when NACO credit was available and the NRM fertilizer supply and credit program was in operation, fertilizer prices in Tan An in December were from VN\$ 170-174 per bag for ammonium sulphate and VN\$ 120 for phosphate tricalcique. Comparable prices one year previous were VN\$ 225 and VN\$ 160, respectively. There is no doubt that these two factors, in effect for the first time in 1958, did much to stabilize the price of chemical fertilizers in the area and prevent the sharp price rises that have been typical in earlier years.

Summary—In reviewing the findings on credit conditions in Khanh Hau, there are many signs of improvement and grounds for optimism. For one thing, it does not appear that the land reform program or the laws devised to weaken the position of the Chinese minority in Viet Nam have had any adverse effect on the traditional local credit structure. Neither large landlords nor professional moneylenders have ever been an important factor in providing loans to these villagers, and any recent curtailment of the activities of these two groups by the government has not restricted credit or brought hardship in the village.

As a second point, the incidence of debt is high, but the size of typical debts is not too large. This is not to minimize the burden even small debts may bring, but there is no sign of widespread massive or overwhelming indebtedness of the sort which, in some countries, reduces debtors to the role of serfs to their creditors.

Interest rates show the characteristics associated with undeveloped rural areas in all parts of the world—"normal" rates of 5 percent per month, effective rates that may go as high as 200 percent per year on loans in kind—but a remarkably high proportion of Loans are made without any interest at all. There is some indication that interest rates decline with the size of Loans and the length of time of Loans, but individual practice varies so widely that this is best described as a general tendency only.

Villagers without land or other collateral have difficulty in obtaining straight commercial loans. Well-to-do landlords prefer to lend their money in towns and seek to avoid trouble and inconvenience by placing Loans where the problems of collection seem minimized. However, friends and relatives from middle and upper class households, but below the level of the rich or well-to-do landowner, provide an important, if limited, source of credit within the village.

Finally, the government's loan program has worked well. It has benefited a substantial proportion of the small landowners and tenants and has been carried through with dispatch and a minimum of complaint. A program of fertilizer credit was also introduced in 1958, and the combined effects of these two credit operations did much to help the typical villager meet his farm needs at greatly reduced cost.

On all these grounds, there are reasons to feel that credit conditions may continue to show improvement, and that this particular problem area, while still an important one, will be less serious than others which the village as a whole must face.

Savings

Information on the size and nature of savings was one of the most difficult areas in which to ask questions or obtain other than vague and evasive replies. This is understandable from several standpoints, but especially because people are afraid to reveal too much about savings lest this information be used in some way which would result in loss to them. What is known about savings, therefore, must be pieced together from other observations and bits of information which became available over a period of time.

It seems highly probable that a. large majority of the village households have no savings at all in the sense of hoards of cash or liquid valuables set aside for emergencies or accumulated to meet specific anticipated needs of a major kind. Most families, of course, will have some small accumulations of cash on hand at any given time and may also own a few pieces of gold in the form of rings, necklaces, or as settings for small bits of jewelry. They may also own goods such as bicycles, pressure lamps, or altar fixtures which would have re-sale value, but these do not constitute savings of the kind identified above. The high proportion of the middle and lower class families who are indebted indicates these households do not accumulate enough income in most years to rid themselves of debt, let alone put aside some of that income in the form of savings. What saving does take place, and thereby becomes the source of much of the borrowing in the village, is centered in the upper class families and a few of the middle class households.

The size of these savings by upper class households will vary from year to year, according to the size of the harvest and the returns from loans or investments in other enterprises. When bad years come and rents are reduced, loans cannot be repaid, interest cannot be collected, and even upper class families will be unable to save much. But even in good years the proportion of households in the village who probably accumulate some savings each year would not exceed 15 percent of total households in the village, and this may be a very generous estimate. The few largest resident landowners in the village, and therefore the most well-to-do, live comfortably and at a level well above the typical villager. Some of them donate generously to village functions, particularly some of the older men who are concerned with accumulating a record of good works before they die. However, these very well-to-do appear to maintain a normal standard of living that is far from ostentatious and also well below their normal income, and it is here that savings accumulate fairly regularly. There is no observable tendency for these households to expand or contract their expenses from year to year in such a manner that all income is always spent, say, for example, in elaborate feasts for other villagers or in external signs of affluence such as enlarging or redecorating tombs, building additional houses, and the like. In other words, where a large majority of the villagers normally cannot expect to accumulate any savings, a small group of village households generally are in a position to do so. There is nothing in the culture to impel them to spend all the income they receive, and after providing a modest but comfortable standard of living for their families they make efforts to save income in excess of these needs.

Physical security is the most important concern for those who have been able to accumulate some savings. Village houses are easily entered, and short of hiding valuables in hollow pillars or burying them in the house or yard, there is no place to keep things safely. A few houses have metal strongboxes, but since they can be easily broken into or carried away, they are more a prestige item for display than a realistic place of safekeeping. Villagers who have relatives living in large towns sometimes keep money or gold in the houses of these relatives. It is also possible to keep money on deposit in a government sub-treasury in My Tho where it would draw a small amount of interest, but no villagers have yet taken advantage of this opportunity. Reluctance to do so may be part of a tendency to avoid becoming involved with governmental procedures if possible. Villagers find "paper work" complicated and difficult to understand, and in addition, in this case, they could earn much higher rates of interest in the village if they had excess funds to lend out.

Savings therefore tend to be channeled into forms or uses where they are physically secure. An important use of savings is to buy land, if this is possible. This is considered the most secure investment of all, for the importance of productive land in a rural community is such that villagers feel certain it will never decline in value. It is secure in the sense that it cannot be stolen by removing it physically, and the great demand for land makes it also a highly liquid asset. Finally, maintenance of the family cult of the ancestors is ensured if the family has land to support the cult, and tradition therefore sanctions the acquisition of land and strengthens the other factors which combine to place a high value on this use of savings.

Lending money at interest is another way in which to utilize savings. As noted earlier, large landowners and landlords prefer to lend to businessmen in the larger towns and lend to small landowners or tenants only on the pledge of land or crops already close to harvest. As a rule, it is not possible to buy small shares in a business, for most Vietnamese merchants or entrepreneurs do not like to participate in large multi-person partnerships. Invested funds therefore take the form of loans, not of shares in business ventures. Further, an effort is made to diversify lending so that loans are placed with only one kind of business at a time.

Those with small amounts of savings may lend to others in the village, both relatives and friends, or participate in a *hoi*. The interest received will be relatively high in these cases, but there may be no interest at all if relatives are the debtors. This is the source of borrowing for middle and lower class households who do not have enough collateral to borrow from the wealthy landowners on a straight commercial basis. Since these small lenders have limited amounts they can put out at interest or to relatives, there is not much concern about diversification at this level.

There are not many signs of visible hoards in the form of gold and jewels. Some children wear small gold earrings; young girls wear gold necklaces on ceremonial occasions; some people have gold teeth or wear gold rings; once in a while bits of jade are seen in rings or earrings. These things are partially a form of savings, but they are also ornamental and are worn with ostentation at times when the owners, particularly young girls, want to look their best, as at weddings. This use of jewelry is most common among the more well-to-do families, but small amounts are worn even by people in poor families. The retention of gold trinkets and jewelry by lower class households would tend to argue that these are more properly ornaments than a form of savings, and that families will borrow to meet household or farm needs before they will sell what little jewelry or gold they possess. The traditional bride price included a gift of gold earrings to the bride, but at the present time lower class households avoid this expense and give symbolic payments, such as areca nut and wine, and some cash. Thus an important stimulus to accumulation in the form of gold jewelry has tended to disappear, although families who can afford to maintain the tradition continue to do so.

In addition to the jewelry, some households hoard gold in the form of flat sheets or in bars, but it is impossible to estimate how much is tied up in this way. One could not detect any widespread feeling of distrust in paper currency as such during 1958-59, and while many people preferred to keep gold instead of cash if they had funds to hold, the desire for gold was far from obsessive. In other words, people do not rush to change paper currency into gold at the first opportunity. Poor households, especially, will often hold any surplus in the form of paddy, which has the advantages of maintaining its value over time, since it is relatively free from spoilage and easy to protect from theft, and of being a fairly liquid asset. In an emergency, the family will always need rice to eat, and their savings will sustain them directly.

By way of summary, the bulk of regular savings in the village are concentrated primarily in the very small percentage of upper class households who have the largest land-holdings. Other households usually cannot manage to save anything from year to year. These savings are largely loaned out, much of them going into nearby towns, but some of them going to villagers. The purchase of land is another outlet for savings that is highly valued. This is less frequently used, however, because it requires someone willing to sell, and land is usually sold only as a last resort in cases of extreme hardship. The willingness to make savings available to others through loans is a very hopeful sign for the future development of a more highly organized series of markets for credit. Further, although there is no strong tradition positively encouraging savings, there is also no strong cultural bar to savings. The main limitation on savings is the low level of a majority of village incomes, and while it is true that some ceremonial spending occurs at the expense of potential savings, this is not the critical factor. Instead, it seems clear that if incomes were to rise there would be increases in consumption of basic items such as food and household articles, but as the experience of most upper class households suggests, there would begin to be savings at modest levels of consumption. A large share of such savings should find their way into productive lending rather than in ceremonial spending or idle hoards of cash, gold, or jewelry.

11

RESPONSES TO INNOVATION AND CHANGE

An important factor affecting the rate of economic development in underdeveloped economies is the willingness with which people accept new ways of doing familiar tasks or undertake both new methods and new tasks. Economic development implies change, and a society receptive to change has a distinct advantage in this respect over one which resists it, other things being equal. Technical advisors have been conditioned to expect resistance rather than acceptance in primitive and peasant societies, and much attention has been devoted to this important point. However, the pendulum may have swung too far in this direction—at least, this appears to be the case in South Viet Nam.

Khanh Hau provided evidence of a number of instances in which new methods and new products had been introduced into the village over the last thirty years. Some of these were accepted; some were rejected. Assuming that this type of historical record is an approximation to what is likely to recur in the future, it affords some basis for generalizing about the conditions under which innovations[1] may successfully be introduced in this part of Viet Nam.

Some Examples of Successful Innovation

Of the several examples of innovational change in Khanh Hau, the most striking has been the enthusiastic adoption of chemical fertilizers in farming, particularly in rice production. These were first introduced in the village around 1930 by a French importing firm. Agents for the firm obtained the names of several leading landowning farmers, and each of these was given a small sample (5 kilos or so) of a phosphate fertilizer and asked to use it on one part of their rice fields, later comparing the results there with those in the surrounding non-fertilized fields. The instructions were simple, the fertilizer sample was free, and the risk to the farmer was negligible. It was an attractive combination, and the farmers accepted the invitation readily.

Results were immediate and obvious. Village farmers who recall the event say that all who participated in the experiment were so convinced by the effectiveness of the new product that they began to use it on all their fields in the following year. Many others were equally impressed and began to apply it at the earliest opportunity. For others the advantages of chemical fertilizer were equally evident, but early adoption was hampered by financial limitations. Small landowners and tenants were not able to buy as much as they wanted or in some cases were not able to buy fertilizer at all.

Farmers in this area had never used natural fertilizers on their crops to any great extent. Night soil has apparently never been used, and animal manure was never available in large enough quantities to be a significant factor in production methods. It is also probable that the quality of animal diet has always been poor, and animal wastes did not make very good fertilizer. The effect of the new chemical fertilizers varied, of course, with the type of soil and the manner in which it was applied, but villagers estimate that its introduction doubled crop yields for most farmers. One farmer even spoke of the advantage as a "net profit" that was half the value of the paddy which the fertilizer added to normal yields, thereby clearly expressing the concept that marginal revenues greatly exceeded the marginal costs and that adoption of the new product was due to recognition of this relationship.

This early success paved the way for the second phase of the introduction of fertilizer, which came about in a completely different way. Again, the original impetus came from French importing firms, but it was a different kind of fertilizer, ammonium sulphate, and it was imported originally for use on sugar cane and in coconut groves. There are two versions of how this first came to be used on rice fields in this village. According to one, a storekeeper in a neighboring village began stocking ammonium sulphate to sell to sugar cane growers, but his store was burned by the Viet Minh in 1946 or 1947. Finding he could not sell this partially damaged stock, he tried some on a portion of his rice field in a blind experiment to find some way to salvage some of his sunk costs. This latter-day variation on the discovery of roast pig had a similarly happy outcome, for the addition of the ammonium sulphate increased yields substantially beyond previous levels. The next year the farmer-storekeeper was using it on all his rice fields, and within two or three growing seasons the news of his accidental discovery had spread throughout the village, and all who could afford to do so were experimenting for themselves. Village-wide adoption followed soon thereafter.

The second version is less dramatic, and according to it, the use of the new type of fertilizer grew out of local experimentation by farmers who had bought ammonium sulphate fertilizer for use on sugar cane but who decided to try using it on rice fields as well. Both version, however, are in substantial agreement that adoption grew out of local initiative and experimentation, and its rapid acceptance reflected its visible contribution to productivity and its complementarity to the earlier happy experience with phosphate fertilizer. Again, limitations on its adoption were largely financial.

A second innovation, more recent than chemical fertilizers, has been the substitution of a Cambodian-style wooden plow for the more traditional Vietnamese plow. This does not represent a change in production methods as did chemical fertilizer, but it illustrates factors associated with change in the type of capital equipment used.

In many ways, the Cambodian and Vietnamese plows are similar, but there is one major difference. Vietnamese plows have wooden shares tipped with metal, whereas the Cambodian model uses an all-metal share. This tends to make the Cambodian plow lighter and gives it a better cutting edge. It is therefore easier to use, lighter to carry, easier to pull, and plows more land in a given time period. It also can plow deeper, although Vietnamese plows go deep enough to satisfy most farmers. This combination of characteristics makes it easier on men and animals and better suited to the hard soils typical of the delta, in addition to its greater efficiency in terms of time saved. There does not seem to be any difference in the useful life of the two models, for this is a function of the quality of materials and workmanship rather than the style as such. The initial cost of the two is also roughly the same, although the Vietnamese plow requires slightly more maintenance because the metal tip needs replacement more frequently than the all-metal plowshare.

The rate of changeover has been less rapid than the adoption of chemical fertilizer, but it has been fast enough to bring about acceptance by a majority of village farmers within ten years. Since it involves replacement of a major capital item, the first to make the change were those who could afford the cash outlay. Many farmers own more than one plow, and some of those who ordered a Cambodian-style plow for the first time did so to provide themselves with a spare. In other words, initial commitment to the new tool was on a partial, experimental basis. Others, financially less able to buy a spare plow, waited until their old one required replacement or major repair, by which time they were able to benefit from the experience of others before making the changeover. Wooden plows require at least partial replacement every four to five years, and this fact tended to set upper limits to the time it took for acceptance of the new model to become general. At present, most farmers in the village have a Cambodian-style plow, and most of the Vietnamese plows one still sees are kept as spares or to use in special cases where individual farmers feel they are more suitable.

A third area of innovation is in irrigation methods. Of the three methods currently in use for getting water from streams into the rice fields—water scoop, water wheel, and gasoline pump—the second is probably the most important. Locally made, the wooden water wheel is the most efficient and economical means available at the present time within the limits set by the diameter of the water wheels most commonly made in the village. Clearly, the mechanical pump offers no advantages under conditions where the two are competing other than the saving of physical labor. The mechanical pump is therefore really a substitute only for the water scoop, and here it is both faster and more economical. Those who can afford the cash outlay for the rental, as opposed to those who must pay the higher opportunity cost in terms of their own labor on the scoop, provide the market for the mechanical pump at the present time. A pump with larger hoses, and therefore larger capacity, would eliminate the present advantage of the water wheel, and the former's main limitation would then be its physical availability. For the present, there is no question but that the villagers accept this innovation—their chief concern is to obtain more pumps, at lower rentals and with greater pumping capacity than the one now in use.

A fourth major innovation has been in threshing methods. Threshing rice in southern Viet Nam has traditionally been done with buffalo, and the heavy animals would either tread, or more rarely pull large stone rollers, over the rice paddy spread on the drying floor in a farmer's yard. This knocked the grains of paddy loose, and the winnowing which followed left a residue of relatively clean paddy. About thirty years ago, farmers in the village began to adopt the new threshing technique of hand beating the cut grain on the side of the threshing sledge, as described in Chapter 4. Villagers were unable to say where the idea came from, but most farm households now use the new method in preference to the old.

The nature of this change is such that threshing now takes place in the fields rather than in the farmer's yard. Since the new method lowers the proportion of empty husks in a given volume of paddy, it possibly increases the volume of milled rice obtainable relative to the former method. It is more burdensome on humans than the older method, which used draft animals, and may even be more costly in terms of opportunity costs. For example, it may take less time to use animals, but this must be weighed against the fact that farmers who are too poor to own their own buffalo provide the necessary manual labor from their own family, thereby eliminating cash outlays. The chief advantage would therefore seem to lie in the combination of increased threshing efficiency coupled with an opportunity to avoid cash expenditures, and not in any reduction in real costs.

The change in threshing techniques has brought a complementary change in the tools used to reap the grain. The new method requires that the grain be cut close to the ground to provide a good handhold for the thresher, whereas the length of the straw is less important if animals are used. This has resulted in a shift to the use of a small curved sickle, replacing the V-shaped cutting blade that was used before.

Finally, there is one example of successful innovation on a community-wide basis. This was the construction of canals in two hamlets in the village, largely under the stimulation and suggestion of the Fundamental Education Center. The Center suggested the canal project to the village council, helped in getting villagers to accept the suggestion, and offered advice on where and how to dig the canals.

The first canal was built in 1957, extending a natural stream to bring fresh water to fields which previously had no source of irrigation. This made it possible to raise two crops of rice a year in some of these fields, although a second crop is also a function of several other things, among them the amount of rainfall and the relative levels of the fields. Nevertheless, the canal made a substantial contribution to productivity, as well as providing a new source of water for bathing, cooking, and drinking and adding a new avenue of transportation.

Although there was little active opposition to the project at first, there was also little enthusiasm. Volunteers were slow to step forward, but eventually a few agreed to dig a portion, and others followed soon thereafter. Digging was assigned to each household on a prorated basis of anticipated benefits, and all labor and tools were supplied by villagers.

The success of the first canal led to the digging of a second canal in the following year, although at that time there was some opposition from landowners who resented the fact that the canal would cut through their lands. This opposition was ultimately overcome, but villagers say that similar attitudes are holding up construction of more canals. In general, such opposition comes from owners of land near the original streams. These people already have a source of irrigation and therefore stand to lose more than they gain from the new canal. At present, the majority sentiment definitely favors more canals, but it is not strong enough to push the new canals through. At a recent meeting of the villagers to consider new projects for the coming year, canal building ranked fifth in order of priority behind such things as construction of a bridge across one of the canals and the establishment of classes to overcome illiteracy among adults.

These represent the major innovational changes which have been introduced into the village and thoroughly assimilated. They can be supplemented by a number of other things which are in the earliest stages of introduction or are less important in terms of productivity effects. Among these latter would be insecticides which have been brought into Viet Nam under the commercial import program of the U.S. aid mission.

In general, insects have not been a major problem in the village, and the use of insecticides has not been as widespread as chemical fertilizers because the need has not been as great. They are available only through private commercial channels, and the burden of introducing them has fallen largely on individual merchants. One unfortunate by-product of this occurred in the village when farmers, seeing the effectiveness of the insecticides on insects in their rice fields, but unaware of its dangers, put the new product on their domestic animals to rid them of pests and body parasites. Several animals died as a result of this uninformed experimentation, and one farmer lost his entire stock of five buffalo.

Despite the genuine calamity this incident brought to some farmers, village reaction was calm and reasoned. Most people felt the affair was due to ignorance on the part of the farmers, and the experience served to make them wary of further experimentation. There was no blind rejection of the new product out of superstition or fear and no indication that it stiffened resistance to change as such. There were, however, complementary complications.

For example, farmers in this area feel that the insect problem has increased over the past two years and is now worse than it has ever been. Some have questioned the coincidence that brought insecticides onto the market for the first time in the same year that insect infestation became serious. They express wonder that the manufacturers could foresee the problem and prepare for it. There was even some feeling that the manufacturers or their agents may have been responsible for the insects in some way, although it is difficult to tell how seriously farmers believe this. A more general concern is that the use of ammonium sulphate fertilizer is somehow related to the increase in insect damage. This view is contradicted by the known facts, for the introduction of ammonium sulphate came long before the insect problem became serious. Nevertheless, the suspicion remains that there is some causal relationship between the two, and this is related to a further feeling that ammonium sulphate is becoming less advantageous over time.

The current attitude toward insecticides is therefore chiefly one of tentative acceptance. Larger farmers tend to use it because damage by insects seems relatively more important to them, and they can afford to buy insecticides. Small farmers do not regard the insect problem as important to them. The initial expense is not high, but repeated applications may be necessary for complete effectiveness. Small farmers are more skeptical than large and must be more convinced of the value of the new product before they are willing to incur the additional cash outlays. Until there is a clear demonstration that the insecticides are beneficial in marginal terms, and unrelated to other farm problems, further spread of their use will probably be slow.

Other examples of willingness to accept change would include the readiness to use inoculation against disease, both for villagers themselves and for their domestic animals, and an increase in the number of brick homes. People use paint to prevent rust in the tins for carrying water, and almost every man in the village owns a mechanical cigarette lighter. Canned foods, plastic items, and ball point pens are also widely used. Some water wheels have been fitted with ball bearings to reduce the physical labor involved in irrigation, and some farmers have begun to make their own concrete fence posts from home-made molds. Even the local diet shows signs of change. Soft drinks, French bread, French ragout, and Indian curry usually appear at village feasts and sometimes in the regular meals of well-to-do families.

Some Examples of Innovation that Failed

Observations are necessarily limited to innovations that have been introduced, tried, and then accepted or rejected by the villagers and do not include innovations which might work but which are unknown. Rejection of, or resistance to, innovation is best understood in cases where there has been an opportunity to consider it actively. In this sense, there have been several instances in which innovations have failed or were rejected.

Most of these involved attempts to introduce new species of domestic animals or new varieties of fruits and vegetables and have already been discussed to some extent. For example, the government extension service introduced imported breeds of swine and poultry to the village, in both cases giving animals to volunteers from the village who promised only to raise them and to repay the government from any subsequent natural increase in the stock. In the case of poultry, the grant was accompanied by detailed instructions on improved feeding, care, and provision for shelter. A kerosene incubator was donated for use in the village, although eggs for hatching had to be purchased from a Ministry of Agriculture field station. Thus, with the exception of eggs, the experiments were relatively costless to the farmer except for feed and labor. Similarly, new varieties of corn and tomatoes were given to some farmers, but here the opportunity cost was somewhat greater, for it involved giving up land that would have been used for other crops. Also, there seems to have been less instruction and advice given than in the case of swine and poultry.

The results of all these experiments were uniformly bad. Many of the swine given to villagers died of a disease which affects local breeds to an equal degree, and this occurred despite inoculations which were made available. Breeding was not controlled, and while villagers state that the offspring of imported and local swine are an improvement over the local strains, it is still too early to tell if the expected degenerative effects of indiscriminate breeding will actually occur. All of the imported poultry died, and here villagers believe the new varieties are more susceptible to disease than local chickens, for the loss occurred even when numerous precautions were taken and the care was superior to that given ordinarily. Results from the incubator were also poor, due largely to poor selection and quality control by the Ministry supplying the eggs, and hatching results compared unfavorably with normal methods. New varieties of corn produced as many ears as local varieties, but each ear had fewer grains, and people found the taste inferior. Tomato yields were less than could be obtained normally using local seed. In addition, there were complaints that some of the seed was defective and worm-eaten.

Reaction in the village was essentially one of conviction that imported varieties are unsuited for local use. Whatever their advantages in other places (and villagers are willing to accept the statement that these same plants and animals do grow successfully elsewhere), they are very skeptical about their usefulness in Khanh Hau. Animal and plant disease is accepted as a fact of life, possibly due to bad luck or as a punishment by heaven for unspecified misdeeds, but basically something to which they must adjust. New varieties do not seem to provide an answer. In the case of swine, villagers continue to believe success is related more to possession of a "hand" (*tay*) or the "lot" or "favor" of heaven (*phan*), which seems to be analogous to the notion of a "green thumb" in gardening. With it, a man can raise any kind of domestic animal; without it, there is little chance for success no matter what new varieties or methods one uses.

The common element in this set of experiences was the failure to make careful tests in advance of innovations to be introduced. The prevalence of animal disease in this area is high, and village farmers have had consistently poor results with their own efforts at animal husbandry. While new varieties can undoubtedly make an important contribution to their economic well-being, it is essential that these be tested thoroughly under local conditions to make certain that there are no unforeseen problems attending their introduction. The problem in this village was compounded further by the poor quality of some of the things introduced (e. g., seed corn and the eggs to be used in incubators), an obvious but, in this village, neglected responsibility of the innovating agency. While these failures have not discouraged villagers from innovation as such, they have probably strengthened feelings that innovations in these important areas are unlikely to work successfully, and the introduction of similar new ideas will probably be more difficult than it was in the past. In this case, the experience with past failures may retard acceptance of new varieties of plants and animals.

The Role of Traditional Institutions

The foregoing provides a body of empirical data of sorts from which to assess the climate for innovations in this village, but examination of local institutions gives some useful supplementary material. On the whole, there seem few obvious blocks to innovation and change due to ritual, taboos, or superstition. Productive activity is free of ritual, except for simple offerings of food and wine at the beginning of the planting season or when starting construction of a new house, and there are no rituals which direct the way work is performed or inhibit the introduction of new work methods. Farmers do tend to avoid starting new activities on days marked "unpropitious" on the lunar calendar, but such days are not numerous and do not constitute an important check to productive activity.

It is true that an important share of resources is diverted into feasts and celebrations throughout the year. The village as a whole celebrates during the four major festivals of the planting season and the feast in honor of the guardian spirit of the village. These are not all of equal size and importance, but each requires expenditures which could be used productively. The same applies to the expenditures made by individual families for the five or six major feasts which they celebrate each year. Weddings and funerals are other occasions which can be elaborate and costly. The advent of the lunar new year requires cash outlays for gifts, new clothing, feasts, firecrackers, candles, joss, altar adornments, and good luck decorations.

However, there are other ways of looking at these expenditures, and all of them have elements of economic rationality as they are actually made. For example, villagers rarely go into debt to carry out their responsibilities to the village or ancestral spirits. In 1958, after a very bad crop year, the expenditures on village festivals were scaled down drastically to relieve some of the cost. The traditional opera performance was canceled, and vigorous bargaining with the village sorcerer reduced his services to the minimum which tradition demands, thereby cutting their cost as well.[2] On another occasion, the sacrifice of a whole pig was eliminated, and only the face and feet of a pig were bought to meet the ritual requirement that these portions of the animal be presented to the spirits. Individual families will reduce the number of feasts, the number of guests invited to each, and the variety and amount of food offered when circumstances demand it. Thus, while villagers will seek to maintain some minimum observance of traditional rites, the actual amounts spent are quite flexible and are largely a function of funds available after estimated needs for the coming year have been provided for. To the outsider, the expense incurred even under these adjustments may appear excessive, but it is important to recognize that adjustments do take place.

Reciprocity in gift giving at weddings and funerals has certain erratic aspects from a strictly economic point of view, for return gifts of cash do not necessarily come in the same year that one gives gifts to others. However, the practice of giving cash at weddings and funerals can be regarded as a built-in saving device for these major expenses. Since the contributions made by guests largely cover the cost of the event, it is not always necessary for individual families to save the entire cost in advance or to borrow when the occasion arises. Contributions made as a guest become a kind of time-payment against the need when one must play host at similar occasions.

Institutions other than ritualistic or traditional practice may affect the scope for innovation, although this village contained few examples of this. One that did was a ruling by the village council that no landowner could operate more than ten hectares of his own land. The rationale for this was to increase the amount of land available for tenants. This could conceivably have adverse effects on productivity, but in actual practice it has not, because only a very few owner-operators held enough land to be affected by the ruling. It thus stands more as an example of how local concern for particular problems—in this case, to create wide tenant opportunities—may result in institutional action which could have unforeseen effects in terms of over-all productivity. Peasant societies, of course, are not unique in this respect.

A final point deals with the basic attitudes which villagers take toward their problems and their position in the society. In this village there is a relatively weak sense of communal identification or community interest, associated with a conservative outlook that is heavily tinged with fatalism. There is a surprisingly individualistic cast to many attitudes, given the communal orientation that has characterized village life in North and Central Viet Nam, and this can have conflicting effects on innovation and change.

Without vigorous leadership, communal activities in Khanh Hau do not seem to get very far. This was evident in the failure to push canal building beyond the successful start which was made and in the failure to establish a successful cooperative in the village or even to make much headway with the idea of cooperation to accomplish minor goals. Concern for one's own household and its problems, for example, is responsible for the frequent and bitter disputes over water rights and water use, and the village contains no examples of unified effort to rationalize the use of water for the benefit of large numbers of farms, even though this is crucial to the production of the major crop.

This individualistic attitude does not make the villagers opposed to change, as the examples of successful innovation attest, but it does mean that they are inclined to think of their problems in terms of their impact on individual households and to be interested in change which will benefit them directly. In the case of small landowners, small tenants, and laborers, this will be further conditioned by an innate conservatism born of practical circumstances. With very small margins of economic security available to them, the risk of the unknown seems very great. The years of war and political unrest have added problems of physical security to those of making a living. Even though present conditions may not be very satisfactory, villagers tend to be interested only in those changes which will bring demonstrably large improvements in their situation, for most changes tend to be costly or require more land than they have or lie beyond their reach in some other way.

Summary

From this evidence of recent experience, and from other observation of institutions and attitudes in this village, a few general conclusions appear valid. This does not mean that similar conclusions would hold even for all parts of Viet Nam, let alone all peasant societies, but they still seem worth pointing up as representative of one particular body of experience.

(1) There are many indications that, in general, villagers in Khanh Hau are reasonably open to new ideas and willing to incorporate new methods. This does not mean that they will accept any and all suggestions offered to them, but it does imply that the initial reaction will not be a

hostile one. The villagers have made some important changes in the past, and they should continue to make them where certain conditions hold true. Rituals, taboos, and superstitions do not constitute an important bar to innovation, and there is evidence of considerable flexibility in the amount of resources devoted to ritual and ceremonial feasting.

(2) Innovations which promise substantial increases in productivity appear most highly valued and have been adopted rapidly after the advantages have been clearly demonstratted. Where replacement of existing capital equipment is involved, the innovation takes place over a longer period of time because many delay making the change until replacement would normally take place. Financing can be a limiting factor in the short run, but where marginal revenues clearly exceed marginal costs, villagers have been willing to borrow in order to use a new product or adopt a new idea soon after it has been introduced. Thus, an improvement in credit facilities or expansion in opportunities to use land would tend to complement the adoption of new ideas. Innovations which promise an increase in leisure or a reduction of physical labor, for example, arouse less interest if this is their only advantage. Similarly, villagers seem unconcerned about acquiring new types of consumer goods, although they are anxious to obtain more of those with which they are already familiar, Modes of dress in the village have changed much less than in the larger towns. There seem to be relatively few community-wide needs or demands, and while communal effort is not unknown, communal values appear to rank below individual ones.

If we could list the factors which seem most related to the acceptance of change, therefore, productivity appears to be most important. Other things being equal, innovations with individual impact take hold more rapidly than those which require communal action.

(3) The workability or advantage of a new idea must be visibly demonstrated before villagers will begin to adopt it, and the demonstration should be carried out by villagers themselves if possible. This is well established in farm

extension work everywhere, but even though it is obvious it requires emphasis again. If the risk to the experimenting farmer is small, and if he can take part in the demonstration at little or no cost to himself, cooperation will be readily offered.

(4) There should be careful pretesting of new products and new varieties under local conditions before they are introduced. A succession of failures, due to lack of or improper testing, may generate long-run skepticism. Although some chance innovations may turn out successfully, as, for example, in the case of fertilizer in this village, there is always the risk that a failure mayhave long-run and wider effects than the specific instance involved in the failure. Despite the delay entailed, careful pretesting is extremely important.

(5) Complementarities are important to innovation in two ways. They extend an original successful innovation into related changes, widening the demand for other new products or paving the way for other new ideas. They also magnify the significance of innovational failures, for poor results with a new product may be related in the minds of the villagers to other recent innovations or may set up complementary expectations of failure in the use of similar new products or methods. Such complementarities can be utilized to accelerate acceptance of innovation over a wide area, but it should be recognized that they also underscore the need to avoid failures through adequate pretesting.

(6) A surprising amount of local experimentation seems to have taken place in the village, some of it successful, but some with disastrous results. This is further evidence of a general climate of opinion favorable to change and new ideas. It also emphasizes the need to make certain that dangers or limitations in the case of new products are fully understood in order to prevent local misuse through uninformed experimentation.

12

AN AGGREGATE VIEW OF ECONOMIC ACTIVITY

Performance and Structure

A deliberate effort has been made throughout this study to avoid any reference to "the village economy" on the grounds that this term implies an integrated, relatively self-sufficient and self-contained economic entity. Khanh Hau is not a "village economy" in this latter sense, but instead is thoroughly tied to the national economy in a number of ways. Further, while the interests and concerns of most village residents are largely with things which take place in the village or affect its people, it does not follow that they identify their own interests primarily, or even extensively, with those of the community at large. This has been implicit in much of the description which has preceded, but the time has come to state this viewpoint specifically and to attempt to substantiate it.

There are, of course, large elements of self-sufficiency in the village in the manner in which people provide themselves with food and shelter. There are also areas of activity that seem conditioned by the resource endownment and the force of tradition more than by the complex price and cost considerations of a sophisticated money economy. Still, the village relies to an important extent on exchange with the more developed commercial sector of the national economy, as the data in Table 12.1 tend to bring out. This shows the sources of expenditure for goods produced in the village and an estimate of the kinds and amounts of goods which are exchanged between the village and the rest of the economy. It is, in fact, an attempt to present a Gross Village Product, analogous in concept to the Gross National Product derived for national economies.

These, it should be emphasized, are simply estimates that have been put together by plausible extensions of bits of known data derived from several sources. Since none of the villagers keeps records, these, in turn, must be expansions of estimates and guesses of varying reliability. Nevertheless,

TABLE 12.1
Sources of Expenditures, Gross Village Produce,
Village of Khanh Hau, in a Hypothetical Year

Source	Amount of expenditure (VN$)	
Consumption		
Rice	2,150,200	
Vegetables	837,564	
Fruit	322,140	
Fish	1,263,600	
Meat	490,880	
Services	1,952,414	
Total		7,016,798
Exports		
Rice	6,183,800	
Vegetables	148,000	
Fruit	148,000	
Meat	1,710,000	
Services	1,000,000	
Fish	100,000	
Total		9,289,800
Imports		
Vegetables	358,956	
Fruit	138,060	
Fish	1,263,600	
Meat	1,963,520	
Manufactured consumer goods	4,448,600	
Other foodstuffs	1,516,888	
Total		10,869,624
Investment in farm equipment	366,000	366,000
GROSS VILLAGE PRODUCT [Consumption + (Exports - Imports) + Investment]		5,802,974

they represent the best information available and as such should be used as approximations to reality, probably accurate with respect to structure and general relationship, if not in verifiable amounts. The terms "export" and "import" are used to refer to goods which are sold outside the village or are brought into the village or purchased by villagers in other towns or market centers. The latter are not limited to goods foreign to Viet Nam, but are all things which are produced outside the village.

Earlier sections described the failure to develop vegetable and fruit cultivation and the relatively undeveloped state of animal husbandry. This also shows in the aggregate figures which indicate that the village exports small quantities of fruits and vegetables and some meat and fish to the market towns, but is a net importer of vegetables, meat, and fish. The large import items, however, are the manufactured consumer goods and the processed foods which do not fall under the categories of fruit, vegetables, meat, and fish. These two items together constitute a measure of the degree to which the village does not provide for its own needs directly out of its own production, for they comprise over one-half of the total imports into the village.

Consumption expenditures represent the value of village production which remains and is consumed within the village. This category also includes services of such people as artisans, village officials, sorcerers, mill operators, and others. The services of peddlers and storekeepers are also added here, because their contribution is considered the same as a transportation service, bringing goods from outside the village into the village for resale. A final item of "other" consumption goods includes the value of woven materials of reed, the thatch for roofs and walls, and a small allowance for the consumption of the few other household items made in the village. On the basis of these estimates, consumption directly from village production constitutes less than half the value of all that is consumed in the village, although in the case of rice and services it is assumed that the village can provide all that is used. In addition, the example assumes that the village provides 70 percent of the vegetables and fruit and half the fish, but only 20 percent of the meat consumed in normal years.

The chief export item is rice, as expected, given the

heavy specialization in its production. Villagers also export small quantities of vegetables and fruits to nearby markets and also much of the meat produced. Occasionally meat is slaughtered in the village, but there are no facilities for refrigeration or preservation if a large animal is slaughtered, and therefore the more common practice is to sell meat animals in the larger towns where there are slaughterhouse facilities. The meat consumed in the village is usually bought in the towns and brought back to the village in small quantities as needed. The export of services includes, for example, the incomes of the village residents who work in Tan An as laborers or artisans, mechanics, and drivers, and the service of school teachers and village officials who live in the village but who are paid from non-village governmental funds.

These figures are based on assumptions which would apply in a "normal" year, and therefore, although many of the estimates made are the results of observations in 1958, they are not presented as applying to 1958 specifically. As shown for this hypothetical year, imports into the village exceed exports from it by more than VN$ 1,500,000.

The adverse trade balance in the hypothetical year is assumed to have arisen because the village need for goods produced outside of the village could not be offset by substitutes produced in the village, and exports of rice and other farm products were not large enough to pay for the imports. This does not happen in every year, but it is very likely to happen in poor crop years like 1957-58 and 1958-59. At such times, village production would be insufficient to maintain the "normal" or "usual" flow of goods from outside, but the need to bring in an aggregate import surplus of goods like clothing and fertilizer would persist. The extent and distribution of debt in the village is further evidence that this problem has arisen in the past, and the persistence of the debt burden would tend to argue that years of export surplus may be relatively infrequent. Thus, the balance of payments problem which arises in the bad crop years means either a reduction in the consumption of the manufactured and processed goods that come from outside the village or an increase in the amount of indebtedness when villagers cannot, or will not, curtail their consumption of imported goods. All hopes for some easing of the debt burden, or for some rise in the standards of living, rest on prospects for a bumper crop of rice to be sold at prices which do not reflect an unfavorable turn in the terms of trade, but the previous chapters have detailed some of the problems which must be overcome if production is to be increased by any substantial margin.

The small amount recorded as investment in the village is an estimate of the farm equipment purchased during the course of a normal year. Since the implements used are largely made of wood, with the exception of some metal parts, they tend to wear out within two to four years. Most investment, therefore, is essentially replacement and not a net addition to existing capital. The canals which the village has built in the last three years represent a type of community capital accumulation, but these cannot be regarded as investments which are normally made each year. Under these assumptions, net village product would be what remained after deleting all investment expenditure, because investment, in any given year, would tend to be the measure of depreciation in the existing stock of capital equipment. Since the construction of capital equipment is a local activity, with the exception of some purchases of implements from other villages, most investment goods are produced in the village itself.

If the consumption expenditures and the imports are added together, the result is an aggregate estimate of village expenditure. This sum, equal to VN$ 17,886,422, converts to an annual expenditure of VN$ 5,519 per capita, or approximately the per capita expenditures for lower and middle class households given in the household budget survey. Since an important part of these aggregate data was based on the household budget findings, this does not constitute proof of the validity of the aggregates in any way. However, the closeness of aggregate and household data makes for consistency between the two, even if they are not completely independent sources of information.

From an aggregate point of view, the village can be considered as export-oriented, dependent on exchange with the commercial economy of the country for an important part of its needs. It faces chronic balance of payments difficulties which can be overcome only in particularly good crop years. At other times, credit and transfers from outside the village provide the means by which import levels are at least partially

maintained. The Gross Village Product makes it possible to identify the ways in which these balance of payments difficulties can
be met—increased export of goods and services to nearby towns
—but unhappily it cannot prescribe the measures by which this
can be accomplished.

Patterns of Cooperation

If the aggregate view of the village shows its link to the national
economy, is it still true that the village organizes its production in
an essentially communal way and that we may speak of the "village economy" in the sense of village-wide cooperative efforts?
Again, the answer seems to be in the negative. Earlier chapters
have shown that what patterns of cooperation do exist are on a base
much narrower than that of the entire village. In the light of the
great interest in community development plans in Viet Nam and
elsewhere in Asia, the relation of the villager to his community in
Khanh Hau and the implications for economic development should
be examined more closely.

The largest group within which there is anything approaching
a genuine sense of community identification and interest is the
hamlet, and even there the number of people is frequently too large,
or the settlement pattern too spread out, to encourage a strong communal spirit. The administrative village is certainly too large for this,
with slow and difficult communication between hamlets. Moreover,
kinship patterns work against close intra-village contact except in
the neighborhood groupings of relatives, and many of the villagers
therefore see one another quite infrequently. It is true that the *dinh*,
the school, and the council house provide village focal points which
draw people for specific purposes, but this would not include all villagers, and some who are drawn do not become very involved. In
short, the village is much too large and unwieldy to be more than
an administrative unit, and it is possibly too large even for that.

The most frequent examples of cooperation are, therefore, found in
units smaller than the hamlet, that is, small clusters of dwellings in more
or less well defined neighborhoods. These may consist of people who are
related to each other—all or part of an extended family—but they may
also be people who simply happened to settle near one another and

who have no close relationship at all. In either case, in lower and middle class neighborhood groups of this kind there is some co-operation and mutual help, and labor is exchanged in farm work, for special tasks like roofing or thatching walls, or in rare joint neighborhood enterprises like building fish ponds. Here there is some sense of identity with a group larger than the household but not necessarily composed of kinsmen. The essential element is proximity and therefore availability for aid and assistance.

However, it is possible to make too much of even this cooperation or limited communal spirit. Although it exists and is important to the lower and middle class households, there remains a large measure of activity that is centered in the individual household —well over half of all economic activity being organized in that way. Economic decision-making is on an individual basis, as is the direction of production and the disposal of the harvest. Cooperation occurs only between lower and middle class households, where the exchange of labor can eliminate the need for cash outlays by farmers who can ill afford them. Other than this, there is little that is communal in an all-inclusive sense.

The failure of a short-lived farmers' cooperative in Khanh Hau is an illustration of this. It faced problems in several respects, financial and organizational, but an important part of the difficulty from the start lay in the lack of real community spirit. People seemed unable to transfer the practice of neighborhood labor exchange to cooperation in a wider sense, over a large area, and with people they knew less well. Disinterest and distrust were major factors inhibiting the success of the cooperative. The lack of communal land in the village is probably significant in this context in a negative way, for unlike villages in the north and central parts of Viet Nam, villagers in Khanh Hau have no background of heavy involvement in the wider community through regular participation in the redistribution of communal land. Without this kind of experience, the reticence and suspicion which attended the formation of a cooperative becomes more understandable.

The canals dug in the village are examples of a communal effort that has been carried to successful conclusion. Yet here the success was dependent largely upon encouragement and direction from the top levels of village local government, backed by the support of the Fundamental Education Center. There was, and continues to be, scattered opposition to the canal building program; the proiect did not come from broad popular demand, and even its success has not sparked support for more of the same.

The lesson in this for future community development or communal projects is that, in this part of Viet Nam, at least, it is unrealistic to expect communal spirit or communal drive to carry through programs on a village-wide basis. Projects which require cooperation, but which are limited to the natural cooperative areas, i.e., hamlets or smaller, stand a much better chance of being accepted and enthusiastically carried out. And perhaps most of all, there should be greater appreciation of the value and potential success of projects which are aimed at the individual households.

Monetization of Economic Activity

Another aspect of economic behavior which reflects this lack of community-mindedness is the high degree to which economic transactions have become monetized. It has already been remarked that barter is a relatively unimportant means of exchange. Neighbors engage in some barter on a very small scale, but the important needs are met by money purchase. This includes things which would at first seem to be free, if not bartered—the thatch for roofs and walls, the manure left by cattle and buffalo, the husks of the rice, the rice straw, and, of course, the labor of men and animals. According to the survey, around 43 percent of all farmers hire labor to some extent, and over two-thirds of all adults hire out as laborers for others. All exchange which takes place in the market centers of Tan An and Tan Huong is for money, and the services of artisans, weavers, mill operators, and traditional physicians and geomancers are paid for in money.

The fact that most transactions are in money does not mean that cash holdings in typical households are large. In fact, one hears complaints that money for transaction purposes is in chronically short supply. For example, there were occasions when members of a household could not supply the change for a VN$ 50 note at the time of some small purchase, and even a canvass of the neighboring houses often failed to produce the necessary smaller notes for change.

Most people receive only small amounts of cash at a time, and they spend most of it quickly in small purchases of things that are needed daily. Still, when the village has a festival or celebration, cash contributions cover a large part of the cost of the feast and entertainment, although villagers also bring food offerings to be served.

Village people are ready to place money values on all items and express curiosity over the cost of things which are unfamiliar to them. They have fairly explicit ideas of the value of the land they own or rent. Many show an awareness of the price differentials which exist between different towns or market centers and indicate a preference for the lower priced sellers. Traditional payments in kind, such as the bride price, are being supplanted in many cases by cash payments, and the solicitation of gifts which takes place at weddings and funerals brings offerings in cash. Rental payments are made in cash, particularly if the paddy is not very good if the landlord is a non-resident of the village, although some rents are paid in kind.

The listing could be continued, but the point can be made without it—although the village presents a picture of a peasant economy in many respects, a surprising volume of transactions takes place in money form, and there is ample evidence that the villagers are accustomed to thinking in monetary terms in expressing the value of items, in contemplating sales or purchases, and in planning future activities. The continuing, and undoubtedly expanding, use of money would imply further weakening of any peasant-communal orientation which may have existed and increasing inter-relatedness with the national economy.

Goals and Incentives

There is, finally, the question of the attitude which villagers would bring to any program designed to spur economic development, at either the local or the national level, and the goals and incentives toward which they currently work. This area is perhaps no more lacking in concrete information than many others discussed in this study, but touching as it does on subjective judgtnents which many villagers have never made articulate in their own minds before, the impressions presented here are offered with greater qualification than in other cases.

Social goals and Western-style economic incentives melt into a blend that, on balance, favors increasing wealth and the accumulation of material goods. A man's social position in the community is determined partly by his income and the kinds of prestige items which he can buy and display. A position in the village organizations depends on his ability to contribute financially to their support. His responsibility to his ancestors and to the other members of his family requires that the family cult be maintained with dignity and proper honor, that the house where the cult is celebrated be substantial and handsome, and that he leave behind the means by which his descendants can continue the cult on the same, or a more elaborate, scale. Provided it is reasonably honest, the society attaches no stigma to any means of achieving these social and economic goals. Merchants are as respected as farmers, although the ownership of land is considered important for cult purposes even if farming is not the primary source of income. The only feature offsetting this otherwise strong set of sanctions for material advancement is the priority given to consumption in the course of maintaining family and village cults. This decreases the amount which could go into more productive use, but it does not eliminate it. Although thrift is not highly valued as such, some people seem to save and to use their savings in lending for productive purposes.

These are admittedly thin reeds on which to rest a judgment on goals and incentives. Nevertheless, to the extent the replies and observations are indicative, the motivation of the villagers is consistent with economic growth and development. This shows up in the social environment, which favors growth and the accumulation of material goods, though not essentially capital goods. It also appears in the desire for more education for the children and the preference that children go into occupations other than farming. Together with the overview of economic activity and the relations with the national economy, the patterns of limited cooperation and household-centered decision-making within the village, and the extent of monetization that exists, one can identify a number of tendencies which all move contrary to the notion of an isolated and self-sufficient "village economy." Institutional friction from this source would not appear to be one of the problems faced in this part of Viet Nam in any effort to stimulate economic development.

13

ECONOMIC ACTIVITY AND THE
SOCIAL SETTING

What has gone before has been, for the most part, descriptive of economic activity in the village of Khanh Hau, with only passing attempts to assess its meaning, if any, in the broader context of village society as a whole and its implications for future economic development. The question remains: are there any generalizations which can be made about the village and its people as a social organism to which the isolated bits of behavior can be related and within which they can be further explained and understood? Is there any synthesis possible in which the contributing points of view of the sociologist, the political scientist, and the economist can become part of a better understanding of village life, free of the confining scope of each discipline when each is applied separately? In short, can something of the breadth of insight toward which the novelist customarily gropes be achieved through the marshaling of data amassed via the techniques of the social scientist? Perhaps not, but the aim of this chapter is to attempt such a synthesis.[1]

The first thing to recognize is that Khanh Hau is a society in transition. A relatively "new" village, the major elements of which probably have an administrative existence of less than 150 years, it was settled by people—refugees, adventurers, soldiers, outcasts—who as they moved southward into the delta area had probably already begun to shed marginal or peripheral elements of the culture of Central and North Viet Nam they had left behind them. As centers of population grew to a size which warranted recognition as a village, relationships and activities within the village took forms recognizably, and understandably, similar to those in Central and North Viet Nam. In many respects, however, they were different. For example, the settlement pattern was more extended, quite distinct from the concentrated, huddled patterns of villages in the north; the differences in soil, climate, and water conditions brought changes in the cycle and methods of cultivation and the kinds of things which were grown; the institution of communal landholdings never achieved significant size, probably because land was relatively plentiful in the early period of settlement, and villagers saw little need to transplant this important means of land tenure from other parts of Viet Nam; kinship groups that were to a large extent starting *de novo* had much narrower circles of relationship to begin with, and subsequently followed the much looser patterns of kinship obligations and ritual observance which are reflected in a rather widespread failure to maintain family geneologies. To the weakening of familiar forms, customs, and traditions that accompanied the move south may be added the additional factor of more direct, and probably more effective, French influence after the mid-nineteenth century. Cochin China, which comprised a majority of the territory that is now South Viet Nam, was a French colony, and unlike the territory to the north, was directly controlled and administered by France. The opportunities for the spread of French (or Western) ideas, attitudes, and behavior patterns were certainly greater there, and a society already in transition was possibly more receptive to all that was new than the more static northern and central parts of the country. For reasons such as these (which are by no means exhaustive) it seems accurate to consider the village of Khanh Hau as a transitional society within this broader framework and in the sense that it shows numerous signs of change from traditional Vietnamese society. Not only has it changed in the past, but it is undoubtedly continuing to change at the present time. It is therefore reasonable to characterize Khanh Hau, and by implication other villages in the region, as amenable to change in (probably) most areas of human activity. Stated negatively, Khanh Hau is not a village whose people are tightly oriented to the past or strongly bound by tradition.

A second point to be stressed follows from the first, and this is simply that the administrative boundaries of the village do not contain a single, unified political, social, and economic unit. Village society is not monolithic or all-embracing in all cases, so that there is no "village economy" in the sense of a self-contained economic organism or set of institutions, nor are the most important social institutions village-wide in their extent. This may be partly due, in the case of Khanh Hau, to the fact that it is today the result of an administrative merger of formerly separate villages, but even the former village boundaries do not delineate coterminous social and economic units. Therefore, care should be taken to avoid thinking in terms of "the village" as somehow a single, homogeneous social grouping for which village-wide aggregates are necessarily the most meaningful measures of behavior. Some activities and some relationships clearly affect a majority of the inhabitants of the village, and some of the institutions accentuate an orientation and loyalty in the village, but the most important events in the lives of people living in the village (in the opinion, at least, of this observer from the outside) either extend beyond the village in scope or are limited to groups or activities that are less extensive than the boundaries of the village or even of the hamlets therein. Thus, heavy dependence on "exports" of paddy from the village and exchange for a wide variety of things not grown or produced in the village has already tied inhabitants of Khanh Hau to the national economy as commercial agriculturists and thereby conditioned them to extend their sights and anticipations beyond their own village; the population pyramid offers strong evidence that young adults have left the village in large numbers in recent years, and while it is not altogether clear why or where they went, ties of kinship now extend well outside the village; the limited size of the patrilineage (including only those related through the male line to a common ancestor in the third ascending generation) and some tendency to follow a patrilocal residence pattern makes for small and fairly tight-knit neighborhoods of villagers belonging to the same kingroup—neighborhoods that are smaller-sized than hamlets and which shape the limited cooperative efforts which do take place in the village. Add to this the fact that years of fighting and insecurity in the delta have awakened some sense of nationality and identification with something more extensive than the village; they have also put heavy strains on intra-village relationships of all kinds and generated bitterness and hostility that does not disappear easily. The net effect of all these factors is to cast considerable doubt on the validity of the view that rural communities in South Viet Nam are essentially village-centered and strongly receptive to anything with a communal or cooperative orientation. Some of the traditionally Vietnamese values and orientations have begun to change as the concentrated effort by the government to stimulate national loyalties and promote economic change filters down to the villagers. At present, the neighborhood residence group, representing an important part of the patrilineage, appears to be the largest-sized effective social grouping, but the individual household is the unit where a majority (and the most important) of the decisions and activities are centered.

This leads to consideration of a third point—the extent to which certain kinds of activity (usually separated as "economic" or "political") are "embedded" in some social grouping. Putting it another way, to what extent are the activities associated with the production and distribution of goods functionally derived from decisions of a social grouping larger than the household or from values and goals not directly concerned with production and distribution as such? A subsidiary question would consider the extent to which these activities are explained by household maximization of income earning opportunities and response to market stimuli. In the realm of political administration of village affairs, does effective administration rely largely on subordinate and super-ordinate relationships existing within traditional village institutions and hereditary status, or can political power be effectively transferred from sources outside the village? Finally, to what extent does prestige and social status stem from income levels or "economic" advantages? The answers to questions like these, as would be expected, are not all clear-cut, but some patterns seem discernible.

It is fairly clear, for instance, that most of the economic activity which takes place in the village is explained by physical limitations of soil, climate, rainfall, and the "state of the arts." That is, the quantities produced per unit of land area mainly reflect the proportions in which the given factor inputs of land and water are combined with labor, the services of crude capital equipment, and varying amounts of fertilizers. Other techniques could probably raise village productivity in agriculture, but these are unknown there, and the means are not at hand to readily demonstrate and explain how they could be used. But even if output per unit of land area doubted, which would place it close to the levels attained in the highly productive rice fields of Japan, the proportionate or greater increase in income which presumably would accompany this would still mean very low standards of living in comparison with living standards in the Western world. The point is simply that the pressure of population on the physical means of production, even with some allowance for improved technologies, is so great that the prospects for major economic development are not bright. Increased attention to the land and its problems will result in some easing of current hardships, but that is the most that can be expected.

There is little evidence that major decisions affecting agricultural activity are significantly affected by factors other than considerations of the effects on total production or on costs in relation to anticipated returns (crude marginal comparisons). Religious practice seems to impinge only in the sense that the success or failure of crops or of animal husbandry is believed to be due, in a major way, to the whim or design of a multitude of supernatural force, and these forces can be displeased by sins of omission and commission in the performance of scheduled rites and ceremonies. There is strong awareness of a basic interdependence between man and nature in the production process, but within the framework of this awareness and the ceremonials which give overt evidence of it there is an area of discretion left to man and his own efforts. What he derives from the soil he works is therefore viewed as the result of his own initiative and the climate and rainfall conditions which nature provides. The findings of this study point to the conclusion that it is this area of discretion left to man that really determines the production patterns of the farmers of Khanh Hau, and that there is little or no evidence that religious beliefs or practices intervene significantly in production decisions, directly or indirectly. What effect exists is probably best exemplified by the case of village attitudes toward raising pigs or chickens—i.e., that some people have a gift for this and do well at it, while others do not. Lacking explicit experience or evidence to the contrary, many households apparently resign themselves and forego this source of income on the grounds that "heaven" would not reward their efforts. In this sense, religion may affect production decisions, but this type of attitude usually comes after some initial effort has failed. Therefore, it would be equally accurate to regard the villagers' attitude as one of conviction that certain kinds of activity do not succeed, and lacking other knowledge, they simply abandon further efforts after trying them once or twice.

Although village farmers make efforts to increase levels of production, and therefore income and consumption, a simple assumption of profit maximization does not seem an adequate explanation of the motives underlying decision—making. Hesitancy to plant a second crop in some cases and the attitudes toward some activities (pig and chicken raising) and some innovations (insecticides) suggest that the minimization of risk and disappointment are also important. The attainable, in economic terms, based on past experience, sets the level of most villager expectations. A clear showing that this can be improved seems to lead to behavior which will adjust to the rise in expectations (e.g., the adoption of fertilizer); repeated failures to meet the old level of attainment seem to result in attempts to find alternatives (e.g., concern over the relationship of fertilizer to plant disease and concern over late rainy seasons) and/or the scaling down of the level of expected attainment (e.g., adjustment to land fragmentation). This is not the behavior of people seeking to maximize all the possibilities for adding to income which might exist, or even those of which they might be aware, but instead is the behavior of people seeking to adjust to what they believe to be the realistically attainable within the limits set by nature and their society. Where failure may mean heavy indebtedness or substantial reduction of living standards which are already extremely low, it is understandable that people shrink from taking major risks and stay within patterns that promise acceptable achievement.

In some respects, economic activity and economic decision-making is "embedded" in other social institutions, but again the major effects seem to be general. For instance, the most dependable source of income and livelihood in the village is land, and most of those owning it have inherited it. Those who buy land, on the few occasions when it is sold, generally are in a position to do so because they already own some land. In this sense, then, access to the land follows the pattern of inheritance to a great extent, although this is not absolute. Fragmentation will probably become more and more important and therefore be a factor conditioning economic activity, but to date it has not reached critical proportions. On the other hand, the obvious willingness and pleasure with which tenants received title to land distributed under the agrarian reform program provided ample evidence that failure to own land earlier was largely due to the lack of opportunity to do so and not because of any considerations of propriety or social eligibility. Further, the system of inheritance has, if anything, a strong egalitarian bias, and through it economic opportunities which are inheritable are diffused and made even rather than recast in basically unequal ways which favor specific kinds of heirs. Even in the case of the artisans in the village, there is no firm pattern of passing on skills to children or even to other relatives. There is some of this, of course, but a measure of basic skill or aptitude for the work seems at least equally important in choosing a successor or partner.

What cooperation occurs in the performance of common tasks, such as transplanting and harvesting, seems to take place in the neighborhood groupings, but is usually limited to the poorest families. To a surprising degree, money payments are made for labor services of all kinds, and to this extent work patterns reflect economic need rather than kinship obligations or considerations of mutual assistance. In the same way, the failure to develop a unified approach to problems of irrigation and the weak sense of communal identification evident in the disputes over canal building or the operations of the agricultural cooperative imply that production activities are more related to the households than to larger social groupings. No examples were found of working groups that are organized by patrilineage, nor were there any examples of other types of economic units organized by patrilineage for the purpose of sharing profits or risks. People do work together with relatives at times, of course, but they associate with others outside the patrilineage as readily for all such purposes, and one cannot conclude that kinship is an important determinant of the composition of groupings formed for economic purposes.

While the productive activities appear to be only partially embedded in the larger social groupings, there are fairly strong material
objectives which attach to the social and cultural values of the villagers. In this category we would place the desire to acquire altar
fixtures and adornments, found in the humblest households, through
the full range of material goals up to and including the acquisition
of *huong hoa* and a substantial brick or frame house, all of which
serve to enhance and honor the cult of the ancestors. The mode
of dress and numerous other prestige symbols, all stemming from
values accepted and recognized throughout the village, require some
command over and productive use of economic resources. It would
be difficult to identify any position or symbol of prestige and status
in the village not at least partially derived from or accompanied by
economic power. Even membership in the traditional council of
notables, to some extent hereditary, requires affluence by village
standards if one is to rise to the highest ranks. All appointed village
officials have some outside means of income, and this probably
contributed to the eligibility of the highest ranking among them.
There are thus adequate grounds to conclude that a man's role in
village society is functionally related, in part, to his income and the
economic power he possesses. To this extent, the drive to achieve,
or retain, the social role to which he feels he is entitled will work
in the same direction as the economic drives to make the most of
his circumstances within the limits suggested above.

The significance of this lies in the implication that "economic"
drives seem present which would give impetus to programs aimed
at increasing production and raising the level of household income. Such programs will have to be brought to the village,
however, or depend on developments outside the village such
as large-scale irrigation projects. Even with these, the possibilities for major improvement in standards of living are limited;
without them the chances are virtually non-existent. Viet Nam
must develop other resources, other forms of production. Her
agricultural base in the rice-producing delta will continue
to make an important contribution to national economic
well-being, but it must be supplemented by development of many

other sectors of the economy, because the upper limits of the agricultural contribution do not appear to be far above the present levels.

Finally, some estimate of the adaptability of Vietnamese in rural communities to the requirements, incentives, and restraints of a modern commercial economy may be drawn from various experiences at the current stage of activity. Signs favorable to ready adaptation would include the entrepreneurial stirrings visible among some of the villagers such as the rice millers and a few of the rice merchants, the growth of independent rice milling throughout the delta, the considerations which go into the planning of agricultural production, the widespread monetization of economic activity and the assignment of monetary values to much in village life, the acceptance of productive innovations in recent years and the willingness to experiment (sometimes dangerously) with new and unknown products, the commercial cast to much of the agricultural activity, and the apparent willingness to leave the village and the countryside if there were some assurance that living standards could really be raised by doing so. All these things and others which the reader may recall for himself would be compatible with a more interdependent, highly organized economy than exists at the present time. Working contrary to this are other attitudes and institutions. For example, the villagers themselves appear to believe that Vietnamese have little talent for commerce and that they distrust each other too much to have successful business relationships. While there is no stigma attached to commerce or industry as occupations, they seem less prestigeful than, say, government service or teaching. It is certainly true that the majority of storekeepers and artisans show little entrepreneurial initiative and little propensity to innovate in their normal activities. Finally, peasant caution—distrust of the outsider from the cities—is not likely to evaporate quickly, particularly in the present insecure environment.

Comparing factors such as these, the balance appears to favor adaptability. It would be unrealistic to interpret this as implying a sophisticated, mobile, and rapidly changing society, for it is not. On the other hand, it gives promise of changing in important ways if the opportunities for doing so are made available. "Economic development" can mean many things to many people. If it means that the resources of land, labor, and equipment are used in different and more productive ways because new uses of labor are uncovered, new kinds of tools and equipment are introduced, new methods of using new or old equipment are presented to people, and these are brought about through possibly greater interdependence and greater indirect exchange of goods and services—if "economic development" is understood to mean these things, rural communities in Viet Nam are not presently on the threshhold of its accomplishment, but the chances for ultimate achievement are extremely favorable.

Appendix

Appendix A

THE METHODOLOGY OF THE STUDY—GENERAL

The study of a rural community by people foreign to its language and culture poses a number of enormous problems from the start, and those who read the final result are entitled to some explanation of the manner in which these problems were handled, with or without final success. In this and succeeding appendices, therefore, the methodology of the study is described for the benefit of those who may want to evaluate the results, as well as those who may be engaged in a similar type of work and who would like to avoid pitfalls and false starts.

The selection of the site of the study followed a period of two weeks during which the members of the study group visited several villages in the rice-growing delta region south of Saigon. The final choice had to meet certain criteria established in advance, or at least come as close as any other alternative. For example, there were still minor security incidents taking place in the spring of 1958, at the time the study was getting under way, and local officials at the provincial level and below were reluctant to permit foreigners to stay overnight in the villages. This meant that commuting from Saigon was inevitable, and one of the criteria was therefore that the site be within reasonable commuting distance from the city. The group also sought a village that would not be a district or canton headquarters but would be of average size, neither rich nor poor for the area, primarily rice producing, and, as far as could be determined in advance, typical of the region with respect to religious practices, methods of production, and administrative structure.

The village of Khanh Hau filled these requirements in all respects, in addition to which it had some special advantages and some definite disadvantages. Of the latter, the most important was the fact that it had been selected as the site of the Fundamental Education Center, which is a training school for teachers. With UNESCO assistance, teachers are trained here to organize community projects so that upon graduation and eventual assignment in rural areas they can spark and direct programs of local improvement. Since the Center had been in the village for about 18 months at that time, there was a possibility that change had been brought to the village to a degree that it was no longer typical of others in the area. Further, the presence of the Center had made it a popular place for official visitors from Saigon, thereby enhancing the possibility that the inhabitants received much more attention than would be the case in other villages nearby and also more assistance in one form or another.

However, a few visits to the village convinced the study group that most of the villagers were quite unaffected by these developments. The program of the Center had not been in full operation long enough to make a substantial dent in local practices, and village contact with official visitors was minimal because they rarely got into the village proper. On the positive side, a very warm relationship had developed between village officials and Mr. Nguyen Van Mung, a staff member of the Center who was then residing in the village and who had numerous contacts among the villagers as a result of his attempts to help and work with them. Mr. Mung became interested in the study and kindly offered to introduce the members of the study group and ease their acceptance in the village by acting as unofficial sponsor. Because of the existing security problem at the time, the question of acceptance by the villagers loomed as a critical one, and the offer of help in establishing the role of the group became a very great advantage in selecting the site. On balance, therefore, Khanh Hau seemed very much like other villages in the area in all respects, but there was the added gain that it promised more rapid acceptance than the others.

From the beginning, the group sought to establish a role for itself as composed of university teachers interested solely in learning as much as possible of life in a Vietnamese rural community. Great emphasis was placed on the fact that the study was not connected with the American aid program in any way and that the villagers could not expect any immediate benefits from it. From time to time the group made contributions to village festivals or special fund-raising efforts, but always in amounts comparable to those given by villagers themselves. Members also gave simple medicines, such as aspirin or malaria pills, to families they came to know well and who were in need of them, donated prizes for the ceremonies at the end of the school year, and gave clothing and candy to the school for distribution to poor children at the lunar new year. However, efforts were made to keep this at a level and in a manner which would be similar to the normal charity of other villagers and never as payment for information received.

In retrospect, it is probably true that most villagers never quite believed the group was composed of disinterested observers and continued to think that some specific benefit might come to the village as the result of our presence. Since this was never promised, there could be no basis for disappointment, but it nevertheless must have been present to some extent throughout. The village council did ask small favors from time to time—the loan of a car to visit district headquarters, to hand-carry a letter to a government agency in Saigon—but they were always within reason. The members of the group tried to avoid being drawn into participation in village decisions, and the village council respected and complied with this position.

The complete study of Khanh Hau is composed of three sections —social (Dr. G. C. Hickey), administrative (Dr. L. W. Woodruff), and economic (the writer). Each member of the group carried on his own investigation, but at the same time shared notes and experiences with the others. To widen the coverage as much as possible, the group anticipated areas of possible overlap and allocated the study of specific topics to eliminate it. Still, in some ways, the members of the group participated together. For example, at village ceremonies the members dressed in traditional costume and took part in the ceremonies along with notables of the village. This was done at the request of the village council, and from all appearances village reaction to this type of activity was quite favorable. Some of the older people assumed that traditional Vietnamese dress was standard in the United States and asked why members of the group did not wear their gowns and turbans more often. Aside from village or school functions, however, each member did his own interviewing, apart from the others, following methods which he decided for himself.

One thing that dominated thinking about the village study was awareness of the recent past as it affected the villagers. The years of war and insecurity made them cautious and suspicious, and it was decided to avoid all questions which touched on political beliefs or loyalties and to minimize questions which dealt with sensitive areas such as savings and crop yields if people seemed uneasy about them. The group decided it would be better to omit whole areas of interest and importance rather than to try for information about them if the attempt created suspicion and distrust. Perhaps the group was overly cautious in this respect, but this accounts for some of the gaps which exist in each of the studies. However, the disadvantages inherent in the decision were fully realized and thoroughly discussed before the study began.

For the first several months of the field work, interviewing was non-directive, and the impressions and information gathered during the early period formed the basis for more direct questioning at a later stage. A common approach was to walk along the village paths or through the fields, stopping to watch people at work and leading into conversation by asking about their current activity. If the person seemed inclined to talk, the conversation could usually be steered into topics that the interviewer wanted to discuss. If the response was negative, the interviewer moved on to something more promising. Most people were friendly and willing to talk, once the nature of the conversation became known, and it was evident that the topic was non-threatening. In this way, too, a number of close acquaintanceships developed with the villagers, and over time many of them became reliable sources of information on a wide variety of subjects. Toward the end of the field work, members of the group tended to seek out the more cooperative and informed of the villagers, by then well known as such, and ask for answers to specific points on which there was incomplete or contradictory information from other sources.

This early background provided the basis on which a sample of twenty families was selected to conduct a family budget survey. People could be asked to assist the group in what was an unfamiliar and unusual task once the group had established a role for itself and, more importantly, once it was possible to select households who would be responsible in keeping the records. It was also important to the larger survey, for the knowledge of village life and village conditions derived from the non-directive interviewing was extremely helpful in making up the questionnaire that was used in the survey. Being aware by then of certain gaps in knowledge about the village, the questionnaire was designed to provide some quantified data in those areas. Finally, the early experience was helpful because every household in three hamlets had been visited at least once in the course of previous interviewing, and villagers therefore had no occasion to fear or suspect the interviewers or the questionnaire. The result was willing cooperation with the survey in almost every household.

The study of economic activity had a further source of information in the village records. Fortunately, these were intact for several years back, and while there are several grounds on which to doubt the accuracy of some of them, in general they were probably fairly reliable. Census data and tenancy data were the best, but the data for rents and yields was subject to qualification. Land records were also accurate, but there was a problem in identifying owners because the names are changed infrequently. The size of the properties was never in question, but actual ownership often was. Tax data and village council budget data were also fairly complete and probably reliable, although all records contained minor arithmetic errors from time to time.

Thus, the basic approach to the problem of data collection for the study of economic activity was to gather all written records and digest these, and at the same time to conduct non-directive interviews as widely as possible. After several months, a family budget survey was started, and finally a questionnaire was prepared, and a sample of 100 households was tested. Throughout the latter stages there was increased reliance on selected informants for checking information obtained in all the other ways.

The time spent on the study was a parameter, not a variable, and once the initial permission was granted there was a maximum of fifteen months in which to complete all field work and present an initial report such as that to which this is attached. This gave enough time to see a complete cycle of rice production and the intervening slack period, as well as time to witness each of the major celebrations which took place during the year. Field work was conducted for about eight months, during which time each member spent three to four days a week in the village and the rest of the time writing notes. There were also other calls on the time of all members of the group for teaching, for administrative duties, and for other research carried on at the same time. The study of the rural community was the major research activity for all, but it was impossible to devote full time to it because of the nature of the other duties all were required to fulfill. This represents an important limitation on the study, as the writer is well aware, but if recognized as such the proper allowances can be made in considering the results obtained.

Appendix B

THE SAMPLE SURVEY

The sample survey was carried out in order to get some quantified data on a wide range of questions, but with particular emphasis on secondary production and farm improvements. It was also designed to get responses to questions that would indicate something of attitudes toward work, toward change, and toward plans for the future. The survey was conducted in the last stages of the field work, after there had been ample opportunity to learn something about the village via other means and therefore to know what que-stions still remained which could be answered by the questionnaire method.

The questionnaire was drawn up in January 1959 and was revised, shortened, and pretested over the period of the next four months. It is included in this appendix for detailed examination, but, in general, it attempted to ask questions only on matters which the head of the household could be expected to know with some accuracy and which he would be willing to answer without distortion or evasion. Thus, for example, it was decided in advance that villagers would be willing to answer questions on their debts but not on the yield from their farms, and the questionnaire therefore contains questions on debt but not on income. The questionnaire was divided into four parts, of which all household heads answered the first three, but only farm operators answered all four. The first section, in part, was filled in by the interviewer before the interview began. Questions were phrased in such a way that the answers would be simple and concrete, a large number of them requiring only "yes" or "no" replies, but in a few cases the questions were left open to see what responses would be given without prompting.

The sample size of 100 households was fixed after discussions with some of the U.S. and UN technical advisors attached to the Institute of Statistics of the Department of National Economy. On the basis of their experience in other parts of Viet Nam, this number is regarded as more than adequate for village sampling purposes. It represents about one-sixth the total number of village households and about one-third the total number of households in the three hamlets from which the sample was drawn. The hamlets of Ap Dinh "A" and "B" and Ap Moi were chosen because they represent a continuous residential area containing about half the village population, the village council house, the school and the village *dinh*. It is as homogeneous a grouping as exists in the entire administrative village, and it is also the most accessible for interviewing purposes.

The sample was stratified on the basis of socio-economic class. These class distinctions rest on a number of considerations, which are dealt with more fully in the companion study by G. C. Hickey, but for purposes of stratifying the sample the sole criterion used was the amount of land a family owned or rented. Thus, upper class households Were defined as all those who own more than 4 hectares or rented more than 5 hectares of rice land; middle class households were those owning between 2 and 4 hectares or renting between 2.5 and 5 hectares of rice land; the lower class households included all those falling below this, even those who had no land at all. The assumption underlying this definition was that those within the limits chosen were in approximately the same economic and social position and that they were distinguished from the other classes in several ways. The relative proportions of the total village population falling within these classes was determined from village land records. A rough check of the reliability of this as a measure of class standing was obtained by comparing it with the percentages of different house types in the village. This latter was available from a survey of house types conducted by Dr. Hickey. In other words, the proportions falling within the social classes, as defined above, and the proportions of houses of brick, frame, and thatch in the village were about the same. The survey later confirmed that there is a relationship between the socio-economic classes as defined and the type of house in which they live. On these grounds, the sample was composed of 12 upper class households, 18 middle class households, and 70 lower class households.

The actual households in the sample were chosen from

the village census records using a table of random numbers. Land-owners and tenants were identified, and a preliminary assignment to a class was given to each household on the census records. A random sample was then drawn from each stratum thus identified in the census data. However, at the time of the interview this preliminary designation was checked by direct question, and if a household was incorrectly identified in advance, the class designation was changed to the correct one. Thus, a few households were found to be incorrectly identified, and replacements for them were drawn again on a random basis.

The questionnaire was originally written in English, but subsequently translated into Vietnamese, and the language used was thoroughly checked to eliminate any type of usage which might be ambiguous or impolite. Although the writer accompanied the interviewers in the pretesting and the initial interviews, the bulk of the actual interviewing was done by two research assistants, both of whom had been connected with the field work for several months and were familiar with the village and the kinds of problems on which further information was needed.

A number of problems arose in the course of the interviewing, none of them of critical importance, but they represent factors to consider in any subsequent interview attempt of this kind in a rural area. The writer is particularly indebted to Mr. Nguyen Van Thuan for reporting on them from his experience. The presence of a foreigner at an interview of this kind, i.e., where a questionnaire is used, is regarded by Vietnamese interviewees as a mixed blessing. On the one hand, it may be considered an honor to the house, and the members react accordingly. On the other, it may make the members of the household more formal and therefore more hesitant to reply fully. This is not necessarily true of the non-directive questioning that took place at an earlier stage, for this was usually done without notebooks, and conversation often ranged over a number of extraneous topics of all kinds, with the result that the atmosphere was much less formal. Again, there is constant need to avoid anything which could be interpreted as threatening, even in the most remote way, for a natural suspicion of strangers had been fortified by war and insecurity.

There are a number of things which are important to the national who attempts an interview of this kind. There is, for example, a language problem, to some extent. Although Vietnamese is standardized throughout the country, there are regional differences of accent and idiom. Villagers often have difficulty in understanding a different accent; in this case the inhabitants of this southern village sometimes had trouble in understanding the language of people who come from the north. It is preferable, therefore, that the national be familiar with the local accent. In this particular study, the interviews were conducted by two staff assistants, one of whom was from the south and whose accent was the same as that of the villagers.

Nationals should also avoid any mannerisms which could be interpreted as overbearing, superior, or impersonal. This can creep in through the language used, and the willingness or unwillingness to spend a certain amount of time in preliminary pleasantries. A pleasant manner and a sympathetic approach win cooperation, but anything which implies that the interviewees are backward or ignorant will turn them indifferent and unresponsive. However, it is equally important that the interviewer avoid extravagant flattery or false heartiness of manner, for the people of the village are sensitive to the motives of the outsider and would react as unfavorably to false good humor as they would to smug superiority. Praise or congratulations, if they are in order and the reason for them comes up naturally, are always welcome, but it must be genuine.

Although it has already been mentioned before, it is worth repeating that the interviews cannot start immediately, but should be preceded by a short period of general conversation, inquiring after the health of family members, recalling some mutual experience, and so on. There was an advantage in this survey in that one member of the interview team had visited each house in the sample on a previous occasion in another context and therefore was already acquainted with the members of the household at least to this extent. This made the "warm-up" period much more natural than it might otherwise have been, for there was the previous experience to build upon.

There was considerable difficulty in locating the households selected for the sample, for the practice of name-avoidance among the villagers meant that many could not identify their near neighbors by the names contained in the census rolls. Further, they could give directions only by local landmarks such as a special tree or bush, a piece of field, a fence, and similar things. It was finally necessary to plot the location of the entire sample in advance with the assistance of the deputy chief of the village, one of the few men who knew the given name and the alias of each household.

Lower class household heads tended to be less precise in their answers than upper class or middle class household heads. This was not always unwillingness to answer, but simply a vagueness of detail on matters which they may have never considered before. For example, an answer of "no" might really mean "not much," and the interviewers would sometimes repeat a question after several minutes to see if there was confirmation of the original answer. If the second reply was different, the interviewer would then try to find out why there was the discrepancy and eventually get an accurate response. This meant departing from the exact wording and order of the prepared questionnaire, but this was permitted on the assumption that the corrected reply would be more accurate than acceptance of the first one offered. Also, as mentioned in the text, some of the poorest families were unable to give specific ambitions for their children, apparently because they had never thought in terms of anything other than a hope for some slight, but unspecified, improvement in their position in life. The more prosperous households, however, often had well defined plans for the future.

The interviews tended to last about 45 minutes for each. In some cases, it was finished in a shorter period of time, but this was rare. The need to spend a small amount of time in general conversation, some problems of communication due to accent differences, and some rephrasing of questions to determine the consistency of responses accounted for the delay, but in a majority of the households this was not excessive.

Finally, it is important that the interviewers enjoy their work, understand what is being attempted, and be sympathetic with the approach. Field work is often hot and dirty, and there are numerous frustrations of all kinds. A person who looks upon the work as "a job" is therefore less likely to accept the working conditions in a frame of mind conducive to effective relations with the people he is interviewing.

VILLAGE STUDY QUESTIONNAIRE

Part I.   External Observations

> INSTRUCTIONS: The following questions can be
> noted down by the interviewer without asking any
> direct questions. This may be done before or after
> the interview itself.

---

1. Identification number of house_____ Hamlet_____

2. The type of house is predominantly:
    Thatched roof with thatch walls   _____
    Thatched roof with wooden walls _____
    Tile roof with wooden walls   _____
    Tile roof with brick walls   _____

3. The house has:
    dirt floors   _____
    cement floors_____
    tile floors   _____

4. Determine the category of the interviewee and check the
    appropriate one listed below:
    landowner   _____
    owner-tenant   _____
    tenant   _____
    laborer   _____
    artisan   _____
    other (specify) _____

5. Check the proper socio-economic classification:
    Class I_____ Class II_____ Class III_____ (ours)
    Class I_____ Class II_____ Class III_____ (actual)

Part II. Family Information

1. What is the main occupation of the head of the household?
   (If the head of the household is a woman, check here ☐)

   Years experience
   on his own

   farmer (landowner or tenant)   _____
   artisan (specify)   _____
   storekeeper   _____
   merchant   _____
   laborer   _____
   other (specify)   _____

2. Does the head of the household also work as:

	Yes	No
hired farm labor	___	___
hired non-farm labor	___	___
rice merchant	___	___
storekeeper	___	___
artisan (specify)	___	___
other (specify)	___	___

3. Does the wife of the family:

   n..a. _____

	Yes	No
work as hired farm labor	___	___
work as hired domestic help	___	___
weave articles for sale	___	___
sell things from house to house	___	___
work as housewife only	___	___

4. Do your grown sons living at home (over 12 years of age):

   n.a. _____

	Yes	No
work as hired farm labor	___	___
work as hired non-farm labor	___	___
work as hired artisan	___	___
do other work (specify)	___	___
continue schooling	___	___

5. Do your grown daughters living at home: n. a. _____
                                          Yes   No

      work as hired farm labor
      work as hired domestic help
      weave articles for sale
      sell things from house to house
      do other work (specify)
      continue schooling

6. How many people in the household work for income?
                   _____ people

7. (a) Did the head of the household attend school?
                  Yes _____   No _____
   (b) If "yes," how many years? _____ years

8. (a) Do all the children in the family who are of school age
       (6-12) attend school regularly? Yes _____   No _____
   (b) If "no," why do some not attend?
      needed to work on farm
      too far from school
      too expensive to send them
      too ill to attend
      do not feel it necessary to send them
      other (specify)

9. (a) Has any member of your household moved away perm-
       anently from Khanh Hau in the last 15 years?
                  Yes _____   No _____
   (b) If "yes," what was his relationship to the head of the
       household?   Son _____   daughter _____
       brother _____   sister _____   grandchild _____
   (c) If "yes," where did they move? (specify) _____
       when? _____
   (d) If "yes," what do they do in their new residence?
   _____

   (e) If "yes," why did they move from Khanh Hau?
   _____

10. (a) Have you ever visited Saigon-Cholon? Yes___ No___
    (b) If "yes," how many times did you go last year? _____
    (c) If "yes," why did you go?
    for amusement _____   to attend national fetes _____
    for business _____   to visit relatives _____
    other (specify) _____

11. Would you move to Saigon if you thought you could find
    work there? Yes ___ No ___ with qualifications _____
    Specify qualifications:

12. Check if the household has:
    safe _____   wardrobe _____
    sewing machine _____   wrist watch _____
    pressure lamp _____   wall clock _____
    portrait photograph _____   marble top table _____
    brass altar fixtures _____   bicycle _____
    set of armchairs and   motor scooter or bike _____
      center table _____   glass front cabinet _____
    plant in chinaware   expensive fountain pen _____
      pottery _____   radio _____
    fresco with Chinese
      characters _____

13. What things would you buy first if you had the money to
    buy them without difficulty?

    INSTRUCTIONS: List at least four items that are vol-
    unteered, and do not attempt to suggest things.
    1.
    2.
    3.
    4.

Part III. Household Economy

1. Does the family have a garden? yes ___ no ___

2. (a) Do you ever sell vegetables? yes ___ no ___
    (b) If "yes," what proportion of your vegetable crop do
        you sell in a good year?
        1/4___ 1/3___ 1/2___ 2/3___ 3/4___ all___
    (c) If "yes," what proportion of your vegetable crop do
        you sell in a bad year?
        1/4___ 1/3___ 1/2___ 2/3___ 3/4___ all___

3. (a) What money income do you get (estimated) for your
        vegetable crop in a good year? _____
    (b) What money income do you get (estimated) for your
        vegetable crop in a bad year? _____

4. Do you raise fruit? yes ___ no ___

5. (a) Do you raise fish? yes ___ no ___
    (b) If "no," why don't you raise fish now?
        no fish pond   ___   no capital   ___
        small homeplot   ___   too difficult to raise ___
        not interested   ___   no time for care   ___
        no water available   ___

6. Since most people in rural areas must borrow money from
    time to time, are you presently in debt to someone?
            yes _____   no _____

7. If the answer to the previous question was "yes," ask all
    the parts to this question. If "no," omit this question.
    (a) Do you have more than one creditor? yes ___ no ___
    (b) Who is (are) your creditor(s)?
        landlord   ___   Tan An moneylender ___
        local storekeeper   ___   hoi   ___
        relative   ___   government   ___
        other (specify)   ___
    (c) Would you mind indicating the amount of debt you
        have? _____
    (d) What is the rate of interest you must pay? _____
        percent per month

(e) What has been happening to the average size of your
debt in the past several years?
increasing ____ decreasing ____ about the same ____
(f) Why is it necessary for you to borrow?

to buy fertilizer	____	to repay old debts ____
to pay planting expense	____	to buy food and
to pay medical bills	____	necessities ____
to pay taxes	____	to pay for
other (specify)	____	ceremonies ____

8. (a) Do you own any water buffalo? yes ____ no ____
   (b) If "yes," how many do you have? _____

9. (a) Do you own any cattle? yes ____ no ____
   (b) If "yes," how many do you have? _____

10. (a) Do you raise pigs? yes ____ no ____
    (b) If "yes," how many do you generally raise per year?
    _____

    (c) If "yes," do you raise them for your own use only?
    yes _____ no _____

11. (a) Do you raise chickens? yes ____ no ____
    (b) If "yes," do you raise them for your own use only?
    yes _____ no _____
    (c) If "yes," do you sell eggs? yes ____ no ____

12. (a) Do you raise ducks? yes ____ no ____
    (b) If "yes," do you raise them for your own use only?
    yes _____ no _____
    (c) If "yes," do you sell eggs? yes ____ no ____

13. (a) Do you buy your own rice? yes ____ no ____
    (b) If "yes," where do you buy it?

village store	____	Tan An market	____
neighbors	____	My Tho market	____
wherever it is cheapest	____	other market	____

14. (a) Do you listen to the radio?
    regularly   _____   seldom   _____
    occasionally   _____   never   _____
    (b) If you ever listen, where do you go? _____

15. Do you read a newspaper?
    regularly   _____   seldom   _____
    occasionally   _____   never   _____

16. If you ever work as a laborer for others, what kinds of labor do you perform in the course of an ordinary year?
    farm work   _____   roof repair   _____
    digging and   mounding   _____
      construction   brick and
      of houses   _____   masonry work   _____
    making   other (specify)   _____
      implements   _____

17. If you work as a laborer, how many months of "regular" work do you get during the course of the year? _____ months (Note: "regular" work means at least 4 to 5 days of work a week, on the average).

18. Do you ever read, or have read to you, publications which tell about ways to improve farming methods?
                     yes _____   no _____

19. What ambitions do you have for your children (i.e., what would you like to see them become in life)?

Part IV. Farm Operations

INSTRUCTIONS: If the answer to Question 1 below
is "yes," ask all the questions which follow. If
the answer is "no," do not ask any further questions.

---

1. (a) Do you own or rent any rice land? yes ___ no ___
    (b) If "yes," how much owned? _____ ha. How much
        rented? _____ ha.

2. (a) Do you hire labor to help you during the year?
            yes _____ no _____
    (b) If you hire labor, do you make any special effort to
        hire relatives before others? yes ___ no ___

3. When you sell your rice, to whom do you ordinarily sell?
    village merchant ____   buyer from Cholon ____
    buyer from Tan An ____   buyer from
    others (specify) ____   village nearby ____

4. Of the rice you sell, when do you sell it?
    immediately   some right after,
      after harvest ____   some later ____
    sell in small   hold until price
      amounts   is best ____
      thoughout year ____   other (specify) ____

5. Where do you prefer to mill your rice?
    Ap Dinh ____ Tan Huong ____ Tan An ____ at home ____
    Other (specify) _____

6. (a) What is the reason for your preference in rice mills?
    least expensive ____   mill owner friendly ____
    more convenient ____   mill gives less
    other (specify) ____   broken rice ____

(b) Which of the following do you own?

plow (Vietnamese)____	plow (Cambodian) ____
harrow ____	water wheel ____
winnowing machine____	shovel or digging
hoe ____	tool ____
saw ____	rice mill ____
axe ____	hammer ____
threshing sledge ____	sickle or scythe ____
roller ____	mortar ____
other (specify) ____	

INSTRUCTIONS: Ask the following question, but then wait for an answer. If you get a reply, write down the main items in the space marked 7(a). If you get no answer, check this box ☐ and then go through the check list in 7(b) marking all items for which you get an affirmative reply.

---

7. In what ways have you changed your methods of farming since you first started on your own?
    (a)

    (b) use chemical fertilizer____ use insecticides____
    changed type of plow____ plant new vegetables____
    plow deeper____ more shallow____ grow new
    fruits____ use more water for irrigation____
    use more____ less____ labor grow new rice
    varieties____ use different threshing technique____
    have not changed techniques at all____

8. How many varieties of rice do you ordinarily grow? ____

9. Do you get two crops of rice per year from your rice land? yes ____ no ____

10. What do you think is the average value of your land at the present time, per hectare? _____

11. What changes have taken place in the amount of land you work since you first started on your own?
    increased ___ decreased ___ stayed the same ___

12. (a) Do you use chemical fertilizer on your rice fields?
                  yes _____   no _____
    (b) If "yes," how long have you used it? _____ years
    (c) If "no," why don't you use it?
              too expensive _____ not much help _____

13. What changes in your farm operations would you make if you had a free choice and money was no obstacle?
    use more fertilizer___   plant more crops
    use a power pump____   of other kinds   ____
    use better seed   ____   buy more land   ____
    use more   use more
      machinery   ____   insecticides   ____
    would do nothing   other (specify)   ____
      differently   ____

14. How much rice land do you operate? _____ ha.

15. Do you rent land from relatives? yes ___ no ___
    partly ___ n.a. ___

16. Is your landlord a resident of Khanh Hau? yes ___
    no ___ n.a. ___

17. Is all your rice land in Khanh Hau? yes ___ no ___

Appendix C

THE FAMILY BUDGET SURVEY

In order to obtain some concrete data on the amounts spent regularly by village households on food and non-food items, a group of 20 households was asked to keep daily records of expenditures or equivalent values of goods supplied from their own farms or gardens. Testing of a form to be used for this began in September 1958, and by October 1958 the actual survey began with a slightly modified budget record form. Records were kept over a period of eight weeks, which included two or three weeks before the harvest of the first rice crops and five or six weeks after it.

Keeping records of this kind was a new experience for villagers, and the selection of the sample therefore involved choosing those who were known to the interviewers and who would be willing to keep accurate records. Thus, the sample was hardly a random one, the selective factors being knowledge of marking and writing and willingness to take part in the experiment. An attempt was made to include all socio-economic classes, but, in fact, the final sample did not contain either any of the very richest or the very poorest households in the village. It did, however, contain a broadly representative group of the three main socio-economic classes. The number chosen, 20, reflects the simple mechanical difficulty of servicing a large number of households. At the beginning of each week, each household was given a form for each day of the following week with instructions to fill in a new form for each day at the end of each day. At the same time, the daily budget forms for the previous week were collected and reviewed on the spot to see if there were any questions or discrepancies to discuss with the head of the household. This collection and distribution of forms was a very time-consuming task, for each call involved a certain amount of general conversation and tea-drinking that tact and village courtesy required. As a result, this would take the better part of one day each week, and the decision was made to limit the number of households in the sample to no more than 20 on the grounds that it would be too time-consuming to attempt more.

The small size of the sample is, therefore, a cause for some concern, but it reflects a limitation of resources. Over the eight-week period, there was an opportunity for unusual or abnormal expenditures to cancel out in each group, with the result that the final impression is probably a valid picture of actual expenditures by households in three socio-economic classes. The need to enlist the cooperation of the household in this type of survey limited the range of village households which would enter the sample, for not all households were willing or able to participate. Again, this is not considered a serious limitation, for as far as can be determined from observation, the households included in the sample had standards of living no different from others in the same socio-economic class.

Some check on the replies was made by appearing in households at mealtimes and observing the size and content of meals. The most probable source of under-reporting, to judge from this type of check, was in vegetables and fish supplied directly, as indicated in the text. However, this is not a major understatement, for, in terms of either value or volume, increasing these items will not change the basic expenditure patterns to a significant degree.

Head of family _____

Occupation _____

Day, month _____

N. B.—Use one separate sheet for each day. For days when nothing is bought, use separate sheets and fill in dates before attaching them to other filled sheets.

ITEMS USED FOR DAILY CONSUMPTION

Items consumed	Quantity	Pro-duced by self	Bought	If bought How much did it cost	Where did you buy it
Rice: ordinary rice					
sticky rice					
Meat: chicken, duck,					
goose, pork,					
buffalo, beef					
Fish and shrimp: dried					
fresh					
Sauce: fish sauce					
soy sauce					
other					
Eggs: chicken, duck					
Vegetables: vegetables					
sweet potatoes					
(Western) pot.					
other					
Fruits: banana					
coconut					
pineapple					
lemon					
other					
Salt					
Sugar: sugar cane					
brown sugar					
white sugar					
Onion, red pepper, pepper					
Peanut oil					
Bread					
Condensed milk					
Ice					
Tea					
Cakes and sweets					
Candies for children					
All other items (list them)					

ITEMS USED DAILY IN FAMILY

Items and products used	(same columns)

Coal
Wood
Kerosene
Other items (list them)
Matches
Candles
Incense sticks and gold paper
Betel nut, betel leaves, and lime
Tobacco and cigarette paper
Beer
Rice wine
Soda, orangeade, root beer, etc.
Chinese medicine, local medicine
Western plain "calico"
clothing printed cloth
material: satin, black satin
          poplin, artificial silk
Tailoring cost
Soaps and toilet articles
Motion picture and theater
Bus and train fare
Book and newspaper
Haircut
Mats, baskets
Conical hat
Fishing equipment
Stationery, pen, and pencil
Glassware, bowls and plates,
  chopsticks, rice cooking pot
Shoes, slippers, wooden clogs
Brooms, cleaning cloths
Other items (list them)

FOOTNOTES

Chapter 1: None.

Chapter 2

1. For example, houses in the village inhabited by illiterate adults are so designated by house numbers of a distinctive color. A new series of literacy classes was scheduled to start in December 1959, with attendance "encouraged by visits of the Self-Defense Corps to the houses of illiterates who failed to attend.
2. Unless otherwise designated, the words "survey" and "survey data" used hereinafter refer to a sample survey of 100 households carried out specifically for this study. Details of the survey are provided in Appendix B, including definitions of the socio-economic class brackets which are used in presenting much of the survey data.
3. This may represent a slight overstatement, since, under the term "relatives," " more than one household could be referring to the same person. For example, the son to one household could be the brother to another, yet both would refer to the same man. From what was known of the households in the sample, however, this overstatement is probably very small.
4. A form of public conveyance used in large towns, cycles carry passengers in the front part of a three-wheeled vehicle propeled by a bicycle-type chain drive, pedaled by the driver.

Chapter 3

1. Yves Henry, *Economic Agricole de L'Indochine francaise* (Hanoi: Gouvernement General de L'Indochine, 1932), p. 109.
2. Ordinance No. 57, October 22, 1956.
3. In addition to this, a landowner may keep up to 15 hectares of *huong hoa* rice land, which is land reserved to maintain the cult of the ancestors. Since the agrarian reform touches only rice land, there is no limit to the amount of other land a person may keep.

4. Although the only people to benefit from the land distribution in Khanh Hau were the former tenants of the large landowner, Ordinance No. 57 provides that refugees, unemployed, and certain small landowners (less than 3 hectares, more than 5 children) are also eligible, in that order, if there is still land available.

5. Approximately US$ 170 to US$ 215 per hectare at an assumed limited access "free" market rate of VN$ 70 = US$ 1.

6. Further evaluation of the land reform program appears below in Chapter 8.

7. Literally, the land used to maintain incense and fire on the family altar. Such land is generally regarded as inalienable, since the income from it is to be used to support the family cult in perpetuity.

8. After three years a landlord may take his land back for cultivation by himself or by a direct dependent 18 years of age or older, or he may remove a tenant for unduly delaying rent payments or failing to pay rents, or for action detrimental to the property. In all cases, the landlord must give the tenant at least six months' compensation for any improvements or installation still useful or productive after termination.

Chapter 4

1. This term is used in referring to the small dikes which separate the fields and retain the water vital to the cultivation of rice.

2. The Vietnamese names which apply to the different varieties and grades of rice are highly localized, and may not refer to the same thing in other parts of Viet Nam. The names used here are those used in Khanh Hau, and no attempt has been made to equate these with terms used elsewhere.

3. The *gia* is a Vietnamese dry measure equal to 40 liters.

4. One such pamphlet is issued by the Societe Indochinoise de Potasse et d'Engrais Chimiques d'Extreme Orient, and is entitled *Nhung Dieu Can Biet Cho Nong-Gia Viet-Nam* [Some Information Useful to Vietnamese Farmers). However, we found no evidence that this kind of material had circulated in the village at any time.

5. The most popular brand is a phosphate tricalcique fertilizer sold under the name *Tran Nong* (containing 30 percent P_2O_5) in 1957 and preceding years. Importation of this brand stopped in 1958, with the result that phosphate tricalcique was available in the local markets under the brand names Than Tai (containing 30

percent P2Og) and *Tarn Tai* (containing 25 percent P2Og). Farmers expressed strong preference for the *Than Nong*, regretted that none seemed available in 1958, but recognized that the *Than Nong, Than Tai,* and *Tarn Tai* were largely interchangeable in all uses. They nevertheless continued to speak of these as different kinds of fertilizer and talked of alternating their application at certain times on the same crop to import sought-for properties in their rice plants. The ammonium sulphate (20 percent nitrogen) comes in at least two brands, *Chim* and *Tien,* but is known locally by the general term of *diem* (sulphate).

6.   It is difficult to get accurate estimates of cost for several reasons which must spring easily to mind. For one thing, farmers do not keep records of cash outlays, and any cost data based on direct interviews would have to depend on their ability to recall past expenses with precision. It is true this method was used to estimate the special non-production expenditures during a year (see Chapter 9), but it still has obvious drawbacks. Another factor is the variation which occurs from year to year due to such things as differences in the volume of rainfall, availability of credit, or the price of fertilizer.

It therefore seemed preferable to make cost estimates by separating rice production into different functions, assigning representative labor time estimates to each of them, and adding estimates for other categories of cost which are based on general knowledge of village practices with respect to credit, rents, and fertilizer use. It was easier to obtain agreement among farmers on the amount of time spent on plowing a hectare of land, for example, than for them to understand and reply accurately to questions which dealt with money costs of production.

7.   See the section on land rental and agrarian reform above.

8.   Kamol O. Janlekha, *A Study of the Economy of a Rice Growing Village in Central Thailand* (Bangkok: Ministry of Agriculture, 1955), pp. 134-40.

9.   *Ibid.*, p. 137.

10.   *Ibid.*, p. 138.

11.   *Ibid.*, p. 124.

12.   Average yield of paddy in Bangchan was estimated at 28. 8 tang per rai for the period 1948-52, which is equal to 104. 2 *gia* per hectare. *Ibid.*, p. 52.

13.   Rose K. Goldsen and Max Ralis, *Factors Related to Acceptance of Innovations in Bang Chan, Thailand* (Ithaca: Department of

Far Eastern Studies, Cornell University, 1957), p. 52.

Chapter 5: None.

Chapter 6

1.   Proportions based on survey data.

Chapter 7

1.   Occupational data cited here are based on the survey of 100 households.
2.   Some occupations have only one or two practitioners in the entire village, and a sample therefore would not pick up all occupations. Short of an occupational census of the entire village, which was not attempted, there was no way to obtain accurate information on the kinds and distribution of occupational skills within the population. Village council records on this score were quite inadequate.
3.   Pierre Gourou, *The Peasants of the Tonkin Delta* [Behavior Science Translations] (New Haven: Human Relations Area Files, 1955), Vol. II, pp. 581 ff. This same type of village specialization is found in villages composed of refugees from the north which have been established south of the 17th parallel since 1954.
4.   *Ibid.*, p. 585.
5.   To illustrate how this works, assume that a farmer needs the services of ten people for three days. The farmer pays the labor contractor VN$ 30, and the laborers pay VN$ 15, or a total of VN$ 45 from all to compensate for the organizing service.
6.   Ordinance No. 53, September 6, 1956.
7.   The factors making for this assumption of an inelastic demand for the milling services include: (a) that this is an important service to village residents; (b) the costs of milling are small because only small amounts of paddy are milled at a time; and (c) hand milling at home is not a good substitute for machine milling, and other rice mills are far enough away that the cost of transportation back and forth would probably equal or exceed the cost of milling a villager's typical order.
8.   A large part of the supply of these woven goods comes from the villages set up to accommodate refugees from north of the 17th parallel.

9. One exception is in the sleeping mats woven for babies. A small design is put into these mats to indicate where the baby's head should go. Local belief holds that to place a baby in a different position, i.e., with the head where the feet normally go, will affect his intelligence.

Chapter 8

1. In one sense, a shift in factor proportions can be considered a "new idea," too, but this leads into problems of definition, resolution of which are of doubtful value for purposes at hand in this discussion.
2. Based on the assumption that 1 *gia* of paddy = 19 kilos.
3. Computed from data provided in United Nations, *Economic Survey of Asia and the Far East*, 1959 (Bangkok: UN, 1960), p. 117.
4. Benjamin Higgins, *Economic Development* (New York: W. W. Norton, 1959), p. 16.
5. This is a crude measure of the size of the work force, but probably accurate enough for comparison purposes. Not all males in these age brackets do actually labor in the fields, and the same would be true for females. However, most of them do, and any overcounting would be more than offset by men and women outside these age brackets who also work but who are not included in this particular definition of the work force.
6. Counting the maximum probable labor input of 60 man-days per hectare multiplied by the area of rice land in the village (925. 9 hectares).
7. Average varieties of paddy sold for approximately VN$ 50 per *gia* (19 kilos in this village) during the harvest of 1958-59.

Chapter 9

1. A discussion of the problem of sample selection and an account of difficulties encountered in collecting and interpreting this data are given in Appendix C, and the reader may refer to this in making his own evaluation of the material presented in this chapter.
2. As in earlier conversions, a "free market" rate of VN$ 70 = US$ 1 is used as approaching, if not accurately measuring, the international exchange value of the Vietnamese currency unit.
3. These corrections are based on the assumption that, on the average, 40 percent of all food expenditures recorded were supplied

in kind by the household themselves—a correction factor derived from replies in the budget records.

4. Per capita daily expenditures were calculated on the basis of the complete budget records for all families, some of which covered a time period in excess of eight weeks. For this reason they are not exactly comparable to the weekly data presented earlier, which covered the eight-week period only.

5. In evaluating these estimates, it is important to bear in mind that they pertain to one village only, and this village is located in one of the most prosperous provinces in Viet Nam. Although Khanh Hau itself is considered one of the less wealthy villages in the province, the figures shown here probably represent levels of expenditure considerably in excess of those which would be found in other parts of Viet Nam. For this reason, these estimates are not intended to be representative of consumption in all parts of Viet Nam, although they are probably comparable to expenditures in other villages in the same part of the delta region.

6. Some per capita income estimates for the period 1952-53 are: Japan—US$ 190; Philippines—US$ 150; Egypt-US$ 120; Pakistan—US$ 70; India —US$ 60.

7. Varieties that are caught or purchased include *ca moi, ca linh, ca loc, ca tre, ca nui, ca ro,* and small shrimp (*tep*) and silver shrimp (*tep bac*).

8. This was the opinion expressed by several staff members of the American aid mission in Viet Nam in conversations with the author. On the other hand, the Pasteur Institute of Viet Nam has recently reported that different kinds of sauce derived from seafood constitute a relatively high degree of protein (20-26 percent) at low prices. The report stated that twenty grams of "*mam*" sauce brought between four and five grams of protides, . 25 to 1 gram of lipoids, and 2 to 3 grams of mineral salts to low income household diets. See *Vietnam Press*, Bulletin No. 154, week ending September 18, I960 (airmail edition), p. 11.

Chapter 10

1. Table 10.8 has eliminated nine cases where the interest rates were indeterminate or where the replies covered more than one loan without specifying adequately the rates applying to the different loans.

Chapter 11

1.   The term "innovation" is used here in the general sense of anything which is done differently and which thereby increases the productivity of available factors of production. Since the scope of observation is extremely localized in this single village, the innovations noted here are limited in their impact to inhabitants of Khanh Hau.

2.   Village sorcerers price their services on a piecework basis, and the total cost varies with the number and elaborateness of the separate rituals which are component parts of the entire service.

Chapter 12: None.

Chapter 13

1.   At this point, the author wishes to acknowledge that in what follows he has drawn heavily from the material presented in the companion volumes initially issued in mimeographed form and written by colleagues in the study of Khanh Hau, *viz.* , G. C. Hickey, *The Study of a Vietnamese Rural Community—Sociology;* and L. W. Woodruff, *The Study of a Vietnamese Rural Community*—Administrative Activity. Both were published in Saigon, in 1960, by the Michigan State University Viet Nam Advisory Group. Rather than footnote page references to these sources, general acknowledgement is offered here for the assistance of these colleagues, both in their writings on the village and their views and observations expressed personally in the course of the study.

Index

For Product Safety Concerns and Information please contact our EU
representative GPSR@taylorandfrancis.com
Taylor & Francis Verlag GmbH, Kaufingerstraße 24, 80331 München, Germany

www.ingramcontent.com/pod-product-compliance
Ingram Content Group UK Ltd.
Pitfield, Milton Keynes, MK11 3LW, UK
UKHW021606240425
457818UK00018B/411